Index Investing

FOR

DUMMIES®

Index Investing
FOR
DUMMIES®

by Russell Wild, MBA

WILEY

Wiley Publishing, Inc.

Index Investing For Dummies®

Published by
Wiley Publishing, Inc.
111 River St.
Hoboken, NJ 07030-5774
www.wiley.com

WILEY

About the Author

Russell Wild is a NAPFA-certified financial advisor and the principal of Global Portfolios, an investment advisory firm based in eastern Pennsylvania. He is one of few wealth managers in the nation who is both fee-only (takes no commissions) and welcomes clients of both substantial and modest means. Wild, in addition to the fun he has with his financial calculator, is also an accomplished writer who helps readers understand and make wise choices about their money. His articles have appeared in many national publications, including *AARP The Magazine, Consumer Reports, Men's Health,* and *Reader's Digest.* He also contributes regularly to professional financial journals, such as *Wealth Manager* and *Financial Planning.*

The author or coauthor of two dozen nonfiction books, Wild's last works, prior to the one you're holding in your hand, were *Bond Investing For Dummies* (Wiley, 2007) and *Exchange-Traded Funds For Dummies* (Wiley, 2007). Before those, he wrote *The Unofficial Guide to Getting a Divorce* (Wiley, 2005) along with attorney Susan Ellis Wild, his ex-wife — yeah, you read that right. No stranger to the mass media, Wild has shared his wit and wisdom on such TV shows as *Oprah, The View, CBS Morning News,* and *Good Day New York,* and in hundreds of radio interviews.

Wild holds a Master of Business Administration (MBA) degree in international management and finance from the Thunderbird School of Global Management in Glendale, Arizona (consistently ranked the #1 school for international business by both *U.S. News and World Report* and *The Wall Street Journal*); a Bachelor of Science (BS) degree in business/economics magna cum laude from American University in Washington, D.C.; and a graduate certificate in personal financial planning from Moravian College in Bethlehem, Pennsylvania (America's sixth-oldest college). A member of the National Association of Personal Financial Advisors (NAPFA) since 2002, Wild is also a long-time member and currently serves as president of the American Society of Journalists and Authors (ASJA).

The author grew up on Long Island and, after living in various places both in the United States and abroad (including France and Morocco), settled in Allentown, Pennsylvania where he lives with his two children, Adrienne and Clayton, along with Norman, the killer poodle. He spends much of his leisure time gardening, bicycling, rereading old Kurt Vonnegut novels, and whispering sweet little nothings in the ear of his partner, Brenda Lange, also a writer.

Wild's Web site is www.globalportfolios.net. His e-mail is Russell@Globalportfolios.net.

Dedication

To Dennis, who in 1981 sold me 100 shares of the soon-to-go-bankrupt Continental Illinois National Bank and Trust Company. You were my first (and last) stockbroker, Dennis, and you taught me everything I ever needed to know about stock-picking.

Author's Acknowledgments

This is the third book for me in the Dummies series, and I've had the pleasure of working with the same great team each time. The team includes the very talented and pleasant Joan Friedman, project editor, and the gregarious and also pleasant Marilyn Allen, my agent. It also includes Stacy Kennedy, acquisitions editor, and a host of other really good editorial, production, and marketing people at Wiley.

New to the team, Ron DeLegge, publisher and editor of www.etfguide.com, was kind enough to do the technical editing, and he did it quite superbly. Check out Ron's syndicated *The Index Investing Show* on radio or podcast: www.indexshow.com. You'll find that I'm a guest on the show from time to time.

I'm very thankful to a number of smart and financially savvy colleagues, especially among my fellow fee-onlys of the National Association of Personal Financial Advisors (NAPFA), who provided helpful input and guidance. Several are quoted throughout the pages of this book.

Thanks, too, to the very helpful staff at Morningstar, especially Mark Komissarouk, and at the Vanguard Group, especially Rebecca Cohen, for sharing their excellent research.

And I'd like to give special thanks to John Bogle, father of index investing, for his enormous contributions to the science of finance, the contribution he's made (indirectly only) to my own personal finances and those of my clients, and for so generously lending his time and expertise to this project.

Publisher's Acknowledgments

We're proud of this book; please send us your comments through our Dummies online registration form located at http://dummies.custhelp.com. For other comments, please contact our Customer Care Department within the U.S. at 877-762-2974, outside the U.S. at 317-572-3993, or fax 317-572-4002.

Some of the people who helped bring this book to market include the following:

Acquisitions, Editorial, and Media Development

Project Editor: Joan Friedman

Acquisitions Editor: Stacy Kennedy

Assistant Editor: Erin Calligan Mooney

Editorial Program Coordinator: Joe Niesen

Technical Editor: Ron L. DeLegge

Senior Editorial Manager: Jennifer Ehrlich

Editorial Supervisor: Carmen Krikorian

Editorial Assistants: Jennette ElNaggar, David Lutton

Cartoons: Rich Tennant (www.the5thwave.com)

Composition Services

Project Coordinator: Erin M. Smith

Layout and Graphics: Reuben W. Davis, Nikki Gately, Sarah Philippart

Proofreaders: Jessica Kramer, Christine Sabooni

Indexer: Ty Koontz

Publishing and Editorial for Consumer Dummies

Diane Graves Steele, Vice President and Publisher, Consumer Dummies

Kristin Ferguson-Wagstaffe, Product Development Director, Consumer Dummies

Ensley Eikenburg, Associate Publisher, Travel

Kelly Regan, Editorial Director, Travel

Publishing for Technology Dummies

Andy Cummings, Vice President and Publisher, Dummies Technology/General User

Composition Services

Gerry Fahey, Vice President of Production Services

Debbie Stailey, Director of Composition Services

Contents at a Glance

Table of Contents

Introduction

So you want to be an index investor. Or perhaps you want to be a *better* index investor. This book is for you — but not for you and you alone. Even an index-investing agnostic has plenty of reason to read *Index Investing For Dummies*. You see, the lessons of index investing — lessons learned since the first index funds were introduced about 35 years ago — are extremely important to *all* investors.

Index investing — investing in entire markets or segments of markets, rather than trying to cherry-pick securities — is the financial world's equivalent of Seward's purchase of Alaska, Henry Ford's horseless carriage, or milkshake-machine salesman Ray Croc's little hamburger stand called McDonald's. It is a stellar example of something that was expected by nearly everyone (including the alleged high wizards of finance) to be a miserable flop, and yet, by almost any measure imaginable, wound up a rave success.

This book explains why index investing has been such a rave success and, more importantly, how you can harness the power of index investing to work for you.

About This Book

By the time you have spent a few hours — pleasurable hours, I certainly hope — thumbing through the following pages, you'll know a lot about index investing, even more than some professional investors. For right now, I'd like to bring home just a few of the virtues of index investing that will make reading this book more than worth your while:

- **Versatility:** Index investing gives you the opportunity to build a portfolio that is well-diversified, extremely low-cost, and fine-tuned to your particular needs. Are you an aggressive investor looking for exposure to small cap stocks, real estate investment trusts (REITs), or commodities? Are you a conservative investor more content with blue chip stocks, U.S. Treasury bonds, or high-grade municipal bonds? It doesn't matter. Indexing allows for all flavors of investment.

✔ **Profitability:** Study after study shows that if you invest in index funds or predominantly index funds, your long-term returns are very likely to far exceed those of most of your neighbors' with their actively managed mutual fund portfolios or individual stock and bond picks. In fact, the odds of an actively managed (cherry-picked) portfolio beating an index portfolio are extremely slim. (I know! I know! You'd think that picking cherries would give you cherry-like returns. Index investing, admittedly, can be as counterintuitive as taking a hot bath to cool off on a steamy August day.)

✔ **Taxability:** Without any question, index investors who buy and hold their index funds (the preferred way to invest in indexes) pay far less to Uncle Sam than do those with mutual fund portfolios, or portfolios of rapidly changing stock holdings. That situation is almost certain to continue to be the case regardless of whether the Democrats or Republicans take control of the White House or Congress, or which football team wins this year's Super Bowl.

✔ **Simplicity:** You can build a portfolio of index funds that will keep you bobbing merrily along in good times and still stay afloat in bad times — and you won't need anything more than this book to do it. In fact, you'll be better off allowing your subscriptions to *Easy Money* magazine and the *Fast Bucks* financial newsletter to lapse. This book, a simple handheld calculator, and patience are about all you need to be a successful investor.

Ready for more?

Dummies books, such as this one, are written so that you can either plow through from beginning to end or, if you prefer, jump from chapter to chapter. Feel free to look though the index (yes, *Index Investing For Dummies* has an index!) for subjects of special interest.

Conventions Used in This Book

To help you cruise the pages of this book as smoothly as can be, I use the following conventions, probably familiar to all veteran readers of books *For Dummies*:

✔ Whenever I introduce a term that is at all jargonish, such as, say, *standard deviation* or *efficient frontier,* the term is set (as you can clearly see) in *italics.* Expect to find a definition or explanation to quickly follow.

✔ If I want to share some information that, juicy as it may be, isn't absolutely essential to profitable index investing, I plop it into a *sidebar,* a darkish rectangle or square with its very own heading, set apart from the rest of the text. (See how smoothly this italics/definition thing works?)

✔ All Web addresses appear in `monofont`; that makes them easy to find if you need to go back and locate one in a jiffy.

Keep in mind that when this book was laid out, some Web addresses may have been broken across two lines of text. Wherever that's the case, rest assured that we haven't put in any hyphens or other thingamabobs to indicate the break. When using one of those broken Web addresses, just type in exactly what you see in this book. Pretend as if the line break doesn't exist.

What You're Not to Read

Unless you're going to be taking a test on index investing, you probably don't need to know everything in this book. Sometimes, I include some fairly technical information that you don't have to know in order to be a very successful index investor. Or I include some tangential info that you may find interesting but that won't really affect your ability to be a successful index investor. In both cases, I tuck this material neatly into the sidebars. Feel free to stop and peruse them, or jump right past and keep moving with the main topics. It's your choice!

Foolish Assumptions

If you're just beginning your education in the world of investments, perhaps the best place to start would be *Investing For Dummies* by Eric Tyson (published by Wiley). But the book you're holding in your hands is only a grade above that one in terms of assumptions of investment knowledge and background. I assume that you are bright, that you have at least a few bucks to invest, and that you know some math (and maybe a wee bit of economics) — that's it.

In other words, you don't need a degree of any sort or years of portfolio management to be able to follow along. Oh, and for those of you who are already fairly savvy investors, perhaps even skilled at building a portfolio of index funds, I'm assuming that you, too, can learn quite a bit by reading this book. (Oh, you know it all, do you? You may know that international stocks have limited correlation to the U.S. stock market, but do you know which kinds of international stocks have the lowest correlation, and so provide the most powerful diversification? You will after reading Chapter 7!)

How This Book Is Organized

Here's a rough idea of what your eyes will be feasting on in the following pages, laid out juicy part by juicy part.

Part I: The (Mostly) Nonviolent Indexing Revolution

What is an index, and how did index funds — baskets of investments that attempt to track indexes — come to pass? Who were the key players, and what motivated them to swim against the strong stream of convention? In this first stop in our adventure, I guide you through a short history of indexing and walk you through the years to the present. You see how indexing has changed over time — in some ways for the better, and in other ways, maybe not. You get a better sense of what makes indexing such a potentially powerful investment tool and how to best wield that tool.

Next, you meet and greet *exchange-traded funds* (or portfolios): the latest (and in some fashions, greatest) way to build an index portfolio. An exchange-traded fund is something of a cross between a mutual fund and a stock, and as of this writing there are more than 700 of them to choose from.

If you have a great sense of curiosity, or a technical bent, this part ends with a discussion of the nuts and bolts of how indexes are actually constructed, and how that construction may make some indexes better foundations for investments than others.

Part II: Getting to Know Your Index Fund Choices

In the second part, this black-and-yellow book starts to get intensely practical. You get a full primer on the differences between the two major choices for index investing: the time-honored mutual fund and the newer and flashier exchange-traded fund. I introduce you to the major indexes on which so many of these funds are based, as well as some of the more obscure indexes. And we look at the people behind the indexes — the builders: who they are, and how much you can trust them.

I give you lots of examples of the different kinds of investments that are commonly indexed: stocks, bonds, and commodities. In each category of investment, you find popular index funds (both the best and the worst) compared, contrasted, and thoroughly evaluated. There's a veritable smorgasbord of index funds out there, but do you know which are the healthiest pickings?

Part III: Drawing a Blueprint for Your Index Portfolio

Continuing along in the practical vein of Part II, this part is where I introduce the recipes for mixing and matching index funds to form the ultimate portfolio. (No, a single index fund probably won't do it.) I talk about brokerage firms, where you'll be housing your index funds. I talk about how many funds you'll need and in roughly what quantity. I talk about what to do if you like the idea of index investing but don't want to limit yourself entirely to index investing. (That's okay, really! There's not a law against it.) I show you how to build a "mixed-marriage" portfolio.

For dessert, I serve up some sample portfolio pies, examples of real portfolios using index funds, or primarily index funds, that you can use as models for your own well-tailored investing strategy.

Part IV: Ensuring Happy Returns

An index portfolio that's just right for you today may no longer be appropriate a decade from now. Things change: your age (alas), health, income, expenditures, and number of kids in college, for example. A portfolio must change along with them. In this part, I outline what kinds of maintenance ensure a smooth-running, age-appropriate, profitable portfolio for years to come.

If you are a do-it-yourselfer, the information you garner in Chapter 16 is essential. If you prefer someone to hold your hand, Chapter 17 reviews the various kinds of financial professionals that you might engage — and those you are probably best off not engaging.

Part V: The Part of Tens

This standard feature in all *For Dummies* books rounds out your index-investing education with a couple of fun but practical lists, plus an interview with the undisputed Father of Indexing, and the man who probably knows more about it than anyone on the planet, John Bogle, founder of Vanguard.

Part VI: Appendixes

In this part, I provide handy-dandy lists of the major indexers and index fund providers, as well as very helpful resources for further information about index investing.

Icons Used in This Book

Throughout the margins of this book, you find cute little drawings in circles. In the *For Dummies* world, like in the cyberworld, these are known as *icons,* and they signal certain notable things going on in the accompanying text.

 Although this is a practical book, you also find some chit and some chat. Any paragraph accompanied by this icon, however, tends to be chitless and chatless — just pure, unadulterated practicality.

The world of index investing — although generally not as risky as some other kinds of investing — still provides plenty of opportunity to get whumped. Wherever you see the bomb, know that money can be lost by ignoring the adjoining advice.

Read carefully! This icon indicates that something really important is being said and is well worth reading twice to allow your noggin to soak it up.

Wall Street is full of people who make money at other people's expense. Where you see the pig face, know that I'm about to point out an instance where someone (perhaps even someone calling himself a proponent of index investing!) may be digging his plump fingers into your pockets.

Where to Go from Here

Where would you like to go from here? If you would like, start at the beginning. If you're mostly interested in, say, stock index funds, you are free to jump right to Chapter 7. Bond index funds? Go ahead and jump to Chapter 8. Commodities? Chapter 9. It's entirely your call. Maybe start by skimming the index at the back of the book.

Part I
The (Mostly) Nonviolent Indexing Revolution

The 5th Wave   By Rich Tennant

"I asked my investment advisor for something that was low cost, easy to manage, and also functions on its own. He suggested an index fund or a robo vac."

In this part . . .

These first five chapters guide you through the history of indexing from its advent through the modern era. You discover the reasons that index investing makes so much more sense than trying to pick cherries or time the markets. You come to understand why index investing was so controversial from the start — and probably always will be! You find out why the great, unwashed masses don't index — and probably never will. (In short, they aren't as smart as you are, and they are more susceptible to Wall Street's propaganda and the silly ramblings of the financial press.) And you are brought up to speed on some recent changes in indexes and index funds that have really changed the nature of index investing forever — in some ways for the better, in some ways, for worse.

Chapter 1

What Indexing Is ... and Isn't

*W*hen John Bogle started The Vanguard Group in 1974 and shortly thereafter introduced the first index fund available to the unwashed masses, the brokerage industry and financial press were less than supportive. In fact, the entire venture was slathered in mockery. "Bogle's Folly," it was called. "Un-American" . . . "A sure way to achieve mediocrity."

Ha!

Bogle wound up getting the last hearty laughs. (You'll find an intimate discussion with this undisputed Father of Indexing in Chapter 20.) Vanguard Investments is today the largest fund company in the United States. A majority of its stock and bond funds are still index funds. Those index funds have gadzillions of dollars in them and long-term track records that put most other funds to shame.

Index investors, with Vanguard and other fund companies, have more than prospered over the past 35 years as the science of indexing has emerged as perhaps the surest way to achieve outsized investment results. While other investors (so-called *active* investors) are busy year-in and year-out metaphorically punching and kicking each other silly, index investors (sometimes called *passive* investors) stand calmly on the sidelines, reaping consistently far greater rewards.

You are about to discover why that is so, how we know it is so beyond any shadow of a doubt, and how you can take "Bogle's Folly" and use it to build the leanest, meanest, smartest portfolio possible. You are also about to find out how a number of pinstriped Johnnies-come-lately (part of the mixed blessing of the exchange-traded fund phenomenon) have terribly complicated the index-investing landscape, making it more important than ever to do your investing homework.

Realizing What Makes Indexing So Powerful

If index investing is nothing else, it is counterintuitive. Without any difficulty whatsoever, I can fully understand why just about the entire brokerage industry and financial press in the mid-1970s thought it was bound to be a flop.

Prior to the mid-1970s, people thought that love beads were cool and bell-bottoms were hip. They also thought that the road to investment success was to be had by hiring a professional manager who could beat the markets. Such a manager, with his freshly minted Harvard MBA, would use fancy algorithms, mile-long formulas, and inside information that no one else could harvest in order to pick individual stocks that would outshine all other stocks. Such a financial wizard could move money in and out of the market at just the right time to catch every ascent and avoid every decline. That was the belief.

Many people — most people, in fact — still believe that such "active management" is the way to win at investing. But prior to 1974, *everyone* believed it. That was before John Bogle came around and anyone bothered to study the matter. (A few academic papers on indexing were written prior to Bogle, and there was even some dabbling at the institutional level by Wells Fargo and American National Bank of Chicago, but the populace was kept in the dark, and the funds' popularity didn't go far.)

Turning common investing knowledge on its head

One of the first studies to raise eyebrows and seriously question the status quo came from a guy named Charles D. Ellis, who happens to be a Harvard MBA himself. In 1975, he conducted a study of the markets and mutual fund performance. Based on his findings, he wrote a groundbreaking article entitled "The Loser's Game." It originally appeared in the *Financial Analysts Journal.* It later was turned into a book, *Winning the Loser's Game,* which was published in 1985 by McGraw-Hill and bore some very rough similarity to the book you are now reading.

In the 1975 article, addressed to fellow investing professionals, Ellis made the following statement:

> *The investment management business is built upon a simple and basic belief: Professional managers can beat the market. That premise appears to be false.*

At the time, mind you, this was akin to telling a group of Jewish grandmothers that chicken soup had no medicinal value. Ellis's position was seen as preposterous. And yet Ellis was willing to spoon out the harsh truth. His careful studies revealed that in the prior decade, 85 percent of institutional investors had underperformed the return of the S&P 500 index.

Ellis's explanation: Investing is a "loser's game." Let me explain what he meant by that, and why it has everything to do with indexing.

Playing tennis — poorly — with your investments

Charles Ellis's term, "loser's game," comes from an analogy he makes to the game of tennis. Picture yourself in a tennis game with your friend, Joe. We'll assume that neither of you is a professional player. Now pick up the ball and smack it. Joe will attempt to smack it back to you. You pray as you lunge for the ball that your tennis racket will connect with the ball and that you'll be able to smack it back to Joe.

If you and Joe are playing a typical game of amateur tennis, points will be gained by one of you simply returning the ball over the net and waiting for the other to make a goof. The harder Joe tries to win — the more *oomph* he puts into each swing — the better his chances of hitting the net or sending the little green ball out of court, and the better your chances of winning the game.

And so, with this analogy, the world was given its first glimpse at the theoretical underpinning of index investing: Allow the other guys to swing away, trying for those cross-court shots, while you content yourself with simply not making mistakes. In almost every case, you'll eventually win.

Not everyone is as smart as you are: Most investors still fool themselves

Although there has been a veritable explosion in the popularity of index investing, especially since the mid-1990s with the advent of exchange-traded funds, the vast majority of investors are still trying to beat the markets — and consistently failing to do so — with actively managed portfolios. There are currently about 1,000 index funds (index mutual funds and exchange-traded funds) available to U.S. investors. That compares to about 6,500 actively managed mutual funds.

The total amount of dollars invested in index funds is about $1.5 trillion, compared to roughly $7.7 trillion in actively managed funds. That translates to about 84 percent of all fund investments being in actively managed funds. And these figures do not reflect the scores of investors who invest willy-nilly in individual stocks, often recommended by their brothers-in-law, who tend to do the worst of all.

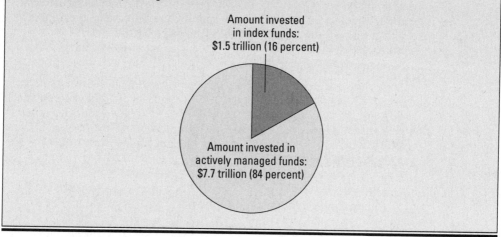

Amount invested in index funds: $1.5 trillion (16 percent)

Amount invested in actively managed funds: $7.7 trillion (84 percent)

Making gains by avoiding mistakes

What Ellis was talking about was investing success through indexing. That is, by "buying the market" rather than trying to cherry-pick securities, you may not profit from putting a big portion of your portfolio into the next Microsoft, but you won't lose by putting a big portion of your portfolio into the next Bear Stearns, either. Instead, you'll own modest positions in both — along with lots and lots of other stocks — and your portfolio will grow, steadily and surely, along with the market at large.

By investing in a fund that tracks an entire index (such as the S&P 500 or the Wilshire 5000), you'll be the guy on the tennis court who simply returns the ball. Your friend Joe, by picking individual stocks or hiring expensive fund managers to do it for him, will be trying to smack the ball within an inch of the net. You'll win. Trust me. You'll win.

More specifically, here's what makes index investing work:

- ✔ **Lower — much, much lower — management costs:** Those professional money managers who run most mutual funds don't come cheap. According to the latest numbers from Morningstar, the average actively run mutual fund now charges an annual management fee of 1.29 percent, and that figure does not include any of the hideous additional sales charges or loads charged by many of those funds. The typical index mutual fund, in contrast, charges a yearly management of 0.76 percent, and almost never any kind of sales charge. The average exchange-traded fund (almost all of which are index funds) carries an expense ratio of 0.56 percent. But many index funds can be had for expense ratios of less than 0.20 percent — less than 1/6 the management fee of an actively managed fund.

- ✔ **Lower everything costs:** It isn't only the management fees that matter. Because they simply mirror indexes, index funds don't have to pay for all kinds of research. They don't have to pay to trade securities. They don't do a lot of advertising. In sum total, Charles Ellis reckoned 30 years ago that the average index fund can be run for about 2 percent less a year than the average actively managed fund. Analysts today say that the 2 percent spread is still a pretty accurate number.

  Now, 2 percent may not sound like a lot, but think about it: If the market returns 10 percent a year over the next X years, your active-fund manager is going to have to get consistent annual returns of 12 percent for you, the poor little investor, in order for you to just break even. Your fund manager is going to have to beat the market by a full 20 percent a year, or you lose. How many fund managers can do that? *Very* few.

- ✔ **Gentler taxation:** Even if your active-fund manager does manage to beat the indexes by 20 percent a year, doing so will likely involve a lot of buying and selling of securities. That brings up taxes. As any owner of an actively managed fund can attest, those taxes can be burdensome. I discuss how burdensome, and talk more about the tax-cost differences between actively managed and index funds, in Chapter 3.

✔ **More honesty, more openness.** Want to avoid unpleasant surprises (in addition to unexpected year-end taxes)? When you invest in an index fund, you won't find your fund managers looking for *window dressing* in December — those last-minute purchases made for the sole purpose of helping the fund's annual returns look better than they actually were. And you won't be enticed to buy an index fund, as you may be enticed to buy an actively managed fund, by a salesman posing as a "financial planner" who stands to make a big, fat commission off you. Nor will you buy a fund with a name that implies one kind of investment (such as U.S. stocks) but invests in all kinds of other things (such as, say, Russian stocks). With index funds, you know exactly what you're getting. There's much more information on these kinds of nonmonetary-related benefits of index funds in Chapter 3.

✔ **Proven results:** Perhaps the greatest reason to buy index funds is that they have such an impressive track record. Maybe you don't want to know why indexing works. Guess what? You really don't have to. Is it important that you understand how the nerves at the ends of your fingers tell your brain to yank your hand away from a hot stove (the neurotransmitters and proteins and all that stuff)? No. The important thing is that the nerve endings and the brain *do* communicate. And with index funds, the important thing is that analysts who have compared and contrasted index fund performance to the performance of actively managed mutual funds generally come to the same conclusion: Index funds are superior.

In Chapter 3, I give you all the cold numbers — return rates from across the investment universe over different time frames — so you can clearly see that investing in index funds is a time-proven, successful strategy.

Not All Indexing Is Created Equal

Although this first chapter — and, in fact, this entire book — may read as something of an ode to index investing, rest assured that I'm not trying to sell you anything. In fact, your having bought this book indicates to me that you were probably sold on index investing long before you and I ever met. More than likely, what you're hoping to get out of *Index Investing For Dummies* are tips to become a better index investor. You won't be disappointed. I promise!

Although it's not rocket science, and it's certainly something you can do on your own, index investing does require some knowledge. Not all indexes are created equal, not all index funds are created equal, and mixing and matching various index funds is crucial to portfolio success. It helps, too, to understand your own financial situation and to pick the optimal index funds for *you.*

Picking your level of market exposure

Some index funds are based on huge indexes, with hundreds or even thousands of stocks or bonds, all across the board. For example, funds that are based on the very popular S&P 500 index give you exposure to 500 large stocks spread out among many industries. A fund such as the iShares Dow Jones U.S. Total Market gives you even a broader exposure to the markets. There are also index funds that in a flash can give you exposure to broad foreign stock markets or the entire U.S. bond market.

Some index funds are narrower, tracking indexes that capture only a sliver of the financial markets. Many of the newer exchange-traded funds fit into this category. Some may track certain industry sectors, such as energy or technology, or industry subsectors such as retail banking or home construction. Others may track certain very specific kinds of stocks, such as those that pay high dividends. An extreme example is the WisdomTree Japan SmallCap Dividend Fund, which tracks an index of small Japanese companies that pay high dividends.

In general, the larger the index tracked by the index fund (in other words, the more securities represented by the index), the greater the diversification and the less the risk to you — but also the less potential return.

Knowing that indexes have various recipes

Some index funds are based on traditional indexes, such as the S&P 500, which allot stocks to the index based on their relative size. But indexes can be formulated any number of ways, and some make a lot more sense than others. Rather popular these days, for example, are equal-weighted indexes (which may or may not make sense, depending on your objective) and fundamentally weighted indexes (which can make enormous sense or not, depending on the economic fundamentals employed). I discuss these options in-depth in Chapter 5 and then elaborate further throughout Part II.

Of utmost importance, regardless of how any index is formulated, is cost. Some index funds cost you very little — in the case of certain index offerings from Fidelity and Vanguard, as little as 0.07 percent a year. (It's even less for institutional investors, should you happen to own an insurance company or bank!) Other offerings from other index fund providers defeat a major benefit of indexing and wind up costing you 0.95 percent in management fees a year.

The entire Part II of this book is devoted to helping you pick the best of the best — in price and all other ways — from the 1,000 or so index funds available.

Selecting what works best for you

Ah, but even when I show you which index funds are better than others, you still have homework to do. That's because some index funds may be perfect for you, and others may be better for someone else. As with any other investment, you have to figure out your financial goals and your level of risk tolerance before you spend your money. The personal aspects of index investing are addressed in depth in Part III.

I am often asked, for example, whether I think a certain index fund is "good." Well, it often depends. For example, an index fund such as the Vanguard REIT ETF (VNQ), which gives exposure to the real estate industry, may make great sense for your one neighbor, the dentist, but little sense for another neighbor who is in the real estate business and already has much of his financial fate tied up in this one industry. The iShares Russell Microcap Index fund (IWC) may make great sense for someone who can justify adding volatility to his portfolio. For someone looking to edge toward more conservative investments, the iShares Lehman Aggregate Bond Fund (AGG) may be a much better choice.

The great news is that you have a wealth of choices among the truly good index funds, so chances are you can tailor the portfolio of your dreams without having to step outside the realm of index investing.

Becoming an Ultra-Savvy Index Investor

Picking the best index funds is a crucial part of being the best index investor you can be, for sure. But there's more to it than that. You also want to know how to mix and match your index funds for maximum diversification. If you want to include a few actively managed funds in your portfolio, you also want to know how to best mix and match those with your index funds. These are areas of discussion that I tackle in depth in the latter chapters of Part III.

You also discover there how to place your fund purchases in the right accounts, be they taxable accounts or tax-advantaged accounts, such as IRAs. The goal, despite your level of patriotism, is to keep your taxes as low as possible and, as a direct corollary, to boost your after-tax returns.

In Part IV, you read about the virtues of buying and holding, and how index funds are the perfect vehicles for a buy-and-hold strategy. Mind you, exchange-traded funds (nearly all of which are index funds) make for great tools if you want to day-trade. But I would suggest doing so only if you have nerves of steel, can take great chances, and are reconciled to losing money! A buy-and-hold strategy makes tremendously more sense, and I show you why.

Investing with realistic expectations

Studies show rather conclusively that long-term investors do much better in index funds than actively managed funds (see Chapter 3 for specifics). Even a rather lazy index investor, one who picks his indexes willy-nilly, is still very likely to wind up in the top 40 percent of investors after 10 years, and the top 20 percent after 20 years.

The truly savvy index investor, one who buys the lowest cost index funds and knows how to mix and match index funds for good diversification, can expect to be in the top 20 percent of all investors over the next 10 years, and the top 10 percent over the next 20 years. These are all ballpark estimates, of course.

A caveat: Index investors of any ilk will rarely be in the top 1 percent of investors, either in the short-run or the long-run. The truly remarkable returns are reserved for inside traders (those who don't wind up in jail); extremely lucky gamblers who bet on small positions and win (thereby avoiding living on the street); and (probably the smallest number) the true stock-picking geniuses, such as billionaire investor Warren Buffett (although Buffett himself has numerous times recommended indexing for most investors).

Becoming an enlightened (and just maybe rich!) index investor

So how to become the kind of savvy investor who will leave 90 percent of other investors in the dust? Read the remaining 300 pages of *Index Investing For Dummies*! Don't be afraid to change your thinking, or the way you've always invested before. Understand that market success — like spiritual enlightenment in the Buddhist tradition — can't be forced. It comes with time and patience, and often going with the flow.

In the Buddhist tradition, your patience and wisdom eventually allow you to become one with the entire universe. In index investing, patience and wisdom lead you to become one with the entire market. It's an exciting and potentially very rewarding journey that John Bogle first charted, and I look forward to taking you there!

Chapter 2

A Short History of the Index and Index Investing

In Chapter 1, I talk a bit about John Bogle, Vanguard, and the birth of the very first index fund. But just as McDonald's needed a cow before it could make a hamburger, and Picasso needed a canvas before he could paint the Mona Lisa, you need an index before you can make an index fund. I now invite you to join me on a trip back in time, back to the late 19th century, when Picasso, who did not actually paint the Mona Lisa (I was just testing you), was a mere lad, and Ronald McDonald wasn't even yet a glimmer in his parents' clownish eyes.

At that time, Charles Dow, a serious-looking, 40-something man with a bushy black beard and wide lapels, got it in his noggin that the world, which already had canvases and cows, needed an index.

The year was 1896. (Harvard historians tell us that nothing else happened that year.) The place was New York City. The time was . . . heck, I don't know.

The Dow Jones Industrial Average: Mother of All Indexes

The Dow Jones Industrial Average, or DJIA — often referred to simply as *the Dow* — is 113 years old as of this writing. That makes it the nation's longest-lived *index,* which is to say a standard measure of the stock market's performance. It's also an enormously popular index. Still.

In fact, any discussion of the financial markets on television or the Internet treats the latest rise or fall in the Dow much as The Weather Channel treats changes in the temperature: No report would be complete without it. Millions of people every day watch the ups and downs of Charles Dow's creation.

The mechanics of the oldest existing index

The T. Rex and brachiosaurus had already died off by the time Charles Dow and his bushy beard came along to give us the Dow Jones Industrial Average, but handheld calculators were still decades in the future, never mind the Excel spreadsheet. Financial indexes — like life itself — were perforce considerably simpler than they are today.

The Dow, for example, started with 12 big companies in 12 important industries of the time (cotton, leather, cattle feed, railroads, and such). The price of a single share of stock in each of these 12 companies was then added up on a piece of paper ($60^3/_8 + 52^5/_8 + 35^7/_8 + 45^1/_2$ and so on), and then the sum total was divided (long-hand, ouch) by 12. On May 26, 1896, the very first day the index was published, the sum of share prices was 491.28, which was divided by 12 to yield *40.94*. That was where the Dow first opened.

Long-lasting popularity

Had CNBC been around back in May, 1896, a very attractive young woman named Martha or Gertrude or Emmeline, with lots of makeup and wearing fashionable puffed sleeves and floral trimmings, would have smiled into the camera and said, "The Dow closed today at 40.94, neither up or down from yesterday's close, since — ha! ha! — the Dow didn't exist yesterday."

Today, the woman's name may be Sue or Becky or Cheng. Cheng can compare the Dow today not only to yesterday's average but to many yesterdays' averages. (She can then interview some balding, boring white guy in a Brooks Brothers suit, who will happily speculate on tomorrow's average.) But the Dow remains essentially the same beast it always was. Indexes such as the Dow, based simply on the price of the stocks that make up the index, divided by the number of stocks, are called *price-weighted* indexes.

Even though Cheng quotes one every 5 seconds, price-weighted indexes are, in many ways, as archaic as the name Emmeline.

Charles Dow: Creator of the index, founder of *The Wall Street Journal*

He was born on a farm in Connecticut in 1851 but had a strong aversion to dirt and manure. So as a very young man, without any formal education, Charles Dow began working as a reporter for various rags in southern New England. He gravitated to business reporting and, at age 29, headed to where the action was: the Big Apple. Granted, it wasn't all that big an apple in those days, but it was a heck of a lot bigger than anything in southern New England.

Dow found work at the Kiernan Wall Street Financial News Bureau, which hand-delivered handwritten financial news blurbs to New York bankers and brokers. After two years at Kiernan, Dow buddied up with a colleague, Edward Jones, and the two 30-something men spun off a competing news bureau called Dow, Jones & Company. They operated out of the

basement of a candy store, publishing a two-page summary of the day's financial news called the *Customers' Afternoon Letter*. It was in that "letter" that the Dow Jones Industrial Average first appeared in 1896.

The two-page flyer, within little time, evolved into a real newspaper called *The Wall Street Journal*, initially selling for two Indian-head pennies a copy. Today, the paper sells for $1.50 a pop. And just weeks prior to my sitting down to write this chapter, the venerable paper was taken over by Rupert Murdoch, the Australian-born financier famous for his crass and cheesy tabloids featuring "sexy sports girls" and up-to-the-minute coverage of the life of Paris Hilton.

One can only wonder what Connecticut farm boy Charles Dow, who never liked manure very much, would think.

Mama has a few shortcomings

Mind you, the Dow never was — if I may use a technical term — the cat's meow. After all, how can a mere dozen stocks represent the entire stock market? And then you add in the price-weighting, and what you have is, basically, cat dander. What's wrong with the way the Dow is weighted? Lots.

Index weightings

I have plenty to say later in this book about the way various indexes are formulated. But for now, I'll ask you to imagine an index with but two stocks, which we will call, for no particular reason, BAG and BOX. Suppose that BAG sells for $10 a share, and BOX sells for $50 a share. If this index were the Dow, the average would be the sum of BAG and BOX ($10 + $50 = $60) divided by the number of stocks in the index (2). Hence, the DJIA would be 30. Now suppose that BAG stock goes up a dollar to $11. You can see that using the same formula, the index will rise to ($11 + $50)/2 = 30.5. The index would be the very same — 30.5 — if BOX rose a dollar, from $50 to $51.

Do you see the problem yet? If BAG goes up a dollar (from $10 to $11) that represents a hefty 10 percent climb in value. If BOX goes up a dollar (from $50 to $51) that represents a climb in value of only 2 percent. Obviously, investors with equal holdings in BAG and BOX would be much, much better off if BAG goes up a dollar than if BOX goes up a dollar. Yet in both cases, the price-weighted index goes up by the same degree: 1.66 percent. So to the extent that an index is a measure of investors' (and the market's) success, the Dow can be a rather crappy measure.

Mother's little helpers

Largely because of these two serious shortcomings — the small number of securities in the Dow and the way it is weighted (although there are other shortcomings to consider later) — the Mother of All Indexes has given way to a number of "children," many of which are superior in a number of ways.

You'll recognize the names of many of these indexes: Wilshire, Morningstar, Lehman, MSCI, FTSE, Russell (hey, that's *my* name!). But the most popular of the post-Dow indexes, by far, is the Standard & Poor's 500 index, commonly known as the S&P 500 or simply *the S&P*. I describe the S&P briefly in the following pages and talk about it, and the other indexes mentioned here, more throughout the book.

The Dow Jones Industrial Average, 1896

When Charles Dow came up with his original index of 12 companies, the following names were as familiar to most Americans as Microsoft and McDonald's are today. Note that General Electric is the only one of the bunch still included in the index. All the others have since died out (such as the U.S. Leather Company); were busted up by (pre-Ronald Reagan) antitrust legislation (American Tobacco Company); or have since been swallowed by other corporations (United States Rubber Company, which became Uniroyal, which merged with B.F. Goodrich, which was eventually bought up by Michelin).

- American Cotton Oil Company
- American Sugar Company
- American Tobacco Company
- Chicago Gas Company
- Distilling & Cattle Feeding Company
- General Electric
- Laclede Gas Light Company
- National Lead Company
- North American Company (electric power)
- Tennessee Coal, Iron and Railroad Company
- United States Rubber Company
- U.S. Leather Company

The Dow Jones Industrial Average, today

The Dow dozen has since become the Dow 30, and you're undoubtedly familiar with most, if not all, of the large U.S. companies that you currently see on the list. The editors at *The Wall Street Journal* shake up the index once or twice every few years and will substitute one company for another. Presumably, their methodology involves more than flipping a coin, but only they are privy to what goes into the decision. The last changes prior to the publication of this book were the February, 2008 additions of Bank of America and Chevron, which replaced old-timers Altria Group (formerly Philip Morris) and Honeywell, and the September, 2008 addition of Kraft Foods to replace American International Group.

- ✓ 3M Corporation
- ✓ Alcoa
- ✓ American Express
- ✓ AT&T
- ✓ Bank of America
- ✓ Boeing
- ✓ Caterpillar
- ✓ Chevron
- ✓ CitiGroup
- ✓ Coca-Cola
- ✓ DuPont
- ✓ Exxon Mobil
- ✓ General Electric
- ✓ General Motors
- ✓ Hewlett-Packard
- ✓ Home Depot
- ✓ Intel Corp.
- ✓ International Business Machines
- ✓ Johnson & Johnson
- ✓ JPMorgan Chase
- ✓ Kraft Foods
- ✓ McDonald's
- ✓ Merck
- ✓ Microsoft
- ✓ Pfizer
- ✓ Procter and Gamble
- ✓ United Technologies
- ✓ Verizon Communications
- ✓ Wal-Mart Stores
- ✓ Walt Disney Co.

Over the years, indexes have come to serve as more than ways of measuring market performance. They have also become common benchmarks that serve to measure the performance of investment managers. And they have come to serve as the foundation for investments themselves — accessible to the investor through *index funds*. An index fund is simply a fund that tracks an index. *Track* is a somewhat fancy word for "ape." If, say, a DJIA index fund is true to its name, it will hold the very same stocks that make up the Dow.

When the inventor of the wheel did his (or her) thing, I'm sure that (s)he had no idea that the invention would one day serve to move millions of people in obnoxiously huge SUVs along the highways and byways of the modern world. When Charles Dow created the first index, I'm sure he had no idea that it would give birth not only to hundreds of indexes, but thousands of investment portfolios upon which millions of people would build their nest eggs!

The S&P 500: The Dow's Undisputed Number-One Son

The Standard & Poor's 500 (S&P 500, or simply *the S&P*) has become as popular with the media, and certainly within the investment world, as the Dow itself. It is clearly a better mousetrap where indexing serves as a measure of the market. It's also a better benchmark against which to measure the performance of investment managers. In fact, it's a superior index all-around than the Dow, but it is not perfect; no index is perfect.

Linear charts and logarithmic charts: What's the difference?

Either way you choose to view it, the long-term growth of the S&P 500 index has been quite impressive. If you look at a *linear* chart (see the first figure in this sidebar), the growth seems even more dramatic than it does on a *logarithmic* chart (shown in the second figure). The two kinds of charts simply use different lenses to view growth.

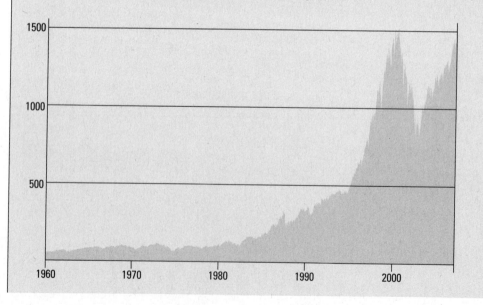

The linear chart measures *absolute* change in price over time. The S&P hardly seems to move up in the early years. That's because there weren't all that many dollars invested in the market. A rise or fall of 10 percent over a year equated to only a few extra bucks won or lost. A rise or fall of 10 percent in more recent days equated to many more bucks won or lost.

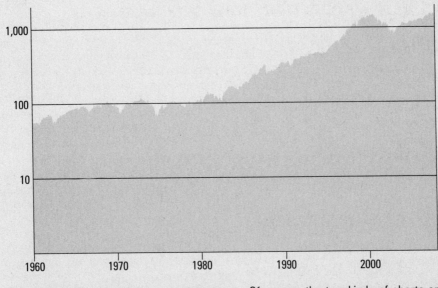

The logarithmic chart measures *percentage* change over time. A rise or fall in the S&P of 10 percent looks the same whether that 10 percent rise or fall occurred 50 years ago or yesterday.

Linear charts, in my mind, are fine for making short-term comparisons. Logarithmic charts, I believe, allow for a more accurate view when measuring performance over decades.

Of course, the two kinds of charts are often used and misused, depending on how the creator of the charts hopes to impress you. If I wanted you to invest in my product, for example, I would likely show you a linear chart when talking about return. I would prefer that you see a logarithmic chart when talking about volatility. It all stems from the very same data, but presentation is everything!

The S&P 500 was born in 1957, making it roughly the same age as the author of this book — old. Unlike the even older Dow, which today includes 30 stocks, the S&P 500 includes — surprise! surprise! — 500 stocks. Very much like the Dow, however, those stocks are predominantly large cap U.S. company stocks. *Large cap* means "large capitalization," which, on Wall Street, refers to a company worth at least $5 billion.

According to Standard & Poor's,

> *The 500 companies chosen for the S&P 500 Index are not the largest companies in terms of market value, but rather, tend to be leaders in important industries within the U.S. economy.*

In the case of certain companies, however, such as the $450 billion Exxon Mobil (the largest company on the list), market value alone would probably warrant a place on the list, even if oil were not such an important industry.

New generation, new mechanics

Unlike the Dow, which is price-weighted, the S&P 500 is an example of a *market value–weighted index.* That means that each stock's weight in the index is proportionate to its market value. Larger, more valuable companies (like Exxon Mobil and General Electric) are given a larger representation in the index than smaller companies (such as American Express and Walt Disney).

The S&P is also (as of 2005) a *float-weighted* index, which means that only those shares of stock that *float* — are available for public sale — are counted in the index. Some rather large companies, such as Berkshire Hathaway, have a good percentage of their stock tied up in private hands and, therefore, may never make it onto the S&P 500. In Chapter 5, and throughout Part II, I discuss how the ways in which various indexes are calculated may greatly affect any investments that track them.

In part because the S&P is so popular and has been around longer than just about all other indexes, its particular method of weighting its components is considered the most "normal" weighting method by most people in the finance industry. And indexes that work like the S&P, or somewhat like the S&P, are commonly called *traditional* indexes.

The S&P today (still) rules the indexing roost

There are *many* investments — both index mutual funds and exchange-traded funds — that track the S&P 500. In fact, there are far more funds that track the S&P 500 (both officially and unofficially) than any other index, including the Dow. According to industry figures, there is more money in index funds that track the S&P — index funds made up of the 500 S&P stocks — than in all other index funds combined!

The S&P is also, far and away, the most commonly used benchmark against which investment managers' performance is weighed. A successful investment manager will have "beaten the index" (meaning the S&P) for one, three, and five years running. Unsuccessful managers "fall behind the index." This is often a silly benchmark for success because large cap U.S. stocks do not represent the entire universe of investments. But it is what it is; lots of things in this world are silly.

As I explain in Chapter 4, the use and misuse of certain indexes (such as the S&P) as benchmarks serves to muddy the waters and often makes the value of index investing more difficult to see. I promise to unmuddy the waters to the best of my ability!

Beyond the Dow and the S&P

As great an improvement as the S&P was over the Dow, no one index can be all things to all people. That's why we have a plethora of indexes, many of which have come into being in the past several years. The silliness I refer to in the previous section can often be eradicated through the use of different indexes for different purposes.

Today, for example, we have indexes that measure collective returns among small cap stocks, value stocks, growth stocks, and stocks in certain industry sectors. I introduce these in Chapters 6 and 7. Other indexes measure returns and serve as appropriate benchmarks in fixed-income markets; I discuss these in Chapter 8. Yet other indexes measure performance and serve as good benchmarks in commodity and real estate markets; see Chapter 9. And there are all kinds of indexes that track markets overseas, too — Chapter 7 offers a sampling.

For just about any index, you can buy a fund today that tracks it. That's especially true since the advent of exchange-traded funds, which in the past several years alone have tripled the number of index funds available. I introduce exchange-traded funds, and fully explain the differences between exchange-traded funds and mutual funds, in Chapter 5.

Indexes of various shapes and sizes

Within each broad category of indexes (large stocks, small stocks, bonds), there are numerous variations of indexes, formulated in numerous fashions to meet different goals. The price weighting of the Dow and the market value weighting of the S&P are only two methods among many for formulating indexes. There are also *equal-weighted* indexes, in which all components affect the index to the same degree. There are *fundamental-weighted* indexes, in which individual components may be given importance by any number of financial considerations, including growth rate or dividend yield. And there are even now some indexes that change so often that they may qualify as *actively managed* indexes. Talk about an oxymoron!

Index investing's icons

Years and years after educated folk realized that the earth was round, most of the world still insisted it was flat. It took Copernicus, Galileo, Magellan, and Columbus to prove otherwise. Today, although most educated folk realize that index investing works, and works well, there are still plenty and plenty of flat-earthers out there. With any luck, Russell Wild's *Index Investing For Dummies* may cause a few of the flat-earthers to see the light. But there have certainly been a few well-read authors and volumes on index investing long before this book was published, or even before this author had ever heard of index investing.

As the writings and experiences of Copernicus, Galileo, Magellan, and Columbus were to the eventual acceptance by most that the earth is round, the writings of Bogle, Malkiel, Samuelson, and Ellis have been similarly powerful in the promotion of index investing.

✔ **John Bogle:** Founder of Vanguard Investments. Wrote his first paper on index investing while a student at Princeton University, from which he graduated in 1951. Bogle has since written, and continues to write, many articles and books on the subject. Followers of index investing sometimes call themselves *Bogleheads,* a term of endearment. Bogle rhymes with *mogul.*

✔ **Burton G. Malkiel:** Princeton University professor. He wrote the book *A Random Walk Down Wall Street* (Norton, 1973), which has become the closest thing index investing has to a bible. Here's a quote from that book: "This complexity suggests that there is no longer any room for the individual investor in today's institutionalized markets. Nothing could be farther from the truth. You can do as well as the experts — perhaps even better."

✔ **Paul Samuelson:** Economist. Nobel Prize winner. Wrote *Economics,* the classic textbook (updated many times) that I used in college. He also wrote "Challenge to Judgment," an article that appeared in *The Journal of Portfolio Management* in the fall of 1974. At that time, Samuelson wrote: "[A]t the least, some large foundation [should] set up an in-house portfolio that tracks the S&P 500 Index — if only for the purpose of setting up a naive model against which their in-house gunslingers can measure their prowess . . . ."

✔ **Charles D. Ellis:** Investment analyst. Wrote the seminal article "The Loser's Game," which appeared in the *Financial Analysts Journal,* July/August 1975. Ellis conducted the first widely covered study on index investing. Here was Ellis's conclusion from that study: "The investment management business is built upon a simple and basic belief: Professional managers can beat the market. That premise appears to be false." The study has been replicated many times.

Indexes also vary by the numbers of companies included (30 for the Dow, 500 for the S&P, 5,000 for the Wilshire 5000, and so on); by the size (capitalization) of the average company in the index; or by how often the index is changed.

I discuss these differences in some depth — and explain how they may affect an index investor's risk and potential return — in Part II. Also covered, of course, will be the ways to find the best index funds to match a particular index.

Indexing gone amok?

In case you're wondering, I am an advocate of index investing and am an index investor myself! That being said, some of the newer indexes and index funds are, to put it bluntly, just plain dumb. I'm talking primarily about indexes that were whipped up specifically so that an investment vehicle (usually an exchange-traded fund) could be sold that would track that specific index. Smart for the seller. Often dumb for the buyer/investor.

As I detail in the next chapter, most index investors are going to be more successful than most non-index investors. But I will qualify this by saying that not all index investing is something to write home about.

Growing Numbers of Fund Companies, More and More Indexing Options

I've talked in this chapter about the history of indexing, how indexes have gotten more sophisticated and varied over the years, and how the number of indexes used by financial professionals has grown from a handful to an Astrodome-full. No surprise, then, that the number of companies offering index funds has exploded as well.

Indexing goes institutional

Prior to the mid-1970s, the only way you could possibly be in index investor was to buy, say, all 500 stocks of the S&P 500 yourself — not an easy proposition at all!

American National Bank in Chicago and Wells Fargo founded the very first index funds, but they were available only to institutional investors, and even among those, there was little interest.

In 1975, John Bogle started Vanguard Investments and offered the first index fund — the First Index Investment Trust (which mirrored the S&P 500) — to the general public.

As Bogle often points out in his writing and speeches, Fidelity Investments Chairman Edward C. Johnson III gave little indication that his brokerage house would ever follow suit. "I can't believe," Johnson told the press, "that the great mass of investors are [sic] going to be satisfied with just receiving average returns. The name of the game is to be the best."

But that attitude didn't last very long — not after Bogle's baby started to appear successful, both in grabbing customers and in showing some rather impressive returns.

Eating crow, and creating new funds

Of course, Fidelity wound up offering not only one index fund but, starting in 1988, many index funds. So did T. Rowe Price, starting in 1990. And Charles Schwab, in 1991. And nearly every other major brokerage house in the world since that time has added at least an index fund or two.

There are now roughly 300 index mutual funds available from dozens of mutual fund companies. And there are about 700 exchange-traded funds available from multiple companies, including Vanguard, Barclays Global Investors (which purchased Wells Fargo indexing operations), and State Street Global Advisors.

Another big player on the indexing scene, Dimensional Fund Advisors (DFA), was started by two of the same men — David Booth and Rex Sinquefield — who built the very first index funds in the early 1970s for American National Bank and Wells Fargo.

In Chapter 10, I offer specific recommendations for where and how to shop for index products among so many sellers.

The five largest index funds

All told, a cool $1.5 trillion is now invested in about 1,000 index funds. But some of those index funds are much larger than others. The five largest index funds alone account for nearly one-fifth of all the money invested in index funds.

Fund	Mutual Fund or ETF?	Purveyor	Index of . . .	Net Assets
SPDR Trust Series 1	ETF	State Street Global Advisors (SSgA)	Large U.S. stocks	$85 billion
Vanguard 500 Index	Mutual fund	Vanguard Investments	Large U.S. stocks	$60 billion
Vanguard Total Stock Market Index	Mutual fund	Vanguard Investments	The entire U.S. stock market	$49 billion
iShares MSCI EAFE Index	ETF	Barclays	Foreign stocks in developed nations	$48 billion
Vanguard Total Bond Index	Mutual fund	Vanguard Investments	The entire U.S. bond market	$30 billion

Chapter 3

Why Indexing Works — and Works So Darned Well

In This Chapter

▶ Appreciating a proven track record of success

▶ Relishing the lowest costs in the industry

▶ Adding up numerous other fringe benefits

▶ Spotting active management's lethal flaws

*I*f you've been to enough financial luncheons, you know that the quality of the meal served has nothing to do with the quality of the product or service being sold. In fact, the opposite is true. Attend a lunchtime lecture given by a salesman hawking high-priced variable annuities of very dubious financial value, and you can expect veal cheeks with herb mashed potatoes, onion–portobello confit, and grilled asparagus in merlot sauce. Attend a lunchtime lecture given by someone selling index funds, and you'll get a hamburger with ketchup, and fries.

Index funds are the better mousetrap and, as such, don't need to be sold. Their track record alone moves them off the shelves. In addition, the people who sell them don't make a large enough margin to afford to serve you veal cheeks — whatever veal cheeks are. Index fund providers usually charge you pennies, or at most dimes, in comparison to the dollars charged by the providers of actively managed funds.

In this chapter, I discuss the very impressive track records of index funds, and I explain how those track records were achieved. Yes, the low cost has very much to do with it.

Lunch, if you're hungry, will be served in 20 minutes.

Clocking Impressive Returns, Year after Year

Measuring the success of index funds is not a precise science. In fact, it is tricky business indeed. Different studies show different results. But we're talking mostly a matter of degrees here. The vast majority of studies that compare active investing to passive (index) investing — and there have been many — come to the same conclusion: Indexing wins hands down.

Of all the number-crunchers in the financial world, those at Morningstar arguably have the most experience. Morningstar is also an independent third party: It does produce indexes, but it sells neither index funds nor actively managed funds. Following are the stats that Morningstar's analysts give as the overall track record for index funds versus actively managed funds over the past 5 and 15 years.

Note that the term *index funds* includes both mutual funds and exchange-traded funds. All figures are current as of December 31, 2007.

Intermediate-term index fund performance results: Good!

Per Morningstar, here are the five-year performance results:

- ✔ Overall average yearly return of all actively managed funds, past five years: **11.83 percent**

- ✔ Overall average yearly return of all index funds, past five years: **13.61 percent**

- ✔ Percent by which the index funds have outshined the actively managed funds in the past five years: **15.0 percent**

- ✔ Value today of $10,000 invested in the average actively managed fund five years ago: **$17,490**

- ✔ Value today of $10,000 invested in the average index fund five years ago: **$18,923**

- ✔ Extra money in the pocket of the index investor, per $10,000 invested, after five years: **$1,433**

Studies, studies, and more studies

One study says that index funds beat actively managed funds 60 percent of the time. Another study says 70 percent of the time. And a third study says 95 percent of the time. Why the huge discrepancies? I found a pretty good answer in the academic *Journal of Financial Planning*, in the November 2007 article "Spotlighting Common Methodological Biases in Active-Vs.-Passive Studies" by David M. Blanchett and Craig L. Israelsen.

Here are why the studies can and do differ, according to the two researchers:

- *Survivorship bias.* How do we account for funds that existed, say, 20 years ago, but have since folded? There are plenty of them out there. Do you pretend they never existed, or leave them out of the study altogether?

- *Weightings.* Do we give each active fund equal measure, or do the funds with more assets count more in determining the average?

- *Share differences.* Some mutual funds come in different share classes (retail, institutional, and so on) with different expense ratios and performance figures. Do we use one share class (which one?) or combine all of them?

- *Index choices.* Which indexes are we picking to match up against the actively managed funds? As I explain throughout this book, indexes vary greatly, as do their performance records.

- *Time frame.* Even a few days' difference in when a study starts and stops can make for large differences in results.

But don't sweat all this small stuff, conclude the authors. Regardless of methodology, most studies still come to the same conclusion: Indexing rocks. "[T]he research conducted for this paper suggests that the possibility of consistently superior active management is the exception, not the rule, and that advisors [this is a journal written for financial advisors] should take a buyer-beware approach when selecting active management for client portfolios," write the authors.

Longer-term index fund performance results: Very good!

Per Morningstar, here are the 15-year performance results:

- Overall average yearly return of all actively managed funds, past 15 years: **7.76 percent**

- Overall average yearly return of all index funds, past 15 years: **9.70 percent**

- Percent by which the index funds have outshined the actively managed funds in the past 15 years: **25 percent**

> ✔ Value today of $10,000 invested in the average actively managed fund 15 years ago: **$30,068**
>
> ✔ Value today of $10,000 invested in the average index fund 15 years ago: **$40,010**
>
> ✔ Extra money in the pocket of the index investor, per $10,000 invested, after 15 years: **$9,942**

Mind you, these are all *pre-tax* figures. Index funds are generally much gentler than actively managed funds in regard to taxes. So after taxes, the differences shown would tend to be much greater (depending on your tax bracket). Again, the laurels go to index funds. The darts go to actively managed funds.

Intrigued?

The reasons for the success of index investing — the heart, really, of why you want to be an index investor — are numerous and varied.

Indexing for Optimal Portfolio Leanness and Meanness

Any discussion of why indexing works must start with the low costs.

Conversely, any discussion of active investing must start with the high costs. Feeding veal cheeks and asparagus in merlot sauce to all those potential customers doesn't come cheap!

I begin now an in-depth discussion of the cost factors and other factors, such as transparency, tax efficiency, and cash drag, that make indexing so logical, so profitable, so sweet.

Keeping your costs to a minimum

Managers of index funds aren't attempting to beat the market by picking cherries or market timing. There is no pretense (yes, pretense, for that's largely what it is) that they know better than anyone else which way the market winds are blowing, or which company stocks will do better in that market. As such, they have less work to do than the managers of active mutual funds. They therefore can charge you a lot less — and they do.

According to 2008 figures from Morningstar, the average actively run mutual fund now charges a yearly management fee of 1.29 percent, and that does not include any additional sales charges or loads, which many actively managed funds carry. The average index mutual fund charges a yearly management fee of 0.76 percent, and the average exchange-traded fund (nearly all of which are index funds) carries an expense ratio of 0.56. Many index funds impose yearly expense ratios much lower — in a good number of cases, less than 0.10 percent.

What does that mean over the life of an investment? *A lot.* All things being equal, if you plunk $10,000 into a fund with gross (pre-expense) returns of 10 percent a year and an expense ratio of 1.29 percent, and that same amount into a fund with a similar gross return that charges 0.20 percent, after 20 years, you'll have $53,136 in the more expensive fund versus $64,870 in the less expensive. In other words (or numbers), the less expensive fund, due partly to the miracle of compound interest, will give you, over two decades, a total greater return of $11,734 on your original investment of $10,000!

Is your actively run mutual fund — gulp! — paying for strippers?

In March 2008, the Securities and Exchange Commission received settlement charges from mutual fund giant Fidelity Investments and from Jefferies & Co., a New York–based brokerage firm. The SEC alleged that Fidelity managers had gotten kickbacks from Jefferies in the form of concert tickets, bottles of wine, travel deals, and even lavish parties with strippers. In exchange for these kickbacks, the Fidelity managers allegedly allowed Jefferies brokers to trade securities held in Fidelity funds — and Fidelity paid a rather generous fee for Jefferies to place those trades.

"This case demonstrates again the SEC's commitment to preventing conflicts of interest from compromising the integrity of the markets," said David P. Bergers, an SEC official, in an SEC press release. "Investment advisers must insist that brokerage firms compete for mutual fund business based on their ability to deliver best execution, not based on personal considerations like event tickets."

In other words, if you owned a Fidelity mutual fund, you were, according to the SEC allegations, indirectly paying for the manager's receipt of all kinds of goodies. Every time Fidelity managers placed a trade, you were potentially scalped. Fidelity consented to the SEC order and paid the fines without admitting or denying the findings.

Mind you, index fund managers also on occasion buy and sell securities — but very infrequently. It is doubtful that the manager of an index fund would receive many invitations to take a trip to Bermuda, attend the Super Bowl, or — if the manager were a single guy — be entertained by dancing naked women.

But it isn't only management fees that are kept to a minimum by the miracle of indexing. There are also trading costs incurred by actively run mutual funds. You never know how much those trading costs are — unlike the management fee, they appear nowhere in the prospectus — but they can be substantial. I'm talking about the *spread,* or the difference between the ask price and the bid price. And I'm talking about fees paid to place trades on any exchange. These are a sad part of doing business on Wall Street, and a mutual fund manager can't avoid the spread or trading fees much more than you can. So that $11,734 difference could turn out to be even larger.

With all the extra fees and costs of active management, coming out ahead of the indexes is akin to winning a race while running in lead boots!

Making your financial life more predictable

If you have but one stock in your portfolio — even a purportedly blue chip, multibillion-dollar darling — then you are taking, in my mind, a huge, unnecessary risk. Remember the venerable Ford Motor Company, trading at nearly $40 a share in 1999? As I write this book, in early 2008, it's trading at around $5.50 (a loss of 86 percent). Then, of course, there's Enron, which went from almost $90 a share to $0 in less time than it takes to say "bankruptcy."

Consider some other companies that were almighty blue chips when you were a kid whose stock is now worth doodly-squat or less: Bethlehem Steel (right around the corner from me), Dow Corning, Eastman Kodak, Sears, Union Carbide, and U.S. Steel. As I'm writing this chapter, a good number of large and powerful finance and home-construction companies have lost two-thirds or more of their value with the decline in real estate prices and the subprime mortgage fiasco.

While index investing can be volatile (how volatile depends on the particular index you track), it has never been nearly as volatile as investing in individual stocks. In the past 50 years, the worst year *ever* for the S&P 500 — an index of America's 500 most influential companies — was 1974, when it clocked a depressing but not devastating return of –26.5. The next year, 1975, it recaptured the entire loss. The relatively recent bear market of 2000, 2001, and 2002 was the only three consecutive years the S&P has declined since the Great Depression. That was followed by three very cheery years.

Of course, any fund whatsoever, either a mutual fund or an exchange-traded fund, will tend to have lower volatility (both downside and upside) than an individual stock. But index funds generally boast the greatest diversification (typically dozens if not hundreds of individual securities) for the smoothest possible ride to riches.

Allowing different — and distinct — baskets for your eggs

If you own two or more mutual funds or exchange-traded funds, you get more diversification than you do by owning just one fund . . . maybe. The problem with many mutual funds is that you aren't always sure what you're buying, and the fund may be subject to *style drift*. That means the manager may be big on large U.S. company stocks one year and something entirely different (say, mid cap stocks) the next year. That drift can result in unfortunate overlap between your various funds — funds that you thought, when you bought them, were separate and distinct.

When the Internet bubble burst in 2000, several funds in the high-flying mutual fund company Janus were simultaneously trounced. It turned out that despite having different names and descriptions, they were holding not only similar stocks but, in many cases, the very same stocks.

With index funds, it becomes much easier to buy tight and distinct "baskets" in which to store your financial "eggs." Buy one index fund that focuses on, say, large growth stocks, and another that focuses on small value stocks, and you know you're getting diversification — a mix of investments that includes some that zig while others zag — and not a lot of overlap.

There is perhaps no better way to diversify and protect your investments than with index funds.

Smacking down Uncle Sam's cut

All index funds, and especially exchange-traded funds, tend to be very tax efficient. Because they do little securities trading, there is rarely a capital gains tax to pay unless you personally happen to sell shares at a greater price than you purchased them. With actively run mutual funds, it's a whole other story. Not only do securities trade within the funds, but they often trade like confetti in the wind. That leads to potential short-term capital gains, which are taxed at the same rate as normal income tax, usually much higher than long-term capitals gains. (*Long-term* generally refers to securities held more than one year.)

Even worse, as a holder of shares of an actively run mutual fund, you may be subject to capital gains earned within the fund even if your shares have decreased in price and even if you personally have done no trading. A lot of mutual fund investors were stung badly at the onset of the bear market of 2000–2002. Not only did their investments sink, but to add insult to injury, they had to pay capital gains tax on profits made by the fund before they even bought into it!

Eliminating cash drag

One rather insidious cost to active management shows up neither on the fund prospectus nor on your tax forms. It is called *cash drag*. In order to buy and sell when he thinks the market is hot or cold, and in order to grab those shares of ABC Corporation at what he sees as the opportune moment, Mr. Active Fund Manager needs cash, and sometimes lots of it. That is why actively managed funds must have relatively large wads of cash sitting around.

According to the latest figures from Morningstar, the average index fund hordes 5.4 percent of its assets in cash. The average actively managed fund hordes 7.6 percent. In other words, if you have $100,000 invested in the average index fund, $5,400 will be in cash at most times. If you have that same amount invested in the average actively managed funds, you'll have $7,600 sitting idly in cash.

How much does that extra $2,200 — or 2.2 percent of your portfolio — drag down your long-term performance? Not to a huge degree, but enough to make some difference. And in some cases, an actively managed fund may well have much more than the average 7.6 percent of assets in cash. I've seen some cases where the cash reserve is as much as one-third of the fund assets. That can create serious cash drag, costing you plenty over time.

A caveat: When the market tanks, you want as much of your nest egg in cash as possible. For that reason, cash drag can be an asset, and actively managed funds often do better in times of market crisis. But I don't see that as a plus, per se, for actively managed funds. Why pay some clown 2 percent a year to hold your cash?! If you need the kind of portfolio protection that cash provides, keep your cash in a money-market account or short-term CD and earn a little on it. Keep your long-term money in funds that keep your money gainfully *invested* — such as index funds.

Assuring greater transparency

Want to avoid unpleasant surprises (in addition to unexpected year-end taxes)? Then you want index funds. With index funds, you won't find the notorious *12-B fees* that enrich the industry and allow mutual fund companies to charge you, the shareholder, for their marketing and advertising. You won't find fund managers looking for *window dressing* in December — those last-minute purchases made for the sole purpose of making the fund's annual returns look better than they actually were. And you won't be enticed to buy an index fund, as you may be enticed to buy an actively managed fund, by a salesman posing as a "financial planner" who stands to make a big, fat commission off you.

With index funds, you always know exactly what you're getting, and you know what you're paying for it. People in the finance world call that *transparency*, and it is a very attractive benefit of indexing.

Theoretical and Real-World Problems with Trying to Beat the Market

Okay, okay, perhaps you're saying to yourself now, actively managed funds are more expensive than index funds, and they result in higher taxes and all that. But still, there certainly are *some* managers out there who are so darned smart that whatever they charge is worth it — whatever shortcomings active management has, they are worth it.

Well, maybe . . .

Granted, some active fund managers have rather impressive track records at beating the markets. There are, alas, very few of them. And how do you find these rock stars of finance? Just as many studies that show the superiority of index investing show that active managers with impressive past performance often show lackluster performance in latter years.

(True, index funds may also do very well in one year and terrible the next, but they don't have high-priced managers who are allegedly there to see that kind of thing doesn't happen.)

Heck, as I'm writing this chapter, three months into 2008 — a terrible time for most markets — I thought I would call mutual fund analyst Morningstar just to see how a few of last year's top-performing mutual funds were doing this year. Ready for some depressing numbers? See Table 3-1.

Table 3-1	How 2007's Top-Performing Mutual Funds Were Performing Two Months Later	
Name of Actively Run Mutual Fund	*Overall 2007 Return*	*Year-to-Date Return, March 5, 2008*
AIM China A	74.94%	−19.23%
Matthews India	64.13%	−19.93%
Fidelity Select Energy Service	55.21%	−47.41%
Nicholas Applegate Emerging Markets	50.71%	−8.60%

There are a number of reasons why active management, although it appears great in theory (*do your homework, and you'll find great buys in the market!*), usually flops in reality. In fact, the theory behind active management — that buying securities is like buying a used car; kick the tires and you'll get those great buys — just doesn't make much sense. Securities are *not* used cars. The New York Stock Exchange (NYSE) and the NASDAQ bear very little resemblance to Bob's Formerly Owned Vehicles.

In the one case (honk honk), you may be able to walk onto the used car lot, check out all 500 cars, and, if you really know cars, buy the one that has been underpriced by the market. You drive home happy. The car lasts you for years. All is good. In the other case, you find a stock that you think is underpriced. You buy it. But in order for you to be happy, the price of the stock has to rise . . . more than the market at large. That's when you find out that the stock you thought was underpriced was perhaps right-priced — or overpriced.

As just about anyone who has tried active management for long enough (oh, yes, yes, that includes me) can attest, if you kick the tires repeatedly, all you're likely to get are sore feet. If you try to get the NYSE or NASDAQ to throw in free mats, you're only going to assure yourself that you'll be driving home in a lemon.

The average investor is very smart and educated

Here, in a nutshell, is why active management is so often a dud, and investing is nothing like buying a used car: All the tires have already been kicked. Numerous times. Securities are not used cars, in that their purchase and sale is ongoing, and your quest to get a better deal than everyone else involves some very, very smart and talented everyone elses.

A strange paradox

Index investing works because the financial markets are quite *efficient*. That means that there are many buyers and sellers, and information flows rather freely, so getting a better deal on a stock than the next guy is next to impossible. Oddly enough, if *everyone* indexed, the market would no longer be efficient, and indexing would no longer work. We indexers NEED active investors who are constantly crunching numbers to make certain that stocks buy and sell at rational prices.

Let me explain.

Suppose you find a fund manager with umpteen degrees, a mind for math, and a deep knowledge of the markets. That manager crunches numbers till the cows come home ("kicking tires"), and he comes up with what he sees as a good stock to buy for your portfolio. He buys that stock. Instead of going up, the stock goes down, as often happens with active management. Can you imagine what possibly went wrong?

Consider where your alleged knight-in-Brooks-Brothers bought the particular "can't lose" stock from. He went to the NASDAQ or to the New York Stock Exchange, and he placed an order. And someone somewhere, through the market, sold him that stock. Why did the seller sell? Probably because he thought the stock was going down, or at least wasn't going to go up as much as other stocks. And — here's the catch — that seller is, in all likelihood, every bit as educated and smart as *your* guy.

In fact, the vast majority of stocks are bought and sold by very highly paid and educated professional fund managers, endowment managers, insurance company and pension managers, and the like. These are, by and large, people who know their stuff. These are no financial fools.

But whenever one of these Brooks Brothers knights is buying, another is selling. When one is selling, another is buying. What I'm describing is known in financial circles as an *efficient* market. There's a lot of knowledge out there, shared more or less equally among potential buyers and sellers. It is extremely hard to get a really good deal.

If you are inclined to pick stocks on your own, I encourage you to ask yourself this one question before sinking part of your life savings into any individual security: *If I buy that stock, someone will be selling it. Why would that someone (very likely a professional trader) be selling — and what makes me think that I'm smarter than he is?* Unless you have a very good answer to that question, you should think twice before trying to beat the market.

Market rigging is rampant

Of course, if the markets were all efficient and the playing field were completely level, you'd have a 50/50 chance of beating the market by picking your own stocks. But I don't believe the playing field is entirely level. Neither you nor the typical professional buyer on Wall Street has a particular advantage — but others do. True "insider" trading, which is illegal, is probably not all that common. But there is a boatload of quasi-insider trading going on out there that makes it very difficult for the little guy, or even the not-so-little guy, to come out ahead.

Consider, for example, two studies:

- ✔ Big executives may donate gifts of company stock to their own family foundations — and get tax deductions for doing so. Research by David Yermack, a finance professor at New York University, found that such donations have an astonishing way of being made just before sharp drops in the company's stock price. In fact, 151 such gifts of more than $1 million were made between mid-2003 and the end of 2005, and stock prices fell relative to the market in about 60 percent of the cases.

- ✔ U.S. senators seem to do as well at market timing as corporate executives. Alan Ziobrowski, a professor at Georgia State University, examined the personal stock portfolios of the top U.S. politicians and found that they tended to outperform the market by 12 percent a year. Most stocks bought by senators — seemingly average stocks before they were purchased — somehow outperformed the market by nearly 29 percent the calendar year after being purchased by the senators. The eight-year study, released in 2004, also found that the high-flying stocks somehow returned to normal after leaving the senators' portfolios.

Moral of story: Buy index funds, and you won't need to worry about certain securities being bought and sold by those in the know, whether captains of industry or Washington elite. One stock may be inflated by their shenanigans; another stock may be deflated. You won't care, because you'll own them both — and lots of others, to boot.

Imitation is the greatest form of flattery

Suppose you buy into an actively managed mutual fund, pay a boatload of cash for the honor of doing so, and then find out that the managers are really indexing the vast majority of your money. In other words, they are running a *closet index fund,* putting your dollars exactly where they would be if you had put them in a real index fund, but charging you two, three, or four times as much. It happens all the time, according to Yale University researchers Martijn Cremers and Antti Petajisto. In fact, a study they did in 2007 came to the startling conclusion that nearly 30 percent of all "actively managed" mutual funds hug the indexes so closely that you may as well be investing in a real index fund.

Why do so many active fund managers hug the indexes? Because indexing works! Why don't they just call their funds index funds? Because they make more money off you by pretending to be active managers!

How do you avoid buying into a closet index fund? If you know what to look for, avoiding this common rip-off isn't all that hard to do. I describe how in Chapter 13.

Chapter 4

Why Everyone Isn't Indexing

An empty head is not really empty; it is stuffed with rubbish. Hence the difficulty of forcing anything into an empty head.

—Eric Hoffer, *The True Believer*

I see NOTHING. I know NOTHING.

—Sergeant Schultz, *Hogan's Heroes*

In 1951, Eric Hoffer, a manual laborer from San Francisco with no formal education, wrote a book that was to become a highly acclaimed classic, both in academia and elsewhere. The book was entitled *The True Believer*. It attempted to explain why large groups of people, even seemingly very smart people, can sometimes do really dumb things.

I'm convinced that if Hoffer were alive today and writing a new edition, there would be at least one chapter devoted to active investing and active investors.

If you know Hoffer, you know that he spends a lot of time decrying the ridiculous thinking (alleged thinking) of fascists. Mind you, I am *not* comparing followers of active investing to people who wear knee-high boots and goose-step in the streets! Active investors — those who choose active mutual funds or try to actively trade stocks on their own — aren't nearly *that* crazy, or dangerous. But they can similarly be subject to delusional thinking and gross illogic. And they can also be highly susceptible to propaganda and manipulation.

I hope I'm not sounding preachy or overzealous (or plum out of my mind), but given the enormous amount of evidence in favor of index investing (see Chapter 3), I find it hard to come to any other conclusion but that active investors — *who outnumber index investors by roughly 5:1* — are often dizzy and confused, or manipulated beyond their senses.

Buy low! Sell high! Beat the market! Sieg heil! "Booyah," as *Mad Money*'s Jim Cramer likes to shout into the camera, as he rolls up his sleeves and touts the stock of the hour.

In this chapter, I explain why and how and by whom many followers of active investing are easily manipulated, and how that manipulation costs them a ton of money.

Booyah!

Caveat: Not ALL active investing is fruity or manipulative or a rip-off — just most of it.

Booyah!

In fact, in Chapter 13, I talk about how active and passive investing can be fruitfully combined. Active investing must be done with extreme caution because it is most often a losing proposition. In terms of overall risk versus return over the long run, it can't hold a candle to index investing.

Booyah!

Worshipping Wall Street

Man is the only creature that strives to surpass himself, and yearns for the impossible.

—Eric Hoffer

With roughly $7.7 trillion invested in actively managed mutual funds — with the average fund charging clients 1.29 percent a year — that gig alone is earning Wall Street more than the GDP of many smaller nations. Add to that the enormous amount of money held at places the likes of Smith Barney and Merrill Lynch and a gadzillion smaller investment advisory firms where commissioned stock brokers call themselves financial planners. At places like these, money is not made by making money *for* clients; it's made by skimming money *from* clients. The more they make, the more you lose.

In total, we find a huge industry — both mutual funds and brokerage houses that actively trade securities — that is built in good measure on the lay public's ignorance. If everyone knew and truly understood the benefits of index investing, Wall Street would very likely morph into something completely different, and the money shows on television would go the way of *Mr. Ed* and *The Munsters.*

As Table 4-1 shows, the differences between actively managed funds and index funds are not hard to see.

Table 4-1	Comparing Index Investing to Active Investing	
	Active Investing	*Index Investing*
Goal	To beat the markets	To match the markets
Number of funds	About 6,500	About 1,000
Money invested in those funds	7.7 trillion	1.5 trillion
Average expense ratio	1.29 percent	0.76 percent
Average return, past 15 years	7.7 percent	9.7 percent
Who promotes the strategy?	Most brokerage houses, commissioned stockbrokers, the gee-whiz financial media, Jim (*Mad Money*) Cramer	The vast majority of academics, many fee-only (non-commissioned) financial planners, Warren Buffett, Russell Wild

With this kind of information readily available, brokerage houses and mutual fund companies must work to maintain the public's ignorance and to ensure the continuation of misconceptions and doubt. Toward that end, they have developed some very slick tricks over the years.

Hiding the fees on financial statements

I see it time and time again . . . A new client comes to me with a "feeling'" that his or her portfolio hasn't been doing especially well. I ask to see the broker's portfolio reports. Here's what I see:

- ✔ A stack of paper, including a detailed list of holdings with the historical returns and historical standard deviations of each holding.

- ✔ Graphs and charts of all shapes and colors showing portfolio returns versus the returns of various indexes over the years.

- ✔ Page after page of cost bases and time-weighted total returns for your portfolio (had your portfolio, such as it is today, been in place five years ago) versus the S&P 500.

In other words, what they give you is a lot of useless and practically meaning-less crap.

I'm not exaggerating.

In the small print of an actual Smith Barney quarterly review report that is sitting on my lap as I type, it says the following:

> *All rates of return on this page are presented before the deduction of management fees.*

Huh? In other words, you have no idea what your *real* rate of return is after paying Smith Barney's fees. And how much are those fees? *Nowhere* in the entire report can you find them, except perhaps on a line that mysteriously tabulates "Contributions/Withdrawals/Fees" as a single item. This purposeful subterfuge has been going on for years and years, and how they get away with it, I have no idea. It amazes and perplexes me that neither the Securities and Exchange Commission nor the Financial Industry Regulatory Authority clamps down on this nonsense.

Furthermore, when you call the Smith Barney broker (as I have asked a number of clients to do, and as I've sometimes done myself) to ask for your fees, you get a mouthful of tuna fish and a few *I'll-have-to-get-back-to-you-on-that*s. Good luck getting a straightforward answer! I'm sure it is a small fortune.

As I show in Chapter 3, in the end, active trading of stocks or bonds typically earns you less than you would earn owning cheap index funds. But you'll never know that reading the full-service broker reports.

Pumping short-term performers

Many active investors allow so-called full-service (read: ridiculously high commissioned) stock brokers to churn them. *Churn* means that securities are bought and sold, and then bought and sold again, with the only apparent benefits going to the churner (and perhaps to Uncle Sam) — very rarely to the churnee.

Many other investors rely on overpriced, underperforming actively run mutual funds to lose money for them, relative to the markets, year after year.

Mutual fund companies are very adept at grabbing investors' money based on all sorts of unfounded promises relayed to the public through repeated adver-tisements in glossy magazines, newspaper spreads, and Web site home pages.

In the past few years, the Securities and Exchange Commission has taken some action — although far from enough — to reduce deceptive advertising in this arena. But a favorite trick of mutual fund companies that persists is the comparison of their funds' performance to completely irrelevant benchmarks. The S&P 500 Index hasn't done very well in the past ten years. For that reason, many active mutual fund companies just *love* to compare their funds' ten-year performance to the S&P 500 . . . even if their funds invest very little in big U.S. companies, the likes of the 500. When compared to more appropriate benchmarks, such as any number of, say, international stock indexes, those same actively managed funds may start to look rather miserable.

Another deceptive practice — pumping short-term performers — continues after years of practice and perfection to give the public a totally false perception that some stock pickers really know their stuff and can handily beat indexing.

Here's how it's often done: XYZ mutual fund company has 20 mutual funds. One invests in, say, large U.S. stocks. Another invests in European stocks. A third invests in the stocks of emerging-market (poor) countries. A fourth invests in oil and gold. Now say, for whatever reasons, the winds of the economy over the past year have blown hard in the face of developed-world stock markets, but emerging-market nations' stock markets and commodities (they often go hand-in-hand) have flown. Chances are good that this company's funds in those areas have done very well. Why? Because up to 90 percent of funds' overall return will be due to the *kind* of investments it makes, rather than the specific security selection.

Let me repeat that: *Up to 90 percent of funds' overall return will be due to the* kind *of investments it makes, rather than the specific security selection.* We know this through years of study. If you look at the best-performing mutual funds of any given year, they will almost always be funds that invest in the same *asset class.* An asset class is a kind of investment — such as large growth stocks or commodities — that tends to exhibit its own behavior, somewhat independent of other kinds of investments.

The XYZ mutual fund company, in its advertisement, doesn't have to reveal that its funds clocked such fabulous returns simply because it was their turn to clock fabulous returns, given the kind of fund they are. Instead, the company takes out full-page advertisements boasting of the performance of, say, its emerging-market and commodity mutual funds, with the strong implication being that its active managers are brilliant.

Nowhere in the advertisement, or only in very small print, does it bother to mention that you would have done even better in an index fund that invests — and invests much more cheaply — in that very same kind of investment. (Yes, there are many such index funds.) And you are left with the false impression that XYZ's almighty stock pickers had something to do with the fund's superlative performance. It simply isn't so.

Tuning In (Tuning Out) the Circus on Television

Far more crucial than what we know or don't know is what we do not want to know.

—Eric Hoffer

I mention Jim (*Mad Money*) Cramer at the onset of this chapter. With his bulging eyes and protruding veins and screaming and yelling and sounds of toilets flushing, the guy would be great entertainment, and a wonderful laugh, if only some investors didn't take him seriously. I'm sorry, Jim, but these are real people investing real money and suffering real consequences when they take your bum tips. I love a good laugh, and I think I have a good sense of humor, but I simply don't find you funny.

Jim Cramer is only the tip of the iceberg, of course. The media's coverage of the markets and exploitation of the public are, by and large, shameful. I know of what I speak here. I was a journalist long before I became a financial planner. There is perhaps no area of the news where the media does a poorer job than in the area of investing.

Making market calls

Jim Cramer picks stocks. Many magazine articles pick stocks or funds. You're familiar with the headlines: "10 Hot Stocks for the New Year!" "Best Funds to Buy NOW!" "Earn 30% in the Next Year!"

Most of us know, deep down, that plunking down $4.95 for a magazine is not likely to make us rich. But such headlines titillate and taunt us into buying magazines, and then tempt us to follow the get-rich-quick advice.

If you think about it, how could a stock tip relayed to potentially millions of readers or viewers possibly have any value? It doesn't. Jim Cramer's track record has been pretty well studied, and it is pretty miserable. (I won't bore you with details. You can do an Internet search and find plenty of independent analyses.)

What's in it for the magazines, the newspaper columns, and Jim Cramer? Why not give reasonable investment advice, such as advising people to buy index funds and to buy and hold their investments rather than trying to quickly trade their way to richness? Why the big tease? Why the toilets flushing and the screaming and yelling?

Mad predictions

Every time you turn on the TV, there's some guy shouting at you, telling you which stock to buy this week to beat the market. These antics help explain why many investors feel they should pick stocks instead of buying index funds. After all, why should they miss out on all the huge profits?

As I was writing this chapter, news broke that the brokerage firm Bear Stearns is facing bankruptcy. "Anything to worry about?" asked a viewer named Peter of *Mad Money*'s Jim Cramer on March 11, 2008.

"NO! NO! NO! Don't move your money from Bear!!!" screamed the host of the show, waving his arms, eyes digging into the camera. "If anything, it's more likely to be taken over!" he added. "That's just being silly! Don't be silly!"

(I suggest watching the clip on YouTube. Search "Jim Cramer Bear Stearns," and you'll find it.)

Six days later, Bear Stearns shares fell by 90 percent. I hope that Peter didn't take Cramer's advice. If he did, he is now feeling silly indeed.

The answer, in short, is that indexing doesn't hold the same entertainment value. Teasing people that they can make big money fast sells publications and air time. Telling people to buy index funds and buy and hold can be boring after a while.

Headlining what's hot

If you look inside the pages of many investment publications, such as *Money*, *Smart Money*, and *Kiplinger's*, you'll find lots of good advice — including the advice to start index investing and stop trying to time the markets and pick cherries. It's usually the cover pieces — designed to sell magazines off the news racks — that truly stink. My advice: If you want to read about money in a magazine, just ignore the cover story!

And keep in mind when you read a story such as one that recently appeared in *U.S. News & World Report* entitled "How to Make Money The Buffett Way" that investors such as Warren Buffett, while they may beat the market, also have way more control over the market than you do. When he buys stock in a company, Buffett often sends in management consultants to change the way a company does business. Can *you* do that?

Not even Warren Buffett can always do that. The billionaire from Omaha has numerous times recommended index investing for most investors.

Also keep in mind that for every Warren Buffett, there are many, many more stock pickers who tried and failed. I'm one! And I know *plenty* of others. It is very, very difficult to pick winning stocks with any kind of regularity. With the costs involved, and taxes, you have to pick winning stocks rather consistently — and sell them at just the right time — to truly beat the markets. Not many people can do that — not many at all.

Patting themselves on the back

One of the reasons that you may find yourself lulled into reading and watching get-rich-quick investment stories is that the producers often praise themselves for making readers or viewers money, giving the firm impression that they've done so and can do it again. Horsedung.

Keep in mind that the same regulations that apply to, say, stock fund prospectuses do not apply to the media. An investment-picking columnist or television trading evangelist can (and often does) say just about anything he wants about his alleged past prowess at cherry picking.

But here's what columnists and pundits and investment newsletters (mustn't forget *those*!) often fail to tell you when patting themselves on the back:

- ✔ **You would have made money regardless . . . and probably more.** Jim Cramer ballyhooed his stock-picking performance over a recent one-year period, exclaiming that his mad-money method had earned 16.2 percent. Great. But when compared to index funds invested in the same kinds of stocks (mostly mid cap with a few foreign stocks), you would have seen a return of 21.8 percent. Throw in the (uncalculated) costs of actually making Cramer's trades and paying the short-term taxes, and your simple index funds' performance would have smashed Cramer's.

- ✔ **Costs are whitewashed.** The cost of trading (commissions, spreads, and so on) can be so high that it makes frequent stock trading almost a guaranteed recipe for failure. *Value Line Investment Survey* newsletter, for example, makes extraordinary claims for its past prowess at earning subscribers high returns.

  From the Value Line Web site, we read the following:

  > A stock portfolio of #1 Ranked stocks for *Timeliness* from ***The Value Line Investment Survey,*** beginning in 1965 and updated at the beginning of each year, would have shown a **gain of 24,470% through the month end of December 2007.**

  > That compares with a gain of 1,355% in the Dow Jones Industrial Average over the same period. **Value Line #1 Ranked stocks outperformed the Dow by more than 18 TO 1.**

  > This gain would have beaten the **S&P 500 by nearly 15 to 1** for the same time span.

Ready to plunk down your $600 a year and start making money fast? Hold on!

Let's check the real-world returns of the Value Line mutual fund (VLIFX), which, according to its prospectus, is run by the very same people and with the very same wisdom that guides the newsletter whose success is trumpeted above. How well has VLIFX done in past years? In other words, how well has the Value Line method worked in real life?

According to Morningstar Principia, pretty darned poorly. The fund's 10-year annual return is now 10.75 percent, compared to 12.40 percent for the S&P 500. Going back 15 years, the fund returned an average annual 6.9 percent, compared to the S&P 500's 9.98 percent annual return. Not only did the fund fail to beat the major index, but the fund was waaaaay more volatile, and you would have incurred waaaay more tax.

✓ **Ooops! Past goofs are simply forgotten.** Some people have no shame. Paul R. La Monica, a CNNMoney.com editor and writer with a syndicated column, makes regular stock picks that appear in my daily paper. Just for fun, I often hang onto his stock tips and see how they've done months after they've made the press. The man's talent at losing money is almost not to be believed. If he invested in his own stock picks (I imagine he's way too smart to do that), he would have achieved bankruptcy a long time ago.

And La Monica isn't alone — consider the Beardstown Ladies, a group of older women from Beardstown, Illinois, who got together to form an investment club in the mid 1980s and claimed to beat the market by leaps and bounds. Their first book on stock-picking, *The Beardstown Ladies' Common-Sense Investment Guide,* was a rave best seller. But then (at the prodding of my fellow Dummies finance author Eric Tyson), independent auditors started to look at the ladies' real-world returns. They found that the Beardstown Business and Professional Women's Investment Club would have seen far, far better returns investing in index funds rather than trying to pick stocks. Even after these independent analysts showed that the ladies' stock picks earned far less than the indexes, that didn't stop the ladies and their publisher from putting out four additional books on picking stocks.

My fave is James Glassman, who wrote a book called *Dow 36,000,* predicting in 1999 that the greatest bull run in market history — the 1990s — had only just begun. Just as the book came out, the market crashed. Glassman just continued to write investment advice columns and hardly made mention of his phenomenal goof, except to occasionally say that his timing may have been a little off.

We're still waiting for Dow 36,000. As I write this, the Dow is trading at about 11,000.

If people like Glassman and La Monica and the Ladies of Beardstown weren't offering pipe dreams and pretending that they come true, I'm certain that more people would be indexing — and earning money rather than losing it.

5 out of 10 experts agree . . .

One of the prime reasons the public at large doesn't believe in indexing is because there are so many experts out there claiming to know which way shares of Microsoft, General Electric, Radio Shack, and every other stock are going. It's hard not to believe that they can actually see the future! Pick up the business section of your paper, read any financial magazine, or log onto any investment Web site, and you'll find story after story in which John Executive, a vice president with SuchandSuch Wall Street Brokerage Firm, is firing off his predictions on the future performance of a particular security or market sector. HA!

Guess what? At any point in time exactly half the experts on Wall Street will say that Microsoft (or any other stock) is going up relative to the market, and exactly half will say it's going down! When the reporter who wrote that story looked for sources, he could have just as easily found a source to support the notion that Microsoft was going up as he could have found a source to support the notion that Microsoft was going down. It's all a game!

Here's how I know that at any point in time the ratio is 50/50: It *has* to be.

The big people on Wall Street who get quoted in newspapers are the market movers and shakers themselves. The vast majority of stocks are bought and sold by institutional buyers: mutual funds, exchange-traded funds, insurance companies, and endowment funds. Very few are bought by Joe Schmoes. If more than half of the institutional buyers thought the price of a stock was headed north, the price would, in fact, go up as a reflection of that optimism. The price would go up to a point where fewer experts would deem the stock to still be a buy. Conversely, if more than half the movers and shakers thought the stock was going down, they would stop buying, and the price of the stock would drop until you got to a point where fewer experts would deem the stock a loser.

Again: At any point in time, the market will be 50/50 as to whether a particular security is going up or down. So when you see that such-and-such an expert predicted that a stock would go up, the reporter who quoted that expert could just as easily have found some expert to say the opposite. Moral of story: Buy the index. Tune out the prognosticators. They don't know what they're talking about.

Delving Deep into the Human Psyche

We lie loudest when we lie to ourselves.

—Eric Hoffer

A few years ago, I attended a large workshop in which participants were asked to rate themselves as drivers. The rating options were *above average, average,* and *below average.* On little slips of paper, we all voted on our own street navigation skills. If I recall correctly, 70 percent of the people considered themselves "above average." Only 5 percent considered themselves "below average." Of course, unless this was an extraordinary group of people (it wasn't), something *had* to be amiss! It was. And should you ask a similarly large group of investors about their own stock-picking stills, I'm certain you'd find that way more than an average number would consider themselves above average.

Returning to our question du jour: Why isn't everyone indexing? It is largely because of *overconfidence in our own abilities.*

Here lies perhaps the biggest reason that everyone doesn't index: It isn't the way we are manipulated and fooled by Wall Street or the media; rather, it is the way we manipulate and fool *ourselves.*

Picking darlings, fixating on numbers

You hear a tip. You buy a stock. The stock goes up. The stock goes down. The stock goes back up. In order to do better than the index investor, you have to buy low and sell high; the timing needs to be right on both ends. To truly do better than the index investor, you need to not only beat the indexes in terms of performance, but you need to do it with comparable risk. And you need to cover all your costs, including the time you spend researching stocks and the money you pay for stock-picking advice. And you need to pull out your money, pay Uncle Sam, and still wind up ahead.

As you can see, active investing presents quite a few hurdles. That's why very few people can do it.

These hurdles are only part of what makes it so very difficult to pick stocks. The other part is the mental games that you (and every other wannabe day-trader) wind up playing. You buy the stock at $5. It goes to $10. Perhaps the stock is bound to go to $20, but goshdarnit, you bought at $5. Who can resist taking such a quick profit? So you do. You lose out on any further gain. Conversely, you buy the stock at $5, and it goes to $2. You don't sell — even though you have bad vibes about the company — because that would mean locking in your loss. You don't sell, and you continue to lose money.

Prices, it has been said, have no memory. The price you paid and the price you plan to sell at are both irrelevant in the real world of investing. But try making them irrelevant in your decision making!

Stock picking also lends itself to fixating on meaningless numbers and, often, falling in love with certain securities . . . for whatever reason we fall in love with anything. You may like the name, the logo, or the city in which the corporation is headquartered. There are so many ways in which emotions can sway clear thinking.

Stock traders are subject to all the same mind games that gamblers in Vegas are subject to, such as the classic *gambler's fallacy* that leads us to believe in "inevitable" sequences: If the market goes down three days in a row, then it *must* go up the fourth, and such nonsense. Markets are largely random, and failure to accept that randomness leads people to not accept indexing as a powerful investment strategy — despite tons of evidence that it is.

If you believe that markets aren't random, I invite you to do a simple little experiment: Search the archives of *The Wall Street Journal*. Pick a date in history — any date. Read the stories about any particular company of which you know relatively little. Try to predict, based on those stories, whether the company stock went up or down in the days and weeks that followed.

Alternatively, go onto a Web site such as Yahoo! Finance (`www.finance.yahoo.com`) and pull up a chart showing the ups and downs of any stock or market sector over the past three months, six months, or year. Make sure this is a stock or market sector you are unfamiliar with. Take a piece of paper and cover the right side of your screen. Now, using only the left side of the screen as your guide, try to predict what's on the right side.

What you're doing in the first exercise, people in the investment world call *fundamental analysis*. That means looking at a company's business to try to predict how well its stock will do. In the second exercise, I'm asking you to do *technical analysis*. That means using charts of stock movements to try to predict how well a stock will do. Neither is as easy as it looks, as these exercises will reveal.

Lots of stock pickers, both amateur and professional, think they can use fundamental and technical analysis to beat the markets. I'm sure that some can, but very, very few! Before you convince yourself that you are one, try my two exercises. I think you'll find them quite humbling!

Keeping track of your own performance

I can't tell you how often new clients come to me with their active portfolios and say, "I haven't done too poorly, really . . . ." But then we start to crunch the numbers and discover how much better they would have done investing in indexes over the years.

It's hard to measure portfolio performance accurately. You need to take account of all your deposits, withdrawals, trading and incidental costs, taxes (most often paid with money from outside the portfolio), and so on. If you think you're an above average investor (as most investors do), it's very easy to prove your point with a subtle, perhaps subconscious doctoring of the books.

If you had simply invested $1 in the S&P 500 in 1926 and allowed it to sit and grow, that $1 would now be $3,100. And as I point out in later chapters, if you are going to invest in one index, the S&P 500 probably isn't the best index to invest in. Had you invested, for example, $1 in a U.S. small cap value index in 1926 (such a beast was only theoretical in 1926, but there are certainly many ways to tap into such an index today), your $1 would now be worth $51,000.

Granted, most people don't have eight decades to invest their money and allow it to grow untouched. Still, I throw out these numbers so you can see that index investing certainly allows for ample creation of wealth.

The long-term track record is one good reason that index investing is well worth considering. And index investing's fabulous track record also, despite all the reasons I discuss in this chapter, makes it odd that only a minority of investors are actually doing it. You, of course, will be in that minority. That means you'll be one of the few investors who thinks he or she is above average who really, truly is above average!

Chapter 5

A New Era Begins: ETFs and Alternative Indexes

As revolutions go, the ETF revolution of the past decade or so has been considerably less violent than, say, the French Revolution. Heads haven't been chopped off, but lots of fees were. The aristocracy wasn't driven from the palace, but the small investor, for the first time in history, found himself no longer at a great disadvantage *vis-à-vis* (that's a French expression) the large and powerful investor.

ETF stands for *exchange-traded fund,* and it is foremost and firstly an index fund. ETFs have all the advantages of index mutual funds — including low costs, tax efficiency, and transparency (you know what you're buying) — with a few additional perks throw in, such as the ability to buy and sell them in a flash, just like an individual stock.

If you're interested in finding out much more about ETFs, you may want to read *Exchange-Traded Funds For Dummies* (Wiley) by Russell Wild. (Hey, that's me!) If you are interested mostly in a snapshot of how ETFs fit into the larger world of index investing, and how they are almost daily making that world even larger, then you're exactly where you need to be. Vive la Révolution!

Expanding the Indexing Universe

Beginning in the mid-1970s, and for 20 years to follow, if you wanted to be an index investor, the only practical way to do so (unless you were very, very rich and could build your own index portfolio) was through index mutual funds. You can still, of course, go that route, and there is nothing wrong with it.

In the mid-1990s, however, ETFs were born, and they have since exploded in popularity. As a result, you now have more than one viable route . . . you have two.

Introducing the new kid on the block

The difference between an ETF (the new kid on the block) and an index mutual fund (the old timer) is not as enormous as many investors seem to think. The words *exchange-traded fund* are frighteningly technical sounding, while the words *mutual fund* sound so soothing and friendly. In reality, one is no more complicated, technical, or unfriendly than the other. They both represent baskets of securities or goods — stocks, bonds, or commodities — that you can buy or sell in one fell swoop.

If you're comparing a mutual fund and an ETF that invest in the very same kind of investment — say, for example, large cap U.S. value stocks — there may be only marginal differences between the two. In most cases, a large cap U.S. value ETF and a large cap U.S. value index mutual fund that track the same index will have very similar costs, return potential, and risk. The differences between two such similar funds are discussed in Chapter 6.

In many cases, however, the ETF and the index mutual fund will *not* invest in the same kind of investment or track the same index. ETFs, you see, just like the Starship Enterprise, have clearly gone where no index mutual fund has gone before.

Tracking indexes that you never knew existed

The very first ETF introduced in the United States — just like the very first index mutual fund introduced about 20 years prior — tracked the venerable S&P 500, an index of stocks of the nation's 500 largest companies. That auspicious introduction came on January 29, 1993. That initial ETF was called the

S&P Depositary Receipts Trust Series 1, also known as the SPDR (or spider) 500. Issued by a company called State Street Global Advisors (SSgA), it traded then, and still trades, under the ticker SPY.

The next ETF to see the light tracked the even older Dow Jones Industrial Average, an index of the nation's most powerful and influential companies as handpicked by a gang of editors at *The Wall Street Journal.* Also issued by SSgA, it trades under the ticker DIA.

Then came a slew of ETFs that invested in industry sectors, such as technology stocks, healthcare stocks, or stocks of petroleum companies. And, at the same time, came ETFs that invested in different regions of the world, such as Europe, the Far East, or the emerging markets, as well as individual countries — Germany, Switzerland, or Canada, for example.

Lately, in an effort to capture more and more narrow slivers of the market (and capture more consumer dollars), ETF providers have given us a huge array of funds that track such industry niches as companies that manufacture medical devices, broker/dealers, and home construction firms. Some of these more narrow indexes may have existed for years, but there were no investment products that tracked them.

Some of the newer ETFs — actually *most of* the newer ETFs, for better or worse — are now tracking indexes that were created specifically just so that an ETF could track them. Talk about the tail wagging the dog! Woof.

Tracking indexes that never existed before

Where ETFs have really changed forever the nature of index investing has been in the creation of indexes that offer the promise — if not the reality — of better investment tools.

These newfangled indexes sometimes reflect the markets like funhouse mirrors reflect your body. They exaggerate here and diminish there, giving us, for example, a version of the S&P 500 where the companies that pay high dividends appear as big as African elephants, and the companies that pay no dividends are portrayed as field mice.

Such distortions, of course, are aimed at garnering greater returns with lesser risk.

In the next section, I outline some of these "funhouse" indexes: how they are created, how they work, and whether they make any financial sense.

Making Sense (or Nonsense) of the Old and New

Before I introduce you to some of the newer indexes and the methodology (and sometimes the touch of madness) behind them, I want to quickly review the older indexes and the traditional methodologies behind them. Then I'll ask you to hold onto your pork pie hats, as I take you on a tour of the new-to-primetime.

Examining the tried and true

As I discuss in Chapter 2, the mother of all indexes, the Dow Jones Industrial Average, and her first-born son, the Standard & Poor's 500, laid the framework for years of indexing to come. Both of the older indexes base their mirroring of the markets on a representative sampling, as do nearly all indexes. (A perfect "entire market" index can't exist for more than perhaps a few hours because new securities are born every day, while others fade away.)

In the case of the Dow, the sampling originally included 12 stocks; today the number is 30. Each stock is given a weight in the portfolio based on the price of the stock.

Since the price of a stock can be somewhat arbitrary, the index, when you think about it, doesn't really make a lot of sense. (Back in the day it was formed, before sophisticated calculators, it made more sense because it was the easiest way to calculate market value with a pencil and paper.) And yet, over the course of history, perhaps just out of dumb luck (I believe dumb luck contributes to a lot in this universe . . . and may even explain the universe itself!), the Dow hasn't done such a terribly poor job of mirroring the U.S. stock market at large. The S&P 500, however, generally does a better job.

The S&P 500 includes 500 stocks that are all given a weighting based on their market capitalization. This — the so-called *cap-weighted index* — has come to be the standard in the industry and what we normally mean when we use the words *traditional index*. Cap-weighted indexes may include any number of companies. Each one is given a weight proportionate to the total dollar value of all stocks issued by the corporation.

Grasping weightings and valuations

If the (fictional) Ace Noodle company issues, say, a million shares, and each share is worth $50, the total capitalization of that company would be $50 million. Ace Noodle would then have twice as much influence on a cap-weighted index, such as the S&P 500, as would another (fictional) company called Amalgamated Fruitcake that was worth only $25 million. If the entire index were to represent, say, $500 million, and Ace Noodle were to shoot up 10 percent, then the index would rise 1 percent (or 1 *point*). If Amalgamated Fruitcake were to rise 10 percent, the index would go up only half a point. Ditto percentage should either Ace or Amalgamated take a tumble.

Most of the common indexes today are cap-weighted indexes, including numerous offerings from Dow Jones Wilshire, Standard & Poor's, Morningstar, Morgan Stanley (MSCI), and Russell.

Within the realm of cap-weighted indexes, there are nuances. Some indexes look at all the stock in existence, regardless of who holds that stock. These babies are called *full cap* indexes.

Other cap-weighted indexes include only shares of stock available to the unwashed masses (people like you and me), excluding shares that are privately held (usually by executive types). These puppies are referred to as *free float* indexes.

Yet others — so-called *constrained* or *capped* indexes — put limits on the degree to which the largest stocks can influence the index. Ace Noodle, for example, might get a 10 percent allocation of the index even if the People's Republic of China were to order a trillion pounds of noodles.

In the next chapter, and throughout Part II, I discuss what these differences in how the indexes are formulated can mean to your portfolio, and how they should influence you in picking the best index funds.

Introducing newer variations (and variations on variations)

Move over, traditional indexes! Well, maybe not quite yet.

The traditional indexes formed the foundation on which index investing, by and large, was based up till a few years ago. Few people complained because index investing has paid off handsomely. But there were indications that one might be able to do even better.

One particular mutual fund company called Dimensional Fund Advisors (also known as DFA), for example, began experimenting years ago with indexes that sought to capture the performance of the entire market but to "lean" toward value (bargain basement) stocks and small-company stocks. These stocks, studies show, have a decades-long performance record that exceeds the performance records of large-company and *growth*-company (popular-but-pricey) stocks.

I talk more about the value and small cap lean in Chapter 7 and throughout Part III. Dimensional, in my mind, has pioneered what has come recently to be known as *fundamental indexing*: indexing designed to capture possible pluses in the market that may contribute to enhanced performance. (Dimensional eschews the term *fundamental indexing* and prefers to refer to its brand of indexing as *enhanced*. So be it.)

Fundamental (enhanced) indexing may have started with Dimensional (whose funds are available only to institutional investors and fee-only financial advisors), but it has branched out in a thousand directions since the advent of ETFs.

Russell's indexing report card

One purpose of an index may be to serve as a foundation for an investment (such as an index mutual fund or exchange-traded fund). With that as its purpose, some indexes do a much better job than others.

Here's a quick grading system for judging whether a particular index is a potential star performer or a dud, and whether that index deserve a berth in your portfolio:

✔ **Does the index make sense?** Broad-based indexes that track entire markets make sense, because most markets go up over time. But what about a very narrow index, such as, say, an index of companies working on cancer cures? Is that really the basis for a solid investment? If one company finds a cure for cancer, its stock is certain to soar. But what of the stock of all the other companies in the index?

✔ **Is there a straightforward and objective selection criteria?** If the stocks that go into an index are picked randomly or subjectively, you are looking at a variation of active management. Active management doesn't have a very successful track record. Indexes put together behind curtains may be best left behind curtains.

✔ **Is the index stable?** If an index changes too often, any investment tracking that index is going to incur both trading costs and extra taxation. Equal-weighted indexes, for example, must trade fairly frequently to remain equally weighted.

✔ **Does the index fit your financial needs?** Some indexes — such as, say, a short-term bond index — are going to come with little volatility and little potential return. Other indexes — such as, say, small cap value stocks, or commodities — will come with considerably more volatility but much greater potential return. One kind of index isn't necessarily better or worse than the other. But your portfolio, based on your personal finances, may or may not warrant a certain level of risk and return. You must find your own risk–return sweet spot and then determine if a particular index helps you or hinders you from achieving it.

✔ **Is the index too hot to touch?** When a certain kind of investment is riding especially high (lately it has been emerging-market stocks and commodities, especially oil), a bevy of new index investments based on that kind of investment is bound to hit the market. But buying into something when that something is red hot is often not such a terribly good idea. *All* investment types go through cycles. In the long run, you want to buy low and sell high — not (as most investors continually do) buy high and sell low!

Figuring Out Fundamental Indexes and Beyond

Dimensional's proprietary indexes identify value stocks by looking mostly at price-to-book ratios. (*Price-to-book* refers to the value of the stock as it relates to the value of the total company's assets.) The lower the price-to-book ratio (the more deeply valued a stock), the greater representation that stock is given in a Dimensional index. There are some good reasons — foremost the history of stock returns — to think that Dimensional's particular brand of fundamental indexing may offer real long-term benefits. I discuss this topic in Chapter 7.

But other fundamental indexes of more recent vintage are using other measurements, such as dividend yield, growth of dividend yield, total company revenue, and price-to-earnings ratios, as criteria by which the indexes are weighed.

Whether buying index funds that track such fundamental indexes will prove wise in the long run is highly questionable and a subject of much debate today among financial experts.

Promoting the uncertain with a positive spin

Fundamental indexing–based ETFs have been advertised extensively in the past couple of years. Many of them have shown great success in garnering outsized performance using *back-testing*. In other words, the indexes are given performance records as if they existed 10 or 15 years ago. Back-testing, as you can imagine, has great limitations. In fact, back-testing, especially if performed by someone who has a vested interest in showing positive results, can be almost worthless.

Silly example: If you wanted to create an index, for example, that "proved" that the Philadelphia Eagles was a better football team than the New York Giants, you could do so. Simply show the two teams' wins and losses, but do so during a time frame when the Eagles were hot and the Giants were not.

Similarly, if you wanted to "prove" that high dividend–paying stocks were a more profitable investment than stocks that typically don't pay dividends (which isn't necessarily the case — trust me), you could choose a time frame in which high dividend–paying stocks soared. That happens to have been the case over the past several years, which may explain why ETFs linked to fundamental indexes that favor high dividend–paying stocks have been selling like hotcakes. (Well, they were at least until the collapse of financial stocks — which tend to pay high dividends — in October, 2008.)

It is simply unknown whether fundamental indexes will wind up as better foundations for index investments than the traditional indexes. I have my doubts. Markets are efficient. If an index of, say, high dividend–paying stocks winds up outperforming all other stocks for a good enough number of years, the market will eventually catch on, raising the price of high dividend–paying stocks to a point that they will no longer have an edge.

As much as I like my practically hometown Philadelphia Eagles, they aren't going to be a top NFL team for all eternity, even though they've had a few good years of late.

Also bear in mind that fundamental indexes, which aim to beat the markets, tend to charge investors considerably more for that presumed edge. Most of the WisdomTree ETFs charge 0.58 percent a year in operating fees, and most of the PowerShares ETFs charge 0.60 percent. That compares to 0.22 percent or less for the majority of Vanguard's traditional-index ETFs.

Getting even with equal-weighted indexes

Another kind of alternative index that has caught on to a great degree of late is the *equal-weighted index.* If an equal-weighted index includes, say, 50 stocks, each stock is worth 1/50 of the index. A large company, such as Ace Noodle, would carry no more weight than would a smaller company, such as Amalgamated Fruitcake.

At first glance, it may seem that such an index would be better diversified than an index in which Ace Noodle would have too much sway. And that may be the case in certain circumstances.

You need to remember, though, that Ace Noodle, being a large and more stable company, is likely to be less volatile than Amalgamated Fruitcake. So giving the latter company an equal weighting will inevitably result in an index that is more volatile than a traditional cousin. When smaller stocks are doing great guns, you'll want an equal-weighted index. When larger stocks are forging ahead, you'll wish you had stuck to the traditional.

You want to keep in mind, too, that equal-weighted indexes require much more juggling than do cap-weighted indexes. If Ace Noodle doubles in size next year, it simply doubles its relative importance in the cap-weighted index. At the same time, unless the entire index doubles, the manager of the equal-weighted index has to sell off a boatload of Ace Noodle stock and buy something else to take its place. Such buys and sells create added costs to the investor and possibly ugly tax consequences.

The leader, at least so far, in equal-weighted indexing has been Rydex Investments. Through Rydex, you can get ETFs that track equal-weighted indexes of all sorts and flavors, including the broad-market Rydex S&P Equal Weight Index ETF (RSP) and any number of equal-weighted industry sector ETFs, such as the Rydex S&P Equal Weight Consumer Discretionary ETF (RCD), the Rydex S&P Equal Weight Consumer Staples ETF (RHS), the Rydex S&P Equal Weight Energy ETF (RYE), and the Rydex S&P Equal Weight Financials ETF (RYF).

The role that such ETFs may play — or not play — in your portfolio is discussed in Chapter 7.

Creating seemingly sociable screened indexes

A variation of sorts on fundamental indexing, *screening* is the process not of picking stocks to include in the index, but rather of picking stocks to exclude. Perhaps the most common use of screening is to weed out companies that are not so much financially undesirable as socially undesirable. By so doing, it becomes possible to be a socially responsible index investor, if one so desires. Granted, "socially responsible" is a subjective term.

The oldest and best-known such index is the Domini 400 Social Index, created in 1990. Investors wishing to track this index can purchase shares of the Green Century Equity Fund (GCEQX).The majority of companies in the index come from the S&P 500. Companies are screened based on their performance records on environmental issues (such as waste disposal, toxic emissions, fines, and penalties), as well as on social issues (such as employee relations, corporate citizenship, product-related issues, and attitudes regarding consumer issues).

The Calvert Social Index Fund (CSXAX), launched in June 2000, is based on the Calvert Social Index. Calvert takes the 1,000 largest companies in the United States and applies its particular brand of social criteria to create the index.

An outfit called KLD Research & Analytics has recently taken the lead in creating screened indexes, some of which are already being tracked by ETFs, and others of which are sure to follow. These indexes include the venerable Domini 400 Social Index (discussed earlier in this section), the KLD Catholic Values 400 Index, the KLD Global Climate 100 Index, and the KLD Global Sustainability Index. It also has created such indexes as the KLD Dividend Achievers Social Index — a combination of socially responsible and fundamental index.

If you want to explore socially screened indexes more, I give some pointers (for stock investing) in Chapter 7 and (for bond investing) in Chapter 8.

Oh — there are also indexes (are you ready for this?) that allow you to invest in companies that are socially *irresponsible!* Yes, you can focus your investments, if you wish, on tobacco, gambling, alcohol, and weapons of mass destruction. Ugh.

Turning the world upside down with inverse indexes

An inverse index is indeed a strange beast. Unlike other indexes, which track the growth of markets, inverse indexes do best when the market shrinks or sinks.

Inverse indexes have been around for some time. They were pioneered by the folks at ProFunds, who ran and still run mutual funds, and now offer ETFs, as well, based on the upside-down beasts. Other major players include Rydex Investments and Direxion Funds.

Funds that track inverse indexes are often touted (by the companies that hawk them) as the perfect diversification tools. After all, if the rest of your holdings are going down, these babies are guaranteed to go up! Whoa . . . not so fast! Yes, having two different investments that zig and zag is the very essence of diversification — a good thing! But you *also* want different investments that tend to go up over time.

Investments tied to inverse indexes have a miserable history of losing money over the long run. You have much better diversification options, as I discuss in Part II. The ETFs based on inverse indexes are for market-timers, and market-timers typically make lousy investors.

Keeping hands completely off with unmanaged indexes

Some may argue that unmanaged indexes are the purest of the pure when it comes to indexes. An unmanaged index starts, like any other index, with an attempt to use sample securities to measure a particular market. The difference between unmanaged indexes and all others is that the unmanaged index remains static . . . always!

That's the deal with HOLDRS, which are index funds very much like ETFs, issued by Merrill Lynch. These are baskets of stocks that, according to Merrill, represent a certain industry sector. There's one, for example, that tracks the biotech industry (BBH), another that tracks the Internet business (HHH), and one that mirrors the semiconductor industry (SMH).

Because these indexes are cap-weighted, and they never change their lineup of companies, they can become very concentrated if one or two companies happen to grow much more than the others.

At the time of this writing, for example, the Internet HOLDR (HHH), created in 1992, is made up of 12 companies. But the last several on the list, including Earthlink and Priceline, make up doodly-squat. More than 86 percent of the index is composed of just four companies: Yahoo!, Amazon, eBay, and Time Warner.

One of hallmarks of a good index is that there should be better diversification than that!

Say, can you really call this an index?!

The very latest wrinkle in indexing is the advent of the so-called *active index*. If ever there were an oxymoron, this is it! And yet, active indexes are spawning an entire second stage of the ETF revolution.

I find it perhaps ironic that the very first actively managed ETF was introduced by Bear Stearns in March 2008 — just as Bear Stearns was on the brink of bankruptcy!

That fund, the Bear Stearns Current Yield Fund (YYY), is based on an "index" of largely bonds and other debt obligations. Although I find the entire idea of active indexing a bit crazy, it may actually have an edge on other kinds of active investing. More on this in Part II.

The great index quiz

Once upon a time . . . financial indexes were delightful and simple things, designed to help measure the ups and downs and sideways of financial markets. There was the venerable S&P 500, the Dow, and a few assorted and sundry others. These indexes tended to be cap-weighted, and they tracked large segments of the market.

In past years, however, we've seen a virtual explosion of indexes. Today, thanks in large part to the exponential growth of exchange-traded funds (ETFs), you can find indexes that track just about anything, constructed in myriad and sometimes oh-so-questionable ways. Many are being birthed for the sole purpose of creating an ETF that can then track the newfangled index. The tail is wagging the dog — and the dog is sometimes getting delirious!

Here, I present a list of a dozen indexes. Most of them are real, with real ETFs that track them. Some of them — well, I just created them for the fun of it; they are pure fantasy. Can you tell the real indexes from the make-believe indexes? (Answers are at the bottom.)

1. **ISE-Revere Wal-Mart Supplier Index.** Ever walk into Wal-Mart and wonder if you could somehow buy shares of the companies that generate most of their sales from the world's most humongous retailer? Well, you can. The FocusShares Wal-Mart Supplier ETF is based on the ISE-Revere Wal-Mart Supplier Index, which tracks the performance of 30 companies that derive a substantial portion of their revenue from Wal-Mart.

2. **The GI/Gender Health Index.** This index invests in healthcare, life sciences, and/or biotechnology companies that have been identified as gastrointestinal/genitourinary/gender health companies. Companies included in the GI/Gender Health Index are engaged in the research, clinical development, and/or commercialization of therapeutic agents for the treatment of a wide variety of diseases.

3. **MSCI Oil Derivatives Index.** This one gauges the performance of companies manufacturing, processing, delivering, or storing petroleum byproducts and other derivatives of oil production. The index includes equities in selected companies that meet the profile, but may also include options and other derivatives of the derivatives, so to speak.

4. **Credit Suisse Global Warming Index.** It tracks a variety of stocks that analysts believe will benefit from the global push toward lower emissions.

5. **Pacific ex-Japan Dividend Index.** This one measures the performance of dividend-paying companies incorporated in the Pacific region, excluding Japan. The index is comprised of companies incorporated in Hong Kong, Singapore, Australia, or New Zealand that meet other requirements necessary to be included in the index. Companies are weighted in the index based on annual cash dividends paid.

6. **ISE-CCM Homeland Security Index.** The U.S. government has put a top priority on counterterrorism, law enforcement, and the securing of its national borders. The top 30 companies at the forefront of such efforts comprise the FocusShares Homeland Security ETF, which is based on the ISE-CCM Homeland Security Index, the fund's benchmark index for the critical homeland security sector.

7. **BARRA North American REIT Index.** This index reflects the performance of real estate investment trusts that benefit from the growth of highway and railroad infrastructure throughout the United States, Canada, and Mexico.

8. **The Fortune 500 Index.** It invests in securities that are known to be held by those investors in last year's listing of the U.S.'s wealthiest people per *Fortune* magazine. The index aims to capitalize on the collective brainpower of the nation's most powerful investors.

9. **The Super Bowl 20 Index.** Companies whose commercials played during last year's Super Bowl and were given most acclaim by television viewers are included in this index. The historical performance of the index (retrospectively) gives solid indication that a favorable showing on America's most-viewed show is a good barometer of annual sales growth.

10. **The CEOpay Index**. It starts with the S&P 500 and eliminates those corporations where the ratio of CEO compensation to the compensation of the average employee exceeds 500. The rationale behind the index, formed in 2007, is that overfed CEOs both bleed a corporation of financial resources and damage employee morale.

11. **Dow Jones BRIC 50 Index**. Designed to provide balanced representation across four markets, this index targets 5 stocks for Russia and 15 each for Brazil, India, and China. Stocks are selected within each country based on size and liquidity, and then the selections are aggregated to form the index.

12. **Dow Jones BRAC 50 Index**. This index is designed to provide balanced representation across three markets, all somewhat tangential to the continental European market. Targeting 20 stocks for Britain, 20 for Austria, and 10 for the Czech Republic, the selections are aggregated based on size and liquidity to form the index.

Answers: 1, 2, 4, 5, 6 and 11 are the real indexes. (But I seriously wish someone would create number 10 as well.)

Part II

Getting to Know Your Index Fund Choices

The 5th Wave   By Rich Tennant

"Eat your cereal. Your father's heavily invested in grain."

In this part . . .

Now that you know the rhyme and reason behind index funds, it's time to stop looking at them as a single entity and to do some comparing and contrasting of the various index fund options. Not all index funds are created equal. Some are born as mutual funds, others as exchange-traded funds. Some track the stock market, others the bond market. Some track investments that may be considered a bit wild and crazy. Most index funds have low expense ratios, but others, alas, are brazen rip-offs. Some are more tax efficient than others. When all is said and done, some are clearly better investments than others. After reading the next four chapters, you will be a true index fund connoisseur.

Chapter 6

The Basic Index Investing Components

*I*ndex investing bears more similarity to U.S. politics than it does to, say, European or Asian politics in that it is largely a two-party system. You can plunk your money into mutual funds (which was the ruling party for many years), or you can invest in exchange-traded funds (otherwise known as ETFs).

Oh, sure, you can invest in something exotic, such as a unit investment trust, just like you can vote for Ralph Nader for president. But you can bet your paycheck that Ralph isn't going to become president because the political landscape is dominated by the Democrats and Republicans. And the investing landscape is similarly certain to be dominated by two prevailing forces for some time to come.

Although not yet nearly as popular as mutual funds, ETFs have caught on very rapidly in the past decade or so. In 2006, while I was writing *Exchange-Traded Funds For Dummies,* investors had about $320 billion deposited in about 200 ETFs. Investors now have more than $650 billion invested in roughly 700 ETFs.

And mutual funds? A couple years ago, the sum total invested in mutual funds was $9.2 trillion; today it stands at roughly $8.5 trillion. At the moment I'm writing this page, the market is slightly up from a couple of years ago, so the majority of this decline is due to the emigration of money from mutual funds to ETFs.

While ETFs are slowly muscling in on mutual funds (I strongly suspect they may surpass mutual funds in the next decade or so), ETFs have already become nearly an equal competitor in the arena of index investing. That's because practically *all* of the $650 billion invested in ETFs is indexed. Of the trillions invested in mutual funds, on the other hand, only a fraction of that — about $840 million, according to Morningstar — is indexed.

In the first part of this kickoff-to-Part-II chapter, I help you understand and appreciate the differences between index mutual funds and ETFs so that you can better "vote" with your money.

The second half of this chapter aims to help you understand the indexes that form the bases for both ETFs and index mutual funds. Those indexes are the foundations on which your index investments — whether ETFs, mutual funds, or Ralph Nader–type investments — lie. Just as even the best recipe still relies on good ingredients, any ETF, mutual fund, or other investment worth your consideration needs to be based on a good, solid, logical index.

After you have a handle on what these investment vehicles are all about, I invite you to cruise the rest of the chapters of Part II, where I help you to pick from among the hordes upon hordes (with more hordes arriving daily!) of index mutual funds and ETFs on the market.

Riding the Index Vehicle

Both kinds of index funds — ETFs and mutual funds — represent baskets of securities. Usually the securities are stocks or bonds, although they could also be commodities such as oil or gold, or something slightly more exotic, like preferred stock.

ETFs differ from mutual funds mostly in how they trade. Whereas mutual funds are purchased directly from a fund company, ETFs trade on the open markets, like stocks. This allows you to do all kinds of fancy things with ETFs that you can't do with mutual funds, such as buying options or shorting them.

(*Options* allow for high leveraging of your investments; you put a modest amount of money down now for the right to buy or sell a stock at a certain price in the future. *Shorting* a fund is a market-timing maneuver that banks on a downfall. If the index that the ETF counter-mirrors loses money, you actually win. Neither strategy is typically very successful for the small, unprofessional investor.)

ETFs also trade throughout the day. You can buy or sell at a moment's notice, and you can buy or sell at whatever price the market brings, whether at 10 a.m. on a Monday morning or 3 p.m. on a Thursday afternoon. Mutual funds, on the other hand, are traded only at the end of the day; you cannot pinpoint your price.

As far as buying and holding either an ETF or a mutual fund (buying and holding is my favorite form of investing, as I discuss in Chapter 16), the differences between the two kinds of funds are largely academic.

The similarities between, say, an S&P 500 mutual fund and an S&P ETF are far greater than the differences. (Some say the same thing about Democrats and Republicans, but let's not go there.)

All the same, knowing a few things about the basic structure for ETFs and mutual funds can't hurt. Follow me!

Investing collectively through mutual funds

A mutual fund is a pooled investment, a repository for money, just like a library is a repository for books.

Lots of investors (so-called *shareholders* of the mutual fund) buy into the pool, and a manager or team of managers — the "librarian" — decides how to best invest the collective money. The managers may invest the money in stocks, bonds, or just about anything else in the hopes of earning shareholders a profit.

Dating back to England in the 1800s, mutual funds today account for the vast majority of household investments in the United States. Most mutual funds today are part of large fund companies, such as Fidelity, T. Rowe Price, or Charles Schwab. Fidelity, for example, is sort of like the Wal-Mart of financial supermarkets. It now offers 350 of its own funds, and many of those come in various classes.

Most, if not all, of the large fund companies offer index mutual funds. Fidelity, for example, offers 20 index funds. Table 6-1 lists the six largest index mutual funds as of this writing.

Table 6-1	The Six Largest Index Mutual Funds	
Name of Fund	*Type of Investment*	*$ Billions Invested*
Vanguard 500 Index	Large U.S. stocks	$114
Vanguard Total Stock Market	U.S. stocks	$92
Vanguard Total Bond Market	U.S. bonds	$56
Vanguard Europe	European stocks	$30
Fidelity Spartan U.S. Equity	U.S. stocks	$27
Vanguard Total International Stock	Foreign stocks	$2.6

Some fund companies, like The Vanguard Group and Dimensional, specialize in index funds. The majority of Vanguard's stock funds are indexed, and nearly all of Dimensional's are.

But about 95 percent of mutual funds, including the majority of those run by Fidelity, Charles Schwab, T. Rowe Price, and others, are actively run. That means that the manager or managers in charge are picking certain securities or trying to time their buying and selling of securities in the hopes of beating the pants off of, rather than mirroring, the markets. They usually don't succeed, but they keep trying.

Mutual funds may be cheap or expensive, well run or poorly run, good investments or bad. Because so much of the nation's money is tied up in mutual funds — they literally *are* the market — it is virtually impossible that the average mutual fund can beat the market. On average and collectively, mutual funds will do about as well as the market, minus their expense ratios and minus the taxes resulting from trades.

In large part because index mutual funds are the least expensive of all mutual funds — in terms of management fees, trading expenses, and taxes — they tend to show better long-term performance than the rest of the pack and, therefore, are generally the better bet for your money.

When you invest in a mutual fund, you either purchase shares directly from the mutual fund company, or you can go to a financial supermarket, such as a Fidelity or a Charles Schwab, and purchase mutual funds from a variety of mutual fund companies through a funds network. Fidelity, for example, in addition to offering its own 350 funds, will allow you to purchase more than 4,000 funds from other companies through its Fund Network. Of those, roughly 1,100 can be purchased without a fee. The remainder will generally cost you $75 to buy. (They cost nothing to sell, if held for at least 90 days.)

For a whole lot more on mutual funds, you may want to read Eric Tyson's *Mutual Funds For Dummies,* 5th Edition (Wiley).

Putting your money into the more modern ETF

Dating back only to the early 1990s, ETFs, like mutual funds, represent baskets of securities. Unlike mutual funds, you don't purchase ETFs from the companies that bundle the securities; you purchase them on an exchange, such as the New York Stock Exchange or the NASDAQ, just as you would purchase stocks.

Until very recently, all ETFs were index funds. Only as I was writing this book did several actively managed ETFs hit the market. It is still questionable whether they will take off and survive. At present, they are miniscule. (I hope they stay that way!)

ETFs tend to carry very low expense ratios, but they do require a commission to buy and sell them. Usually, the commission is small (perhaps $10 or so). Any brokerage house or financial supermarket will allow you to buy and sell any ETF. They are unlike mutual funds in that regard. You cannot necessarily purchase any mutual fund through any brokerage house.

Table 6-2 shows the six largest ETFs as of this writing.

Table 6-2	The Six Largest Exchange-Traded Funds	
Name of Fund	**Type of Investment**	**$ Billions Invested**
SPDR Trust Series 1	Large U.S. stocks	$85
iShares MSCI EAFE	Foreign stocks, rich countries	$47
iShares Emerging Markets	Foreign stocks, poor countries	$25.5
PowerShares QQQ	U.S. stocks, mostly large growth, lots of technology	$20
SPDR Gold Trust	Gold	$20
iShares S&P 500	Large U.S. stocks	$18

As far as index investing is concerned, ETFs offer a much wider variety than do mutual funds. That's because even though there are more mutual funds than ETFs, only about 5 percent of mutual funds are index mutual funds (the remainder are actively run funds). And of the index mutual funds, many track the same indexes, such as the S&P 500. There are, in fact, *dozens* of index mutual funds that track the S&P 500!

In contrast, you can buy an ETF that tracks every index imaginable, from entire stock and bond markets to narrow industry market niches, and from large geographical regions (such as Asia and Europe) to individual countries (large and small). ETFs also allow you to buy investments that track both traditional indexes (such as the S&P 500 or the Dow) and all sorts of newfangled indexes based on myriad algorithms and investment theories. Table 6-3 gives you a taste of the variety you can sample, as of September, 2008.

Table 6-3	A Variety of ETFs That Track a Plethora of Indexes
Type of Index Tracked	*Number of ETFs*
Broad stock market	29
Commodities (gold, silver, oil, and so on)	38
Foreign currencies	24
Bonds	54
Global and foreign	130
Inverse/leveraged	66
Industry sector	137
U.S. stock, by size (large cap stocks, micro cap stocks, and so on)	90
Specialty (high-dividend, socially conscious, and such)	55

For much more on ETFs, you may want to read *Exchange-Traded Funds For Dummies* (Wiley) written by, ahem, me.

Facing off: Mutual funds versus ETFs

Let's forget for a moment about which index you wish to track. It doesn't matter whether it is stocks or bonds, U.S. or foreign securities, something high-flying like tech stocks or ultraconservative like Treasuries. There are certain things you should look for in *any* index fund, whether it's a mutual fund or an ETF.

Here are some of the key questions you need to ask yourself in deciding whether you want a mutual fund or an ETF portfolio — or some combination thereof:

 ✔ How well does the investment vehicle track the index?

 ✔ What kind of expenses are we talking about?

 ✔ What tax consequences are you likely to encounter?

✔ Do you need up-to-the-moment pricing?

✔ How transparent is the fund? (Do you know exactly what you're buying?)

✔ Do you need the fancy stuff, like the ability to buy options or short the fund?

In some cases, such as if you think you require options, your choice between a mutual fund and an ETF will be clear: You'll need an ETF. In most cases, however, it will be a judgment call. Neither index mutual funds nor ETFs are necessarily better than the other. In each of the chapters that follows, I try to point you to specific funds that beat the pack. They may be mutual funds, or they may be ETFs.

Often, what's better for you will depend on your particular circumstances. ETFs, which tend to be a bit cheaper than mutual funds, are often your best option for buy-and-hold investing. For money that is regularly invested in small amounts, or for an investment that you may need to tap with any regularity, mutual funds may be better, as you can avoid the commissions charged on ETFs.

Because ETFs tend to be a bit more tax-efficient than mutual funds, they may also be a better bet, all other things being equal, in a taxable account.

Table 6-4 spells out some of the similarities and differences between these two investment options.

Table 6-4	Mutual Funds versus Exchange-Traded Funds	
	Mutual Funds	*ETFs*
Do they offer index investing options?	Yes	Yes
Can you get an instant diversified portfolio?	Yes	Yes
Can you find an inexpensive fund?	Yes	Yes
Do you pay a fee or commission to make a trade?	Sometimes	Yes
Can you buy/sell options?	No	Yes
Can you short?	No	Yes
Is there continuous trading and pricing throughout the day?	No	Yes
Is there a minimum investment?	Usually	No
Are there redemption charges for early withdrawals?	Often	No
Are the funds tax-efficient?	Yes	Yes
Can you make or lose money?	Yes!	Yes!

Spotting Rare Birds in the Index Investing Forest

Not all index funds are mutual funds or ETFs. There are two other options worth knowing about, even though they are far less common. These are exchange-traded notes and unit investment trusts.

Exchange-traded notes (ETNs)

According to Barclays Bank, the outfit that spearheaded ETNs, these are "senior, unsecured, unsubordinated debt securities . . . designed to provide investors with a new way to access the returns of market benchmarks or strategies." In other words, they are strange ducks indeed.

Technically, when you buy an ETN (which you do on an open exchange, just as you would an ETF) you are buying a debt instrument sort of like a bond. If the issuer goes under — poof! — you lose your money. Otherwise, you get a "rate of return" — somewhat similar to interest on a bond but much less predictable — that is linked to the index the ETN is tracking.

Unlike ETFs, most of the ETNs in existence track commodity and currency indexes. The issuer may do all sorts of fancy maneuvers to track these often difficult-to-track indexes, but all that matters to you (as long as the issuer remains solvent) is that you get a rate of return equal to any growth (or shrinkage) in the value of the index. I talk more about ETNs in Chapter 9. Yes, they can sometimes make for good investments.

Unit investment trusts (UITs)

A UIT most resembles a mutual fund with an expiration date. You buy into a UIT, often as you would buy into a mutual fund, and you become a shareholder of a basket of securities — stocks or bonds, usually — that were either hand-picked by a manager or that represent an index.

Some UITs mature in relatively short periods of time — say, within 5 years — at which point you take your money and go home. Others may not mature for as much as 30 years. Some of these longer-duration UITs are traded on exchanges and bear much resemblance to ETFs. In fact, they bear so much resemblance to ETFs that they are often referred to as ETFs, and I may do so myself later in this book.

Exchange-traded portfolios/products

Because UITs can resemble ETFs (and so can ETNs), some media, such as *The Wall Street Journal,* have recently coined the phrase *exchange-traded portfolios* to describe all basket-like investments that trade on exchanges, whether they are true ETFs, ETNs, or UITs. I've also seen the term *exchange-traded products* bandied about of late. (Fortunately, *exchange-traded portfolio* and *exchange-traded products* carry the very same initials, so you'll see them often referred to as ETPs.)

The term *exchange-traded portfolios/products* may also include closed-end mutual funds, which similarly trade on exchanges but, as far as I know, never track indexes. All closed-end mutual funds are actively managed. The more typical mutual fund, the kind of mutual fund we usually refer to when we speak of mutual funds, is technically known as an *open-end* mutual fund. The open-end funds do not trade on exchanges. Because closed-end funds are not index funds, I do not discuss them further in this book.

Meeting the Major Index Makers

The biggest and brawniest of all indexes is the Standard & Poor's 500. More investment dollars are linked to the S&P 500 than to all other indexes *combined.* I'm not saying that you shouldn't invest your money in the S&P 500, but there's no question in my mind that most people (and institutions) do so out of sheer laziness. There are many indexes out there, and many of them may make better foundations for your investments than the Big Kahuna.

In this section, I introduce you to the indexes that form the foundations for much index investing, and I invite you to meet the major index makers.

Standard & Poor's

As the producer of the world's most oft-quoted index, by far, Standard & Poor's — a division of McGraw-Hill — enjoys the catbird seat among index makers and shakers.

The S&P 500

S&P's flagship product, the S&P 500, forms the foundation for four ETFs — including the oldest and largest ETF, the SPDR Trust Series 1 (ticker SPY) — and no fewer than *74* distinct index mutual funds. All together, those funds are valued at more than $1.53 trillion. (That's more than the gross domestic product of Canada!)

So what exactly does this behemoth of an index measure? Although it tracks the ups and downs of only 500 stocks (out of more than 8,000 publicly traded stocks in the United States), those 500 stocks represent approximately three-quarters of the value of the entire U.S. stock market.

The S&P 500 is a *market capitalization* index: Larger company stocks get to play a more important role in the index. The current top five companies are ExxonMobil (3.96 percent of the index), General Electric (2.9 percent), Microsoft (2.22 percent), AT&T (1.95 percent), and Procter & Gamble (1.76 percent).

The 500 companies in the index — although they are all good-sized companies, for sure — are not the 500 largest companies in the land. Rather, they are chosen by their standing within their respective industries; each one supposedly is a leader. Two common misconceptions about the S&P 500 are that it is a mirror of the entire stock market (yes, but a little bit like a funhouse mirror) and that it is an index of all giant companies (close, but no cigar — about 10 percent of the companies in the index would be considered mid cap, not large cap).

Other S&P products

Other popular S&P indexes include the S&P 100 (a subset of the S&P 500 focusing on the largest companies), the S&P Mid Cap 400, the S&P 600 Small Cap Index, and the S&P 1500 (which combines the S&P 500 with the Mid Cap 400 and the 600 Small Cap). S&P also offers the S&P Total Market Index, with about 4,500 companies, including teeny weeny microcaps.

Can you create your own index fund?

In a word, *no.*

Academics have gone back and forth for years arguing about how many stocks you would need to have in your portfolio to attain true diversification — the kind of diversification you can have in a flash by investing in an index fund. At a bare-bones minimum, you would need, I believe, at least 30 stocks, with no one stock comprising much more than 3 percent of your portfolio, to say you are truly well diversified.

But even then, your "well-diversified" portfolio would represent only, say, U.S. stocks. In order to have a portfolio so well-diversified as to include U.S. and foreign stocks, stocks and bonds, and commodities (not to mention exposure to growth stocks and value stocks, large caps and small caps), you'd have to have dozens upon dozens of securities.

Even if you had the money to invest in such a portfolio, the hassles of rebalancing and the resulting trading costs would make it very hard to come out ahead. Why not spend, if you wish, as little as 7/100 of 1 percent a year to own index funds (the cost of several Fidelity and Vanguard index funds)?

That's obviously the way to go — even if you are super rich.

In addition, S&P offers a number of international indexes that form the basis for many of the SPDR brand of ETFs issued by State Street Global Advisors (SSgA), one of the leading ETF producers. And the firm produces style indexes (large growth, small value, and so on) used by ETF leader Barclays iShares for many of its domestic stock offerings.

S&P has also of late begun to produce a number of equal-weighted indexes — both for broad markets and for industry sectors — that certain smaller ETF providers, such as Rydex, are using to base their investment products. The firm is also busy producing various fundamental, or economic-weighted, indexes used by such ETF providers as RevenueShares.

Russell's review

Popularity, alas, is great if you are a rock star but not so great if you are an index.

Given the huge amount of dollars invested in the S&P 500 index funds, a company that joins the S&P 500 index inevitably sees an immediate influx of cash, bidding up the price of the stock. If a company leaves the S&P 500, just as soon as that is announced to the public, the price of the stock inevitably takes a little plunge. The end result of this activity is that managers of S&P 500 funds are often forced to buy higher and sell lower than they should — and shareholders in the funds lose. We're not talking a *lot* of loss here — some analysts says 1/5 of 1 percentage point a year — but why have to suffer that loss at all? Other indexes are broader (better diversified) than the S&P 500, and their lack of such extreme popularity will add to your bottom line. I would not necessarily avoid S&P 500 funds (some of them, due to economies of scale, have very low management fees), but I wouldn't put them at the top of the pack, either.

As with all cap-weighted indexes, the S&P 500 and its ilk may give too much weight to companies that have grown too big for their britches. Over time, some of the newer, fundamental indexes may outperform. But even if the indexes outperform, it is still highly questionable whether the funds tracking the indexes (which are more expensive than the S&P funds, and generally will have greater turnover) will similarly outperform.

The S&P equal-weighted indexes, as well as some of its fundamental or economic indexes, are interesting products. I wouldn't rush to buy a fund based on an equal-weighted or other fundamental index, however, without fully understanding the ramifications. Many people don't.

An equal-weighted index, for example, treats small cap companies the same as it does large cap companies. That egalitarian approach means that an investment based on such an index will offer greater long-term potential return but will also carry more risk (volatility) than an investment based on a conventional index where the largest stocks have the greatest sway. Investments based on equal-weighted or other fundamental indexes versus conventional indexes also require more turnover, resulting in higher costs and possibly greater taxation.

Dow Jones/Dow Jones Wilshire

In Chapter 2, I dub the Dow Jones Industrial Average (DJIA) the "Mother of All Indexes." The DJIA dates back to 1896 and, since that time, has been quoted more times than Shakespeare, Will Rogers, and Confucius combined. The DJIA, which originally consisted of 12 of the nation's most influential and trendsetting companies, now consists of 30, all hand-picked by the editors of *The Wall Street Journal*.

The DJIA

The DJIA is price-weighted, which is a very strange way to construct an index. Stocks with higher prices tip the basket more than the others. Although it made sense 100 or so years ago (before the advent of electronic calculators, or even ballpoint pens), such a strategy really makes little sense today. And neither does an index made up of only 30 stocks that purports to represent the entire stock market.

The DJIA is an anachronism. It is a dinosaur. It is not representative of the entire stock market by any means and doesn't even do a great job of representing large companies! And yet it continues to be quoted, every single day, as a matter of bad habit. (Could it be — shock! — because *The Wall Street Journal* is a Dow Jones newspaper?!) So be it. There are a handful of ETFs and index mutual funds that track the DJIA, but I wouldn't put them on the top of my list for most people's portfolios.

Other products

Dow Jones, however, produces several *thousand* other indexes that track every conceivable slice and sliver of the U.S. stock market, along with the stock markets of other nations.

In 2004, Dow Jones partnered up with the folks at Wilshire Associates, a California firm that had been producing its own popular indexes for a good number of years, to co-brand a series of indexes that measure the market at large. These include the Dow Jones Wilshire 5000, which aims to capture the return of the entire U.S. stock market — and does so rather well. And it includes the Dow Jones Wilshire 4500, which is essentially the Dow Jones Wilshire 5000 minus the S&P 500. The DJW 4500 is a very common measure for all the mid cap and small cap stocks of the land.

Unlike the clunky and anachronistic DJIA, the Dow Jones Wilshire 4500 (which, at the moment, actually contains more than 4,900 stocks — go figure) and the Dow Jones Wilshire 5000 (which currently has more than 5,400 stocks) are both market cap–weighted. And unlike the DJIA, which replaces companies only when the editors of *The Wall Street Journal* are having a slow day and feel like issuing a press release, the Dow Jones Wilshire indexes update monthly.

At present, the five largest holdings in the DJW 5000 are ExxonMobil (3.32 percent of the index), General Electric (2.2 percent), Microsoft (1.6 percent), Procter & Gamble (1.4 percent), and AT&T (1.4 percent). The top five in the DJW 4500 are Genentech (1 percent of the index), The Mosaic Company (0.5 percent), Bunge (0.4 percent), MasterCard (0.4 percent), and McDermott International (0.4 percent).

Dow Jones, like S&P, has recently gotten into the business of producing fundamental indexes based on various economic factors, and some of these are packaged in the form of ETFs. The iShares Dow Jones Select Dividend Index, for example, is both an index and an ETF that tracks the index, which over-weights companies that pay relatively fat dividends.

Russell's review

The DJIA is not the best index for your investments to track. On the other hand, if you already own an ETF or mutual fund that tracks the DJIA, you could do worse — don't panic! Read Chapter 7 and decide if another stock index fund — perhaps based on a broader (more diversified) and more logically weighted index — may suit your purposes better.

If you're going to have only one U.S. stock index to base your investments on, the Dow Jones Wilshire 5000 is a pretty good choice — not optimal, but pretty good. The Dow Jones Wilshire 4500 is not at all a bad representative of mid cap and small cap U.S. equities. I reveal optimal choices in Chapter 7!

Lehman Brothers

Personally, I'd just as soon be a tamer of lions with attitude than try to create a fixed-income index, so I'm glad Lehman Brothers is in business to do it for us. Indexing bonds is much, much trickier than indexing stocks. The reason: There are only several thousand public issues of stock being offered in the United States versus literally *millions* of bonds.

A large company like Johnson & Johnson or Coca-Cola, for example, may issue one, two, or possibly three kinds of stock. But such a company may issue hundreds of series of bonds, each with its own coupon rate, callability features, and guarantees. The U.S. government and government agencies collectively issue more bonds than McDonald's makes hamburgers. And then there are the many, many municipalities that sell bonds to raise money for road repairs and bridges and such.

Lehman Brothers, the producers of such popular bond indexes as the Lehman Aggregate Bond Index, figures out how to take representative samples from the enormous bond universe and turn them into a workable index. Bless them.

The Lehman Aggregate Bond Index is far and away the nation's most popular and broadest index for fixed-income securities. It tracks the performance of the entire U.S. investment-grade (high quality) bond market, which includes U.S. Treasury bonds, agency bonds, corporate bonds, and mortgage-backed securities.

At present, there are three ETFs and several dozen mutual funds that track the Lehman Aggregate Bond Index. Lehman offers hundreds of other indexes that track everything from high-yield (junk) bonds and municipal bonds to Treasury Inflation-Protected Securities and convertible bonds.

Russell's review

If you're going to have only one bond holding, by all means, owning an ETF or index mutual fund that tracks the Lehman Aggregate Bond Index isn't a bad way to go — provided you want a taxable bond portfolio, you're using the fixed-income position to generate cash, and you can handle a bit of volatility. The average maturity of the index is 6.5 years, which means that the value of any fund tracking the index will have its ups and downs.

You may need something less volatile, or you may want a fund that provides either a higher potential return or tax-free interest payments. Such fine-tuning of your bond portfolio is the subject of Chapter 8. There, you'll find suggestions for many bond index funds that track, in many cases, Lehman Brothers indexes of various sorts.

MSCI Barra

The "MS" in MSCI stands for Morgan Stanley, and the investment banking house is a majority shareholder in this firm, which is famous for, among other things, its global indexes.

MSCI produces indexes that track the performance of both stock and bond markets in nearly every nation on Earth, including 23 developed markets (England, France, Japan), 25 emerging markets (Russia, Brazil, India), and 20 of what the MSCI folks call *frontier* markets (Kenya, Croatia, Sri Lanka).

A good portion of non-U.S. ETFs, including most of those issued by industry leaders Barclays and Vanguard, track MSCI global indexes. Vanguard also uses MSCI indexes for many of its domestic equity funds, both ETFs and mutual funds.

What makes for a superior index?

All indexes are not created equal. Where it comes to investing — and picking an index upon which to base an investment strategy — the following are signs that the index you've chosen to track is a winner or a loser:

What securities are included in the index?

✔ *Winners:* Inclusion of securities in the index is determined by an objective means, and that means is clearly spelled out and based on a crisp set of criteria that all can see.

✔ *Losers:* Securities in the index are chosen by men in funny hats who read tea leaves and use tarot cards.

What are the securities chosen meant to represent?

✔ *Winners:* The securities represent an entire market, or a good chunk of a market that may be defined as an *asset class*. In other words, the basket of securities has certain characteristics that set it apart from anything else in your portfolio. Examples may include large cap growth stocks, real estate investment trusts, or commodities.

✔ *Losers:* The securities represent a tiny sliver of the market or have no real distinguishing characteristic that sets them apart from any other investments you may hold. Examples may include all companies whose CEO is named Fred or companies that issue dividends on the second Tuesday of each month.

How often does the index change?

✔ *Winners:* Updated at least annually to reflect changes in the market. But not updated so often as to create unnecessary turnover leading to excess expenses and negative tax consequences.

✔ *Losers:* Updated when the men in funny hats feel like it.

What kind of weighting method is used?

✔ *Winners:* It's generally best that the index is cap-weighted according to the investible portion of companies (float-weighted) — but there may be exceptions.

✔ *Losers:* Weighted by some seemingly random or fleeting element, such as the price of the stock or the astrological sign of the CEO.

If the index is tilted to juice investment returns, just how is it tilted?

✔ *Winners:* The index uses long-term historical data to find market segments that outperform. Example: A broad stock market index that tilts toward value (bargain-basement) stocks.

✔ *Losers:* The index uses very recent market performance to concentrate on whatever happens to be hot at the moment. Example: A stock market index that tilts toward companies that are making money off national security initiatives.

MSCI indexes are cap-weighted, but they purposely allow for ample fudge room before bumping a company from one category and moving it into another. This results in instances in which you may occasionally find, say, a mid cap company in a large cap index. You may also find certain companies whose stock appears in both a value index and a growth index.

The downside to this methodology is that you wind up with somewhat nebulous indexes with possible crossover. The upside is that the indexes necessitate limited turnover, which can reduce trading costs and taxes to those who invest in funds that track MSCI indexes. (Hey, no index is perfect; they *all* have pros and cons.)

Russell's review

Provided the fund management fees are low, funds based on MSCI indexes should be considered gems, although not necessarily Hope diamonds. In Chapter 7 where I outline my suggestions for specific stock ETFs and index mutual funds, you'll find that many MSCI index–based funds make it to the top of the list.

Russell

Although they don't have the same household familiarity as either Standard & Poor's or Dow Jones, the Russell indexes are where most financial professionals look to measure the performance of the broad U.S. stock market.

Although Russell produces dozens of global indexes — with a particular emphasis on Japan (the Russell/Nomura indexes) — this index provider is best known for its U.S. indexes, especially the Russell 3000, the Russell 1000, and the Russell 2000. Here is how they work:

Each year, on May 31, the folks at Russell rank U.S. common stocks from largest to smallest, using market capitalization but on a strictly *free-float basis*. (They ignore all stocks held in private hands that are very unlikely to be bought or sold anytime soon.) After they've calculated the entire list, they divide it up as follows:

- ✔ **The broad market:** The largest 3,000 stocks become the Russell 3000 Index.

- ✔ **The large cap and mid cap market:** Within the broad market, the top one-third — the largest 1,000 stocks — become the Russell 1000 Index.

- ✔ **The small cap market:** The remaining two-thirds of stocks become the Russell 2000 Index.

Within each of these size categories, Russell further breaks up the world of stocks into value and growth, and the methodology it uses to do so (largely price-to-book ratio) makes eminent sense, even though it has been attacked of late for being old-fashioned.

Many ETFs, including a good number of Barclays iShares domestic stock ETFs, use the Russell indexes as their foundation.

Russell's review

There is good rhyme and reason behind Russell's lineup of indexes. (Plus, the name is excellent, don't you think?) As I tend to like broad indexes on which to base investments, I naturally lean toward Russell as a solid base for any index funds chosen for a portfolio. Russell indexes, especially when combined with the prowess of Barclays at producing index investment products, make for especially smart portfolio choices.

Getting to Know Some of the Secondary Teams

The minor leagues of indexing is where you are most likely to find things done in a nontraditional manner. Hold onto your hats as I introduce you to some players in the field you many not be familiar with. The following outfits produce indexes that have a substantial number of funds tracking them, so you should familiarize yourself with their names and basic styles. In the following several chapters, I may recommend either ETFs or index mutual funds that use their indexes.

FTSE

FTSE is to the United Kingdom what Standard & Poor's is to the United States. It is an independent company owned by the *Financial Times* and the London Stock Exchange. Its flagship index, the FTSE 100, is often used to represent the British stock market, much as the S&P 500 represents the U.S. stock market. But just as S&P produces many indexes aside from the S&P 500, so does FTSE produce many indexes aside from the famous FTSE 100. In fact, it produces more than 100,000 indexes covering all sorts of asset classes in nearly every country of the world.

In the United States, FTSE has become a leader in the production of *fundamental* indexes: indexes that use various financial criteria to build investment portfolios designed to (they hope) outperform conventional indexes. For example, FTSE produces a host of industry-sector indexes (utilities, healthcare, consumer services, and so on) in which the companies included, and their weights in the index, are chosen by their book values, income, sales, and dividends.

Several purveyors of ETFs — most notably PowerShares and Vanguard — have chosen to base a number of index investment products on FTSE indexes.

Morningstar

From the company most famous for its independent analysis — and star ratings — of stocks and stock funds, Morningstar indexes cover everything from the broad stock market to small market sectors, as well as bonds and commodities.

Perhaps most particular to Morningstar indexes is the strong emphasis on style investing. You may be familiar with the Morningstar "grid" that breaks the universe of stocks into large, mid cap, and small stocks, as well as value, blend, and growth stocks. Many financial professionals, including the handsome guy writing this book, like to look at their portfolios in terms of the Morningstar grid. We therefore tend to like indexes that (in the words of Morningstar) "can be used for precise asset allocation and benchmarking, and as efficient tools for portfolio construction and market analysis."

Barclays iShares issues a series of ETFs based on Morningstar indexes. They've been around for several years but have not become enormously popular. Nonetheless, they are among the better ETFs you can buy, in terms of both following a highly reasonable index and carrying low management expenses.

Dimensional

Dimensional Fund Advisors, also called DFA, has been around since 1981 and has become an undisputed leader in index investing. The name isn't nearly as well-known as Vanguard's because Dimensional sells its funds only to institutions and fee-only (non-commissioned) wealth managers. I myself use Dimensional, in addition to Vanguard index funds and various ETFs. Dimensional produces its own indexes and does so brilliantly.

Here's what's unique about Dimensional: The firm embraces years of academic research that tell us certain kinds of stocks and bonds tend to show higher performance per unit of risk. Most notably, value stocks — stocks that sell at low prices compared to the innate value of the company — tend to kick butt over time. Small cap and microcap stocks similarly tend to yield higher returns per unit of risk than do large cap stocks. Based on this research, Dimensional's indexes, even those that measure broad markets, tend to lean toward small cap and value.

This is something very few other producers of indexes seem to grasp or, even if they do, orchestrate as well as Dimensional.

On the bond side of things, Dimensional's quasi index-based funds scour the developed fixed-income world looking for the highest yields. It's a unique approach that has served Dimensional's investors well.

The only problem with Dimensional is that the fund expenses, while reasonable, are still considerably higher than some other index products on the market. And if you have to work through a fee-only advisor, that, too, will add to your expenses. Together, it means that Dimensional products, although excellent, are not a slam-dunk for your portfolio.

I weigh in more on Dimensional index funds in Chapter 7.

WisdomTree

Under the tutelage of investment gurus Jeremy Siegel (author of *Stocks for the Long Run* and esteemed professor at Wharton) and Michael Steinhardt (former hedge-fund king), an upstart company named WisdomTree is producing ETFs and the indexes behind them. WisdomTree's propriety indexes are weighted according to both company earnings and the issuance of dividends. In essence, the company is taking a crack at redefining value stocks using a new methodology to pick them. Instead of using the traditional book-to-value and price-earnings ratios used by most financial types, WisdomTree is looking more at a company's profitability and trends in cash disbursements to shareholders.

Will the newer methodology bring better returns for investors? Only time will tell. Seigel and Steinhardt are very smart guys, for sure. But there are also financial powerhouses who still swear by more traditional methods of indexing.

If all else were equal, I'd be quite keen on WisdomTree ETFs. But because they tend to carry slightly higher costs than other ETFs, they also carry a risk that should the new methodology not prove clearly superior, investors could lose out. Time will be the judge.

Chapter 7

Investing in Stock Indexes: Your Gateway to Growth

. . . .

In This Chapter

▶ Recognizing the importance of stocks in your portfolio

▶ Appreciating that not all stocks — or stock indexes — are the same

▶ Achieving diversification in your equity portfolio

▶ Understanding the basics of style investing

▶ Choosing the best index funds for your stock holdings

▶ Knowing what options are best to avoid

. . . .

*Y*es, the heading to this chapter is 100 percent on the mark — stocks are indeed your "gateway to growth." BUT, hey (you already know this, I'm sure, but a reminder won't hurt), the gate swings *both ways*. Invest in the wrong stocks, or invest at the wrong time, and your nest egg can get seriously scrambled.

Just ask grandma and grandpa about that little picnic called the Great Depression. Or ask anyone who was invested in stocks during the much more recent three-year bear market of 2000–2002. Or look at your own portfolio's less-than-anything-to-write-home-about performance in even more recent days. (I write this three-quarters of the way through 2008, when the S&P 500 is down more than 11 percent year-to-date.)

Indeed, the gate swings both ways, and if you aren't careful, it can knock you on your financial butt.

 Index investing can't protect you entirely from market downturns. If you are invested in stocks — any stocks — most bear markets will still leave teeth marks in your portfolio. But investing in stock index funds can greatly lessen the severity of the bites. And by investing wisely in stock index funds along with, say, bond index funds (see Chapter 8) and commodity index funds (see Chapter 9), you can sometimes turn bear bites into cub bites.

Diversification, you see, is one very important way to lessen the inherent risk in a portfolio that has a lot of stock. (Any portfolio poised for growth *should* have lots of stock.) And there is no better way to achieve diversification than through index funds.

In this chapter, I focus on stock index funds (which comprise about 90 percent of all index funds) and discuss the many options — good, great, and not-so-great — available to you.

Understanding the Whys and Wherefores of Stock Investing

Stocks go up. Stocks go down. But over the long run — sometimes you may need to wait till the very long run! — they go up. That's why you want stocks in your portfolio. If you can stomach the inevitable volatility, you want predominately stocks. (See recommended percentages in Chapters 11 and 15.)

Stocks are nothing magic. They are little more than certificates (real paper-and-ink certificates in the old days, virtual certificates today) that verify you are a partial owner in a company. As a partial owner, you are due a portion of any dividends issued by the company. You are also due to share in any increase in the price of the company's stock. A stock's price may increase because the company itself becomes more valuable (as evidenced by sales and profits and patents and such), or it may increase simply because the market suddenly thinks the stock should be worth more, whether sales and profits are going up or not.

Of course, if the company starts to lose money or goes under, or the market simply loses faith in a stock, the dividend payments will dry up faster than a sponge in the microwave, and the value of your holdings (the price of your shares) will drop.

Distinguishing individual stocks from stocks in the aggregate

An individual company stock — even for a company as large and powerful as McDonald's or Coca-Cola — is subject to the whims of the market. That includes the market for burgers and soda, as well as the stock market itself.

But in the aggregate, stocks are much less subject to whims. As long as the economy at large is doing well, most company stocks will do well. That's because industry is the largest component in our economy.

To put it in other words, if you invest in a large basket of stocks, you will very likely see good return on your capital as long as capitalism is thriving. That's not to say that capitalism will thrive forever. It won't. Sooner or later, the sun will explode, taking even McDonald's and Coca-Cola with it. But the current economic system, despite many problems, doesn't seem on the verge of collapse. (One of the tips I provide later on — in Chapter 16 — is to tune out the mass media coverage of the markets, which is forever forecasting imminent collapse.)

We invest in stocks because stocks have a long history of superlative performance, and we assume that the future may look something like the past. And, despite what we may hear on CNN, scientists tell us that we have about 5 billion more years until the sun explodes.

Separating the two kinds of risk

The risk you take investing in stocks comes in two varieties. When you invest in an individual stock, say McDonald's, you risk that the company itself will be hurt either by something it does wrong or something beyond its control that nonetheless crushes its stock. The company may offer a new product or product line (lizard burgers, for example) that the public simply hates. Or the CEO may have a heart attack (from eating too many lizard burgers with fries). Or there may be an expensive lawsuit brought by a rival company or an angry supplier or customer (who choked on a lizard bone). This kind of risk is known as *nonsystemic* risk.

The other kind of risk — the *systemic* version — is the risk that the entire economy will falter or that stock valuations will plummet simply because the public at large (after watching too much CNN) gets cold feet and decides to shove all its investment dollars under the mattress (or put it into Treasury bonds and CDs). This kind of risk is much more dangerous to investors.

Investing in stock indexes wipes nonsystemic risk off the map. When you are an index investor, you free yourself from the stupidity of individual CEOs and the vicissitudes of a fickle investing public that may like a certain stock one day and not the next.

Unfortunately, index investing can't do a whole lot to eliminate systemic risk.

But here's the good news: Over the long run, you get compensated for systemic risk. Investing in a high-risk market (like small cap stocks or emerging-market stocks) has historically paid off very handsomely.

Investing in less risky markets, like blue chip stocks, has paid off handsomely, but less so. The higher the risk, the higher the return — as long as we're talking about systemic risk! Nonsystemic risk, on the other hand, brings *no* concurrent reward. None. Zip. *Nada.*

If McDonald's brings out a lizard burger, and you hold McDonald's stock, you lose. There is no up side.

By investing in index funds and eliminating nonsystemic risk, you essentially increase your anticipated return per unit of risk. And that's a very good thing! That's one of many reasons that indexing makes such a sweet investment strategy.

Appreciating past performance

In Figure 7-1, I present a bird's-eye view of how stocks of large companies and small companies have performed in the past 20+ years. What's shown here are the rolling 36-month returns of two stocks indexes: the Russell 2000 (small stocks) and the S&P 500 (large stocks). As a point of comparison, I also show you how well bonds — the obvious alternative to stocks — have done in the same time period. (Chapter 8 talks all about bond indexes.)

Keep in mind that history is history. Just because stocks have seen an average annual return of about 10 percent over the past 80 or so years is no guarantee that they will do so in the future. We simply don't know.

Taking a cautionary approach

Note that such long-term charts as Figure 7-1 — I'm sure you've seen similar charts before — can be a wee bit misleading, giving you something of a false sense of security. Few people can invest their money for 20+ years. Many of us build sizeable nest eggs by the time we're, say, 55 or so, and then hope to head to retirement within, say, the next 10 years. If we're only a few years away from retirement, swings in the stock market can make or break us.

For that reason, investing in stocks, in the eyes of most financial types, is a no-brainer for the young who have lots of time to see their investments grow (or to replace those investments should they go *poof*). For older investors, mixing stocks with other, more conservative investments is the way to go. I talk about this subject more in Chapter 11 and then provide sample portfolios in Chapter 15.

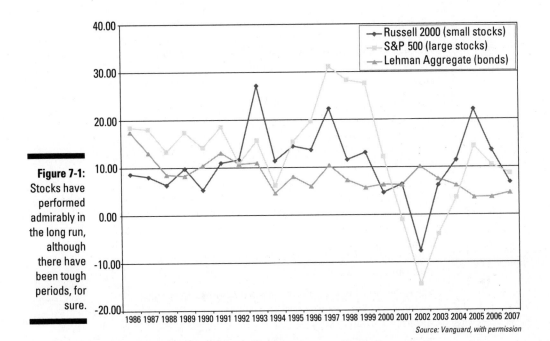

Figure 7-1:
Stocks have performed admirably in the long run, although there have been tough periods, for sure.

Source: Vanguard, with permission

For the remainder of this chapter, I want to focus in on your choices in stocks, and stocks alone.

Investing in Stocks the Right Way

Within the world of stock investing, there are ways to invest brilliantly and ways to invest dumbly. I've seen both.

Here are some general guidelines for intelligent and profitable stock investing. Note that choosing stock index funds will help you achieve many of these guidelines!

✔ **Be in it for the long haul.** You don't know where the value of your investment will be in one, two, or three years. Stock markets are volatile. Only invest money in stocks that you aren't going to need for at least several years to come.

✔ **Don't tinker too much.** Buying and selling stock can be expensive, with commissions and *spreads* (the difference between the ask and buy price) eating into your profits, and taxes eating up whatever is left. Resist the urge to day-trade, or anything close to it. Buying and holding saves money, and a penny saved is . . . you know.

✔ **Watch what you pay the experts.** Mutual funds are great ways to own stocks. So are exchange-traded funds. And sometimes, having a professional broker or financial planner to guide you can be very helpful. But always watch your bottom line. Fund management fees and advisor costs should be scrutinized. Are you really getting what you're paying for?

✔ **Diversify to the hilt.** At a minimum, you should have a good mix of U.S. and international stocks. Preferably, you should not only have a global mix, but you should also have large-company and small-company stocks, and value and growth stocks. And your stocks should be spread among various industries.

✔ **Be tax conscious.** Use tax-advantaged accounts, such as 401(k)s and IRAs, to stash whatever assets you can. Stocks that throw off lots of dividend income or stocks that can be expected to appreciate greatly can profit you a lot more if Uncle Sam's hands can be kept away. Certain kinds of stocks — such as real estate investment trusts (REITs) — are notoriously tax-inefficient and should always be kept in tax-advantaged accounts.

✔ **Be risk-appropriate.** All stocks are potentially volatile and offer a crack at appreciation. Some stocks, however, are riskier (more volatile) and allow for greater growth. Know one kind of stock from another, and know what your personal level of risk should be. Generally, stocks in smaller companies and less advanced countries offer greater potential for return and the highest odds of taking a belly flop.

✔ **Achieve balance in your portfolio.** Know that even an optimally diversified stock portfolio will still carry risk. Few, if any, investors should have everything in stocks. Seek to balance your stock portfolio with bonds, commodities, and cash.

✔ **Buy low, sell high!** One of the biggest mistakes that investors make is bailing out of stocks when the going gets rough, then loading back up on the stocks when the going is grand. You don't want to do that! Be better disciplined. If you feel that your portfolio deserves, say, a 60 percent allocation to stocks, get it there, and keep it there. Yes, that may mean buying more stock just when others are selling, and selling when others are buying. You'll clobber those others' returns over the long run!

✔ **Buy and hold, but don't ignore.** Set yourself up with a solid portfolio strategy, but don't forget to revisit it from time to time. You'll be getting older, your income will change, your expenses may vary, your domestic situation may change . . . All of these factors can warrant a tweaking of your original plans.

Choosing Wisely among Many Stock Index Funds

Your choice of stock index funds is enormous — and growing. (A select list of index mutual funds appears in Appendix A, and a select list of exchange-traded funds appears in Appendix B.) If I were to review every single index fund, this book would run over 1,000 pages! In the following sections, I review only some of my very favorite stock index funds (and give dishonorable mention to a few of my least favorite).

Note that there is no such thing as a "perfect" index or index fund. I try to give you a good idea of what comes close to perfect in this chapter, but much depends on your personal circumstances. I get into all that personal stuff — your investment style, your risk tolerance, your tax bracket, your career, your age, and so on — in Part III.

Home of the brave: Broad U.S. stock market index funds

For most investors living, working, and spending their hard-earned cash in the United States, taking a somewhat sizeable stake in the U.S. stock market makes enormous sense. A healthy financial exposure to the largest economy on the planet makes sense even in the portfolio of a Brit or a Japanese. And to a U.S. citizen, it makes even more sense. That's because high inflation and stock market performance are somewhat correlated. If inflation zooms, chances are good (but not guaranteed) that the stock market will zoom, and your portfolio will protect you from poverty.

How much do you want to invest in the broad U.S. stock market? It currently represents 38 percent of the global stock market. I recommend that your total stock position be somewhere in the ballpark of 50 to 60 percent U.S. stocks. You want at least 40 percent international stock to diversify your portfolio. Even though most U.S. investors have recently poured money into foreign stocks (for all the wrong reasons — they were chasing recent performance), most of them still could stand to have more invested abroad.

As for the 50 to 60 percent of your portfolio that you want in U.S. stock, it may belong in a broad-market index fund. For modest stock portfolios ($20,000 or under), a single broad-index U.S. fund combined with a single broad-index international fund is often the best route to go. Many mutual funds have minimum investments of $2,500 or so, but some of the best, unfortunately, have minimums of $10,000. If you go with an exchange-traded fund, there will never be a minimum, but trading costs can add appreciably to your total investment costs if you try to split less than $20,000 too many ways.

Following are some broad U.S. stock market index funds worthy of consideration.

Mutual funds

Fidelity Spartan Total Market Index Fund (FSTMX)

Indexed to: Dow Jones Wilshire 5000 Index. The fund holds about 3,370 of the 5,400 stocks in the index.

Expense ratio: 0.10 percent

Average cap size: $28.0 billion

P/E ratio: 15.8

Minimum initial purchase: $10,000

Minimum initial purchase in IRA: $10,000

Top five holdings: Exxon Mobil, General Electric, Microsoft, AT&T, Procter & Gamble

Notes: This fund tracks a *very* broad index (that's good!) and is a true low-cost leader among index funds. If you can amass $100,000, you can then move the money to the Fidelity Spartan Total Market Advantage Class version — the very same fund, but with an absolute rock-bottom industry fee of 0.07 percent a year. Fidelity, I believe, has lowered the prices on a few of its broad index market funds for the main purpose of taking away index customers from index-investing leader Vanguard. You can take advantage of this price war!

Vanguard Total Stock Market Index Fund (VTSMX)

Indexed to: The MSCI U.S. Broad Market Index, which captures 99.5 percent of the value of all the publicly traded stock in the United States. The fund typically holds the largest 1,200 to 1,300 stocks in its target index (covering nearly 95 percent of the MSCI index's total market capitalization) and a representative sampling of the remaining stocks.

Expense ratio: 0.15 percent

Average cap size: $34.5 billion

P/E ratio: 16.9

Minimum initial purchase: $3,000

Minimum initial purchase in IRA: $3,000

Top five holdings: Exxon Mobil, General Electric, Microsoft, AT&T, Procter & Gamble

Notes: If you qualify for Vanguard Admiral Shares, you can have this very same fund for a total of 0.07 percent a year, the lowest in the business (on a par with Fidelity). You qualify for the Vanguard Total Stock Market Index Fund Admiral Shares (VTSAX) if you have $100,000 or more invested in the fund, or if you've owned the fund for at least 10 years and have a balance of $50,000 or more. Alternatively, you can buy the same fund in ETF version, pay 0.07 percent, and not have to have any minimum amount invested (although you will pay a trading fee).

T. Rowe Price Total Equity Market Index Fund (POMIX)

Indexed to: The S&P Total Market Index, which boasts a lineup of roughly 4,500 stocks, cap-weighted.

Expense ratio: 0.40 percent

Average cap size: $31.1 billion

P/E ratio: 16.7

Minimum initial purchase: $2,500

Minimum initial purchase in IRA: $1,000

Top five holdings: AT & T, Bank of America, Chevron, Exxon Mobil, General Electric

Notes: This is a very similar fund to both the Vanguard and Fidelity options. Note the higher expense ratio but the lower minimum investment. T. Rowe Price has a tradition of being friendlier than most large brokerage houses to the smaller investor.

Exchange-traded funds

Vanguard Total Stock Market ETF (VTI)

Indexed to: The MSCI U.S. Broad Market Index, which captures 99.5 percent of the value of all the publicly traded stock in the United States. The fund typically holds the largest 1,200 to 1,300 stocks in its target index (covering nearly 95 percent of the MSCI index's total market capitalization) and a representative sample of the remaining stocks.

Expense ratio: 0.07 percent

Average cap size: $31.0 billion

P/E ratio: 16.7

Top five holdings: Exxon Mobil, General Electric, Microsoft, AT&T, Procter & Gamble

Notes: This is the ETF version of Vanguard's Total Stock Market Index Fund. At 0.07 percent (versus about twice as much for the mutual fund), the ETF is clearly a better way to go for most folks. Of all the total-market funds in the business, this will be the optimal choice for many investors, both for its breadth of investments and its super-low cost . . . not to mention a high degree of tax-efficiency.

SPDR DJ Wilshire Total Market ETF (TMW)

Indexed to: The Dow Jones Wilshire 5000 Index. The fund holds about 1,020 of the 5,400 stocks in the index.

Expense ratio: 0.20 percent

Average cap size: $30.6 billion

P/E ratio: 13.8

Top five holdings: Exxon Mobil, General Electric, Microsoft, AT&T, Procter & Gamble

Notes: This is essentially the same fund as the Fidelity Spartan Total Market Index Fund (FSTMX) — but at exactly twice the cost. I sometimes use this fund as an example to illustrate that ETFs aren't always cheaper than mutual funds. Of course, this ETF doesn't carry a $10,000 minimum, as does the Fidelity mutual fund. It may also prove to be slightly more tax-efficient over time.

What does the P/E ratio mean?

We financial people just love ratios, and perhaps no ratio is as often quoted as the P/E, which is short for Price/Earnings.

To get the P/E, you start with the company's total earnings over the past year, and divide that number by the total number of shares of stock issued by the company. The resulting figure represents earnings per share, represented by the letter *E*. The upper number of the equation — P — represents the market price of the stock. When a P/E is applied to a fund, it represents the aggregate of all the P's and all the E's in the fund portfolio.

Generally speaking, the lower the ratio (the higher the earnings in relation to the price of the stock), the more "valuey" a stock or a portfolio. That's often a good thing because valuey stocks and portfolios, over the course of history, all things being equal, tend to appreciate more over time. Growth stocks and growth funds typically have higher P/E ratios than value stocks and funds. (In fact, "growth" and "value" are often defined by the P/E ratios.) For a well-diversified portfolio, you want both.

iShares Dow Jones U.S. Total Market (IYY)

Indexed to: The Dow Jones U.S. Index, which aims to represent the top 95 percent of U.S. companies based on float-adjusted market capitalization, excluding the very smallest and least-liquid stocks. IYY consists of approximately 1,500 stocks used as a representative sampling.

Expense ratio: 0.20 percent

Average cap size: $32.3 billion

P/E ratio: 19.8

Top five holdings: Exxon Mobil, General Electric, Microsoft, AT&T, Procter & Gamble

Notes: ETF industry leader Barclays iShares knows how to produce index funds, and this is indeed a well-greased product, on a par with the similar SPDR ETF (TMW) in terms of both breadth and expense ratio. Both of these securities, however, exceed Vanguard's ETF (VTI) and Fidelity's index mutual fund (FSTMX) in cost, and I doubt you will get any extra juice for your money.

Microsoft and McDonald's: Large cap U.S. stock index funds

Big and beefy, U.S. *large cap* stocks (the term generally refers to stocks of companies worth at least $5 billion) are the single biggest component in most people's portfolios. If your total stock portfolio is over $20,000 or so, and the total amount you have allocated to U.S. stock is above $10,000 or so, I recommend that you consider splitting your domestic holdings into large cap and small cap, rather than dumping everything into a total market fund.

Why?

By splitting your holdings, you gain the ability to rebalance your portfolio every year or so. (I explain rebalancing in Chapter 16.) And by doing that — by adding to down positions and drawing from up positions — you can perhaps juice some added return from your portfolio. As your portfolio gets larger, you may want to slice and dice your domestic stock holdings into several categories, but for a start, large cap and small cap work quite nicely.

Large cap stocks tend to do better in certain times (remember the 1990s?). Small caps tend to perform better in the long haul, but with considerably more volatility. I suggest proper proportions of each in Chapters 12 and 15. Here, I present some of the large cap funds most worthy of consideration.

Mutual funds

Vanguard Large Cap Index Fund (VLACX)

Indexed to: The MSCI U.S. Prime Market 750 Index, a diversified index of stocks of the most humungous U.S. companies, both value and growth.

Expense ratio: 0.20 percent

Average cap size: $47.5 billion

P/E ratio: 16.6

Minimum initial purchase: $3,000

Minimum initial purchase in IRA: $3,000

Top five holdings: Exxon Mobil, General Electric, Microsoft, AT&T, Procter & Gamble

Notes: With $100,000, you can move to the Admiral Class of this fund (VLCAX) — the very same beast but with a yearly fee of only 0.12 percent. Or, if you want the ETF version of the same fund, you can purchase the Vanguard Large Cap ETF (VV), which has an expense ratio of only 0.07 percent.

Fidelity 100 Index Fund (FOHIX)

Indexed to: The S&P 100 Index, which is a subset of the S&P 500. (Would you believe that the 100 largest stocks in the S&P 500 constitute 60 percent of the S&P 500 and 45 percent of the capitalization of the entire U.S. stock market?!)

Expense ratio: 0.20 percent

Average cap size: $105.1 billion

P/E ratio: 15.3

Minimum initial purchase: $10,000

Minimum initial purchase in IRA: $10,000

Top five holdings: Exxon Mobil, General Electric, Microsoft, AT&T, Procter & Gamble

Notes: The Fidelity Spartan 500 Index Fund (FSMKX) is more popular and cheaper (0.10 percent annual management fee), but if you want a large cap fund that is truly large, the Fidelity 100 is the way to go. At 0.20 percent, the fee is reasonable, and this fund gives you excellent diversification if matched with a small cap index fund.

Exchange-traded funds

Rydex Russell Top 50 ETF (XLG)

Indexed to: The Russell Top 50 Index, which includes approximately 50 of the largest companies in the land.

Expense ratio: 0.20 percent

Average cap size: $139.8 billion

P/E ratio: 15.3

Top five holdings: Exxon Mobil, General Electric, Microsoft, AT&T, Procter & Gamble

Notes: If you want BIG — really BIG — this is the fund to choose. The expense ratio is fine. The Russell indexes are well constructed. There's nothing to lose here — unless large caps get clobbered.

Vanguard Large Cap ETF (VV)

Indexed to: The MSCI U.S. Prime Market 750 Index, a diversified index of stocks of the most humungous U.S. companies, both value and growth.

Expense ratio: 0.07 percent

Average cap size: $47.5 billion

P/E ratio: 16.6

Top five holdings: Exxon Mobil, General Electric, Microsoft, AT&T, Procter & Gamble

Notes: This is the ETF version of Vanguard's Large Cap Index Fund (VLACX). The ETF has a considerably lower management fee, but, of course, you have to pay a commission to buy and trade it. Like all ETFs, there is no minimum investment.

iShares S&P 100 Index Fund (OEF)

Indexed to: The S&P 100 Index, which is a subset of the S&P 500.

Expense ratio: 0.20 percent

Average cap size: $104.9 billion

P/E ratio: 15.3

Top five holdings: Exxon Mobil, General Electric, Microsoft, AT&T, Procter & Gamble

Notes: This Barclays product is essentially the ETF version of the Fidelity 100 Index Fund (FOHIX) — same expense ratio and everything. Which is the better bet? There isn't going to be much difference, really. If you have the $10,000 to invest in the mutual fund, and you already have your money parked at Fidelity, I'd say it's going to be pretty much a wash. If you have less than $10,000 to invest, or if you're using another brokerage house (which will probably charge more for the Fidelity mutual fund than the ETF), go with the ETF.

Small is beautiful: Small cap and micro cap index funds

In the parlance of Wall Street, small cap stocks are stocks in companies worth $250 million to $1 billion, and micro cap stocks are with companies valued at $50 million to $250 million. (Compare these figures to large caps, which are companies with more than $5 billion in capitalization, and mid caps, which are everything in between.)

Over time, small cap stocks clearly outperform larger company stocks. (Think Microsoft as a young company versus Microsoft today.) According to the latest figures from Morningstar, one dollar invested in large company stocks at year-end 1925 would have grown by now to $3,250. One dollar invested in small company stocks would have grown by now to $15,100. That equates to an average compound annual return of 10.4 for the large stocks and 12.5 for the small stocks.

Small stocks are also more volatile than large stocks. If you're familiar with standard deviation, the most popular way that volatility is measured, large company stocks have a long-term standard deviation, per Morningstar, of 20.0 percent versus 32.6 percent for small company stocks.

It pays to have both large company and small company stocks in your portfolio because they tend to do better (or worse) at different times. A perfect example comes from the dot-com explosion of the 1990s, when large cap stocks were flying high, versus just a few years later, when small caps raged ahead. Note the dramatic difference in compound annual return between these two five-year periods:

	1994–1998	*2000–2004*
Large company stocks	24.06	–2.30
Small company stocks	13.16	14.32

Source: Morningstar

Following are a few small company stock index funds well worth your consideration.

Mutual funds

Vanguard Small Cap Index Fund (NAESX)

Indexed to: The MSCI U.S. Small Cap 1750 Index, which represents the universe of small cap companies in the U.S. market. The index targets for inclusion 1,750 companies (sometimes it may be slightly more or less) and represents about 12 percent of the capitalization of the U.S. stock market.

Expense ratio: 0.23 percent

Average cap size: $1.5 billion

P/E ratio: 17.8

Minimum initial purchase: $3,000

Minimum initial purchase in IRA: $3,000

Top five holdings: CF Industries, Flowserve, Respironics, BE Aerospace, Terra Industries

Notes: This is a good all-around small cap index fund, although it isn't as small cap as it could be. With $100,000 invested, you can move to the Vanguard Admiral Shares version of this fund (VSMAX) and pay only 0.13 percent a year in operating fees. Or, you can choose the ETF version (VB) and spend only 0.10 percent.

Bridgeway Ultra-Small Company Market Fund (BRSIX)

Indexed to: The CRSP 10 index. The fund uses approximately 550 stocks to closely — but not exactly — mirror the performance of the CRSP 10, which is the smallest of the smallest of publicly traded companies. CRSP, by the way, stands for The Center for Research in Security Prices, which is associated with the University of Chicago's Graduate School of Business.

Expense ratio: 0.65 percent

Average cap size: $338 million

P/E ratio: 16.8

Minimum initial purchase: $2,000

Minimum initial purchase in IRA: $2,000

Top five holdings: iShares Russell 2000 Index ETF, iShares Russell 2000 Value Index ETF, Amedisys, Twin Disc, Hurco Companies

Notes: This is a quasi-index mutual fund, but that's about all you're going to find in the arena of very small-company mutual funds. That's okay. Bridgeway's reasonable costs (compared to some other managed small cap mutual funds) and index-like approach make this a good — although not great — choice for small cap exposure.

Exchange-traded funds

Vanguard Small Cap ETF (VB)

Indexed to: The MSCI U.S. Small Cap 1750 Index, which represents the universe of small cap companies in the U.S. market. The index targets for inclusion 1,750 companies (sometimes it may be slightly more or less) and represents about 12 percent of the capitalization of the U.S. stock market.

Expense ratio: 0.10

Average cap size: $1.5 billion

P/E ratio: 17.8

Top five holdings: CF Industries, Flowserve, Respironics, BE Aerospace, Terra Industries

Notes: This is the ETF version of Vanguard's Small Cap Index (mutual) Fund. The low fee on this ETF makes it a very serious contender for best of the bunch if you're going with an ETF portfolio and want exposure to small cap U.S. stocks. Note, however, that the cap size is considerably larger than some other options in this category.

iShares Russell Microcap (IWC)

Indexed to: The Russell Microcap Index, which measures the performance of the micro cap segment of the U.S. equity market. It makes up less than 3 percent of the U.S. equity market and includes 1,000 of the smallest securities in the small cap Russell 2000 Index.

Expense ratio: 0.60 percent

Average cap size: $327 million

P/E ratio: 16.0

Why no mid cap stocks?

You'll notice that I recommend large cap stock funds and small cap stock funds, but no mid caps. The reason: You don't need them. Other investment gurus may turn red in the face at such a suggestion, but so be it. Mid cap returns and risk are, well, midway between large cap and small cap. Almost always. So why include them in your portfolio? Most large cap and small cap funds are somewhat fluid and give you a smattering of mid cap anyway. Sector funds — like REITs — are predominantly mid cap. You don't need to go out of your way to incorporate this middle-of-the-road style into your portfolio. Having large and small company stocks will give you better diversification. Adding mid cap funds generally only complicates matters and raises your overall expenses.

Top five holdings: Cepheid, Arena Resources, Concur Technologies, Savient Pharmaceuticals, Argo Group International Holdings

Notes: Barclays' microcap offering is quite a bit more pricey than the Vanguard fund (or several other ETF small cap offerings), but if you want ultra-small, IWC is the obvious ETF choice. To diversify away from a predominantly large cap portfolio, the added cost may be worth it. In addition to better diversification and probable greater performance than the Vanguard fund, you will also, however, undoubtedly see much greater volatility . . . HUGE volatility.

C'est bon: Developed world index funds

In recent decades (and my guess would be for decades to come), the total return on stocks in the United States and other developed countries has been rather similar. Why would it be otherwise? Risk and return, we know from years of studying the markets, tend to go hand-in-hand. The economic strengths and political environment of the United States, Canada, England, France, Japan, and Australia would seem to be roughly on a par.

As I discuss more in Part III where I address portfolio allocation, it would be nothing short of crazy to have all your eggs in one (national) basket. Non-U.S. stocks make up 62 percent of all the world's stocks. I recommend that about half (and no less than 40 percent) of your total stock allocation be non-U.S. (I would suggest that 62 percent be non-U.S. except that non-U.S. funds tend to charge more, and there is currency fluctuation to be concerned with. As a U.S. resident, you also have domestic inflation to contend with. If inflation rages, the stock market will generally do well, offering you some protection from rising prices.)

International diversification makes enormous sense. As you can see in Table 7-1, although the long-term return of most Western nations' stock markets is comparable, the differences year-to-year and decade-by-decade can be large. And those differences can mean a much, much smoother ride for your entire portfolio.

Table 7-1	The Compound Annual Return for Various Regions' Stock Markets			
	1970s	*1980s*	*1990s*	*2000–2007*
United States	5.9	17.5	18.2	1.7
European markets	8.6	18.5	14.5	7.1
Pacific markets	14.8	26.4	0.5	2.6
World	7.0	19.9	12.0	3.4

Source: Morningstar

One caveat: Some investors believe in country-picking, akin to stock-picking. (ETFs make that easy. You can buy ETFs that mirror the markets of countries from Belgium to Chile and Hong Kong to the Netherlands.) But country-picking, in most instances, is no more successful than stock-picking. There's no way for you to know that the Canadian stock market will do better than the Swedish stock market next year. When choosing international index funds, think broad. Think *regions* — Europe, Pacific, emerging markets — rather than Austria, Australia, and Brazil.

Mutual funds

Vanguard European Stock Index Fund (VEURX)

Indexed to: The MSCI Europe Index, which is made up of common stocks of companies located in Austria, Belgium, Denmark, Finland, France, Germany, Greece, Ireland, Italy, the Netherlands, Norway, Portugal, Spain, Sweden, Switzerland, and the United Kingdom.

Expense ratio: 0.22 percent

Average cap size: $50.4 billion

P/E ratio: 13.8

Minimum initial purchase: $3,000

Minimum initial purchase in IRA: $3,000

Top five holdings: BP, HSBC Holdings, Vodafone Group, Nestle, TOTAL

Notes: With $100,000, you can buy the Vanguard Admiral Shares version of this fund (VEUSX), with an annual expense ratio of only 0.12 percent — the same expense ratio as the ETF version (VGK).

Vanguard Pacific Stock Index (VPACX)

Indexed to: The MSCI Pacific Index, which consists of common stocks of large companies located in Japan, Australia, Hong Kong, Singapore, and New Zealand.

Expense ratio: 0.22 percent

Average cap size: $19.6 billion

P/E ratio: 16.3

Minimum initial purchase: $3,000

Minimum initial purchase in IRA: $3,000

Top five holdings: Toyota Motor, BHP Billiton Ltd, Mitsubishi UFJ Financial Group, Nintendo, Commonwealth Bank of Australia

Notes: A good, broad, reasonably priced fund to capture market returns in developed nations of the Far Orient and South Pacific. If you qualify, you may be able to purchase Vanguard Admiral Shares of this fund (VPADX), which carry a management fee of only 0.12 percent — the same as the ETF version of this fund (VPL).

Exchange-traded funds

Vanguard European ETF (VGK)

Indexed to: The MSCI Europe Index, which is made up of common stocks of companies located in Austria, Belgium, Denmark, Finland, France, Germany, Greece, Ireland, Italy, the Netherlands, Norway, Portugal, Spain, Sweden, Switzerland, and the United Kingdom.

Expense ratio: 0.22 percent

Average cap size: $50.4 billion

P/E ratio: 13.8

Top five holdings: BP, HSBC Holdings, Vodafone Group, Nestle, TOTAL

Notes: This is the ETF version of the Vanguard European Stock Market mutual fund (VEURX) . . . only it's cheaper, and there's no minimum. As international ETFs go, this is one of the least expensive, and it tracks a broad index. Note that you are getting no small cap exposure with this fund. Small cap international exposure will need to come from elsewhere.

Vanguard Pacific ETF (VPL)
Indexed to: The MSCI Pacific Index, which consists of common stocks of large companies located in Japan, Australia, Hong Kong, Singapore, and New Zealand.

Expense ratio: 0.12 percent

Average cap size: $19.6 billion

P/E ratio: 16.3

Top five holdings: Toyota Motor, BHP Billiton Ltd, Mitsubishi UFJ Financial Group, Nintendo Co, Commonwealth Bank of Australia

Notes: This is the ETF version of the Vanguard Pacific Stock Index mutual fund (VPACX) . . . only it's cheaper, and there's no minimum. Note that you are getting no small cap exposure with this fund. Small cap international exposure will need to come from elsewhere.

iShares MSCI EAFE Small Cap (SCZ)
Indexed to: The MSCI EAFE (Europe, Australasia, Far East) Small Cap Index, which tracks small capitalization stocks in developed non-U.S. nations. The five top countries represented are Japan, the United Kingdom, Australia, Germany, and France.

Expense ratio: 0.40 percent

Average cap size: $1.6 billion

P/E ratio: 11.9

Top five holdings: Sagami Railway, Confinimmo, Cairn Energy, Incitec Pivot Ltd., Café de Coral Holdings Ltd.

Notes: This offering from Barclays is a very good bet for international small cap exposure. Small caps in various nations tend to cater to local markets and so have significantly less correlation to each other than do large cap company stocks. For example, a modest-sized bank in Toyko that lends Yen to businesses only in Japan may be unaffected by even large market tremors that may occur in Europe or North America.

A calculated risk: Emerging-market stock index funds

Whoooeee . . . Stocks of emerging-market (read: We *hope* they are emerging-market) nations can yield high returns, but they can be very volatile. These are stocks of companies based in countries like Brazil, Russia, India, and China (often called the *BRIC* nations — these are the largest emerging markets), as well as Turkey, Chile, Taiwan, and Korea.

You want emerging-market stocks in your portfolio to some limited degree, mostly because they tend to have limited correlation to U.S. stocks — less correlation than other international stocks.

Mutual funds

Vanguard Emerging Markets Stock Index Fund (VEIEX)

Indexed to: The MSCI Emerging Markets Index, which is made up of common stocks of large companies located in emerging markets around the world. The top five nations represented are China, Korea, Brazil, Taiwan, and India.

Expense ratio: 0.37 percent

Average cap size: $20.0 billion

P/E ratio: 18.3

Minimum initial purchase: $3,000

Minimum initial purchase in IRA: $3,000

Top five holdings: OAO Gazprom, China Mobile Ltd., Samsung Electronics, América Móvil, Petroleo Brasileiro

Notes: There aren't many indexed options out there when it comes to investing in emerging markets. But you don't need many. This one will do just fine. If you've got the bucks ($100,000), you can qualify for the Vanguard Admiral Shares of this fund (VEMAX), which charges 0.28 percent a year in management fees. The ETF version (VWO) charges but 0.25 percent.

Exchange-traded funds

Vanguard Emerging Markets (VWO)

Indexed to: The MSCI Emerging Markets Index, which is made up of common stocks of large companies located in emerging markets around the world. The top five nations represented are China, Korea, Brazil, Taiwan, and India.

What the tickers on index funds designate (nothing much!)

Perhaps Wall Street lacks creativity, but *all* open-end mutual funds — indexed or not — have tickers with five letters, and the last letter is always an X. Thus, the Vanguard Emerging Markets Index Fund is VEIEX, and the T. Rowe Price Total Equity Market is POMIX. Exchange-traded funds, on the other hand, typically have three letters in their tickers. Thus, the iShares Russell Microcap ETF is IWC, and the Rydex Russell Top 50 ETF is XLG. These three-letter ETFs may trade on any exchange. A handful of ETFs that trade on the NASDAQ happen to have four-letter tickers. The most popular of these is the PowerShares QQQ (an ETF that tracks the top 100 stocks of the NASDAQ) that uses the ticker QQQQ.

Expense ratio: 0.25 percent

Average cap size: $20.0 billion

P/E ratio: 18.3

Top five holdings: OAO Gazprom, China Mobile Ltd., Samsung Electronics, América Móvil, Petroleo Brasileiro

Notes: This is the ETF version of the Vanguard Emerging Markets Index (VEIEX) mutual fund, one of the only indexed emerging-market mutual funds. Among ETFs, there are a few options, but Vanguard's is at the head of the pack (largely for its low cost).

Value and growth: Slicing the cake with style funds

When your stock portfolio gets large enough (ballpark $30,000), you may consider breaking up your holdings by style as well as cap size.

By *style,* financial types are referring to *value* and *growth*. Value stocks are bargain-basement stocks, usually in slow-growing industries like utilities, natural resources, and banking. Growth stocks are often popular and may be expensive, and they belong to hot companies usually in glamour industries like technology and pharmaceuticals.

Value and growth tend to move in different business cycles, as Table 7-2 demonstrates.

Table 7-2	Compound Annual Returns of Growth and Value Stocks			
	1970s	*1980s*	*1990s*	*2000–2007*
Large cap growth stocks	2.4	15.6	21.4	–2.8
Large cap value stocks	7.7	18.1	15.8	4.2
Small cap growth stocks	8.6	14.4	13.1	2.6
Small cap value stocks	14.9	20.3	14.5	13.6

Source: Morningstar

Owning both won't give you the diversification of, say, stocks and bonds, or even domestic and international stock. But if you can afford to carry both in your portfolio and keep them separate, you should. Not only will you gain diversification, but you'll be able to squeeze out extra return over the long run by rebalancing your portfolio every year or two (see Chapter 16).

If you're going to split up your portfolio into the four major style groups — large value, large growth, small value, and small growth — following are some good funds to use. Note that you can divide up your domestic holdings into value and growth and, although there are fewer options for doing so, you also can — and should — divide up your international holdings.

Large value mutual fund

Vanguard Value Index Fund (VIVAX)

Indexed to: The MSCI U.S. Prime Market Value Index, a broadly diversified index predominantly made up of value stocks of large U.S. companies. The fund holds about 380 stocks.

Expense ratio: 0.23 percent

Average cap size: $57.3 billion

P/E ratio: 13.6

Minimum initial purchase: $3,000

Minimum initial purchase in IRA: $3,000

Top five holdings: Exxon Mobil, AT&T, General Electric, Chevron, Johnson & Johnson

Notes: Good P/E ratio, diversified holdings, low price . . . what's not to like? With $100,000 to invest, you can switch to Vanguard Admiral shares (VVIAX) and incur only a 0.11 percent annual management fee. Or you can buy the ETF version of this fund (VTV), which also carries an annual expense ratio of 0.11 percent, no minimum investment, and, at least theoretically, perhaps a tad more tax efficiency.

Large value exchange-traded funds

Vanguard Value ETF (VTV)

Indexed to: The MSCI U.S. Prime Market Value Index, a broadly diversified index predominantly made up of value stocks of large U.S. companies. The fund holds about 380 stocks.

Expense ratio: 0.23 percent

Average cap size: $57.3 billion

P/E ratio: 13.6

Top five holdings: Exxon Mobil, AT&T, General Electric, Chevron, Johnson & Johnson

Notes: This the ETF version of the Vanguard Value Index mutual fund (VIVAX). There's nothing fancy about this fund. It's a good, solid, core investment that fits most people's portfolios like a glove.

PowerShares FTSE RAFI U.S. 1000 (PRF)

Indexed to: The FTSE RAFI U.S. 1000 Index. The index is designed to track — sort of — the performance of the largest U.S. equities, selected based on the following four fundamental measures of firm size: book value, cash flow, sales, and dividends. PowerShares claims it's a better way to index.

Expense ratio: 0.76 percent

Average cap size: $34.4 billion

P/E ratio: 14.7

Top five holdings: Exxon Mobil, General Electric, Kraft Foods, Chevron, Wal-Mart

Notes: The FTSE RAFI methodology presents a new, comprehensive way of looking for value in stocks. Will it prove lucrative in the long run — lucrative enough to overcome an expense ratio considerably more than some of the traditional value alternatives (such as Vanguard's)? That could be the case, and PowerShares has some smart proponents, but I wouldn't bet the bank on it.

Large growth mutual fund
Vanguard Growth Index (VIGRX)

Indexed to: The MSCI U.S. Prime Market Growth Index, a broadly diversified index predominantly made up of growth (fast moving) stocks of large U.S. companies. The fund holds about 420 stocks.

Expense ratio: 0.22 percent

Average cap size: $39.5 billion

P/E ratio: 21.0

Minimum initial purchase: $3,000

Minimum initial purchase in IRA: $3,000

Top five holdings: Microsoft, Google, Cisco Systems, Apple, Intel

Notes: This is an excellent choice for large cap growth exposure, especially given the low expense ratio. That ratio can be lowered still — to 0.11 — if you qualify for the Vanguard Admiral share class of this fund (VIGAX). You can also purchase the ETF version of this fund (for a commission) and enjoy the same 0.11 expense ratio, with no minimum purchase.

Large growth exchange-traded funds
Vanguard Growth ETF (VUG)

Indexed to: The MSCI U.S. Prime Market Growth Index, a broadly diversified index predominantly made up of growth (fast moving) stocks of large U.S. companies. The fund holds about 420 stocks.

Expense ratio: 0.11 percent

Average cap size: $39.5 billion

P/E ratio: 21.0

Top five holdings: Microsoft, Google, Cisco Systems, Apple, Intel

Notes: This is the ETF version of the Vanguard Growth Index fund (VIGRX). In the area of index mutual funds, Vanguard is often a slam-dunk. With ETFs, you have choices, but Vanguard is still a very good one. Note that the current lineup of stocks makes this almost a technology-sector fund.

iShares Morningstar Large Growth (JKE)

Indexed to: The Morningstar U.S. Growth Index, which tracks the performance of stocks (673 of them) that are expected to grow at a faster pace than the rest of the market as measured by forward earnings, historical earnings, book value, cash flow, and sales.

Expense ratio: 0.25 percent

Average cap size: $47.3 billion

P/E ratio: 20.0

Top five holdings: Microsoft, Intel, Cisco Systems, Google, Apple

Notes: This ETF has a higher expense ratio than does Vanguard's but offers potentially better portfolio diversification, given its greater average cap size. Morningstar also promises no overlap between its indexes: You'll never find the same holding in both small value and small growth, which I like a lot. Note when buying the Morningstar iShares funds that they aren't traded as frequently as are some other ETFs, so you may want to purchase them using a limit order rather than a market order. See Chapter 10 for a discussion about trading ETFs.

Small value mutual fund

Vanguard Small-Cap Value Index Fund (VISVX)

Indexed to: The MSCI U.S. Small Cap Value Index, a broadly diversified index of value stocks of smaller U.S. companies. The fund holds about 930 stocks.

Expense ratio: 0.23 percent

Average cap size: $1.46 billion

P/E ratio: 15.1

Minimum initial purchase: $3,000

Minimum initial purchase in IRA: $3,000

Top five holdings: Whiting Petroleum Corp., URS Corp., SAIC Inc., Puget Energy Inc., Rayonier Inc. REIT

Notes: The Admiral Shares version of this fund (VSMAX), if you qualify, lowers your annual expense ratio to 0.13 percent. The ETF version (VBR) carries an annual expense of 0.12 percent. Any way you go, it's hard to lose. This fund is a very good way to gain exposure to small value stocks. In the long run, small value stocks will probably wind up as your best-returning asset class.

Small value exchange-traded funds

Vanguard Small Value EFT (VBR)

Indexed to: The MSCI U.S. Small Cap Value Index, a broadly diversified index of value stocks of smaller U.S. companies. The fund holds about 930 stocks.

Expense ratio: 0.12 percent

Average cap size: $1.46 billion

P/E ratio: 15.1

Top five holdings: Whiting Petroleum Corp., URS Corp., SAIC Inc., Puget Energy Inc., Rayonier Inc. REIT

Notes: Whether you choose the mutual-fund version of this ETF (VISVX) or the ETF itself, it's hard to lose. This fund is a very good way to gain exposure to small value stocks. In the long run, small cap value stocks will very likely turn out to be your best-returning asset class.

iShares Morningstar Small Value (JKL)

Indexed to: The Morningstar Small Value Index, which measures the performance of small cap stocks (305 of them) with relatively low prices given anticipated per-share earnings, book value, cash flow, sales, and dividends.

Expense ratio: 0.30 percent

Average cap size: $950 million

P/E ratio: 13.1

Top five holdings: Whiting Petroleum, Tenet Healthcare, Unit Corp., BJ's Wholesale Club, Senior Housing Properties Trust

Notes: This fund has a higher expense ratio than Vanguard's small cap value offering but a lower P/E ratio and small cap size for better diversification. Morningstar also promises no overlap between its indexes: You'll never find the same holding in both small value and small growth, which I like a lot. Note when buying the Morningstar iShares funds that they aren't traded as frequently as are some other ETFs, so you may want to purchase them using a limit order rather than a market order. See Chapter 10 for a discussion about trading ETFs.

Small growth mutual fund

Vanguard Small-Cap Growth Index Fund (VISGX)

Indexed to: The MSCI U.S. Small Cap Growth Index, a broadly diversified index of value stocks of smaller U.S. companies. The fund holds about 930 stocks.

Expense ratio: 0.23

Average cap size: $1.64 billion

P/E ratio: 21.6

Minimum initial purchase: $3,000

Minimum initial purchase in IRA: $3,000

Top five holdings: Cleveland-Cliffs, Priceline.com, Illumina, FLIR Systems, Bucyrus International

Notes: Small growth probably won't be your best-returning asset class, but it is still worth having in your portfolio, for sure. This Vanguard offering is a super choice. If you qualify for the Admiral Shares version of this fund (VSMAX), the expense ratio drops to 0.13 percent. The ETF version of the fund (VBK) is only 0.12 percent.

Small growth exchange-traded funds
Vanguard Small Cap Growth ETF (VBK)
Indexed to: The MSCI U.S. Small Cap Growth Index, a broadly diversified index of value stocks of smaller U.S. companies. The fund holds about 930 stocks.

Expense ratio: 0.12 percent

Average cap size: $1.64 billion

P/E ratio: 21.6

Top five holdings: Cleveland-Cliffs, Priceline.com, Illumina, FLIR Systems, Bucyrus International

Notes: This ETF version of the Vanguard Small-Cap Growth Index Fund (VISGX) is one of the best small growth ETFs available, both for its breadth and its economy.

iShares Morningstar Small Growth (JKK)
Indexed to: The Morningstar Small Growth Index, which measures the performance of small cap stocks (approximately 300 of them) that are expected to grow at a faster pace than the rest of the market as measured by forward earnings, historical earnings, book value, cash flow, and sales.

Expense ratio: 0.30 percent

Average cap size: $930 million

P/E ratio: 23.6

Top five holdings: FTI Consulting, Kirby Corp., Alpha Natural Resources, LKQ Corp., ITC Holdings Corp.

Notes: This fund costs more than the Vanguard offering but has a smaller average cap size and higher P/E for better diversification. Morningstar also promises no overlap between its indexes: You'll never find the same holding in both small value and small growth, which I like a lot. Note when buying the Morningstar iShares funds that they aren't traded as frequently as are some other ETFs, so you may want to purchase them using a limit order rather than a market order. See Chapter 10 for a discussion about trading ETFs.

International value ETF

iShares MSCI EAFE Value (EFV)

Indexed to: The MSCI EAFE (Europe, Australasia, Far East) Value Index, which includes approximately 550 value company stocks from across the developed world.

Expense ratio: 0.40 percent

Average cap size: $38.7 billion

P/E ratio: 9.7

Top five holdings: BP, HSBC Holdings, Vodafone Group, TOTAL, Toyota Motor Corp.

Notes: This Barclays international value ETF (along with its sister international growth fund) is the way to go if you want to split your foreign stocks into value and growth. I'm not crazy that MSCI allows for overlap between funds (you may find the same stock in both sister funds), but I have no other complaints about this reasonably priced, well-diversified security. And yes, it is a very good idea to split your international stock holdings — as well as your domestic stocks — into value and growth.

International growth ETF

iShares MSCI EAFE Growth (EFG)

Indexed to: The MSCI EAFE (Europe, Australasia, Far East) Growth Index, which includes approximately 560 growth company stocks from across the developed world.

Expense ratio: 0.40 percent

Average cap size: $30.4 billion

P/E ratio: 15.1

Top five holdings: Nestle, Nokia, Roche Holding, Telefonica, GlaxoSmithKline

Notes: This Barclays international growth ETF (along with its sister international value fund) is the way to go if you want to split your foreign stocks into value and growth. I'm not crazy that MSCI allows for overlap between funds (you may find the same stock in both sister funds), but I have no other complaints about this reasonably priced, well-diversified security. And yes, it is a very good idea to split your international stock holdings — as well as your domestic stocks — into value and growth.

Diversify using both style and industry-sector funds

If you take the advice I give in this chapter and divide your stock portfolio into large cap, small cap, value, and growth, does it still make sense to have any industry sector funds? Yes, it may.

Certain industry sectors, like technology and financial services, are a huge part of our economy. Any of your style index funds are sure to include a large chunk of either. Breaking the sector out further and buying a technology index fund or financial services index fund isn't going to add a lot of diversification. But smaller sectors may be worth overweighting by buying separate index funds.

Real estate investment trusts (REITs) are one example, and I discuss those in depth in Chapter 9. But there may be others. Energy, for example, often moves out of lockstep with the rest of the stock market. (Use the Vanguard Energy ETF [VDE] or the Energy Select Sector SPDR [XLE].) And consumer staples — toilet paper and beer and such — have a way of staying buoyant even in the worst of times. (Use Vanguard Consumer Staples [VDC] or the Consumer Staples Select Sector SPDR [XLP].) Limit your exposure to either sector to no more than 20 percent of your domestic stock portfolio.

On rare occasion, if an industry sector — even a narrow industry sector — seems impossibly beaten down, I might condone allocating a small percentage of your equity pie and taking a shot on that sector using a sector index fund. This is one of two kinds of active management that I think are worthy of consideration. The other is very carefully choosing index fund–like actively managed funds for part of your portfolio. I talk about both in Chapter 13.

Energy, technology, health care, and more: Splitting the pie by industry sector

Some investment gurus champion industry sector funds as a way of slicing and dicing the stock market pie, rather than using cap size (large stocks and small stocks) and style (value and growth). There is nothing terribly wrong with the industry sector approach, although I prefer to use style and size. I prefer cap size and style because it necessitates holding fewer funds (four versus a dozen or more for the U.S. side of your portfolio), and the funds tend to have lower operating expenses than industry sector funds.

If you decide to choose industry sector funds, search for the very same qualities in an index fund that I have suggested all along: broad diversification (within each industry group), low costs, transparency (make sure you know exactly what you're buying), tax efficiency (low turnover), and good diversification among sector funds.

You can find a handful of technology and real estate index mutual funds, but if serious index sector investing is your game plan, ETFs are the way to go.

You have several choices in fund company lineups:

- **Vanguard** industry-sector ETFs include the Vanguard Consumer Discretionary ETF (VCR), the Vanguard Consumer Staples ETF (VDC), the Vanguard Energy ETF (VDE), the Vanguard Financials ETF (VFH), and seven others. They all carry an expense ratio of 0.22 percent, and they represent broad industry groups. **Overall rating: A**

- **SSgA's Select SPDRS** include the Utilities Select Sector SPDR (XLU), the Technology Select Sector SPDR (XLK), the Industrial Select Sector SPDR (XLI), and half a dozen others. Like Vanguard's ETFs, these are well-diversified funds with a modest expense ratio of 0.23 percent. **Overall rating: A**

- **SSgA** also offers a lineup of S&P SPDRS that include the SPDR S&P Biotech ETF (XBI), the SPDR S&P Homebuilders ETF (XHB), and the SPDR S&P Metals and Mining ETF (XME). These have expense ratios of 0.35 percent and tend to represent more narrow slivers of the stock market. **Overall rating: B**

- **Barclays iShares** offers ETFs in many industry sectors, including the iShares Dow Jones U.S. Healthcare ETF (IYH), the iShares Dow Jones Transportation ETF (IYT), and the iShares Dow Jones U.S. Pharmaceuticals ETF (IHE). The categories tend to be as broad as either the Vanguard ETFs or the SPDRs but carry an unnecessarily high expense ratio of 0.48 percent. **Overall rating: B**

✔ **PowerShares** also has a complete lineup of industry sector ETFs, including the PowerShares Dynamic Banking ETF (PJB), the PowerShares Dynamic Insurance ETF (PIC), and the PowerShares Dynamic Semiconductor ETF (PSI). These are narrow in scope, use questionable methodologies to form the indexes, and cost 0.60 percent a year in management fees. **Overall rating: C**

✔ I would advise you to avoid **Merrill Lynch's** HOLDRS ETFs, which tend to have very concentrated holdings, complicated pricing, and purchase requirements. **Overall rating: C-**

✔ Also avoid the **HealthShares** series of industry-sliver ETFs that include the HealthShares Emerging Cancer ETF (HHJ), the HealthShares Autoimmune-Inflammation ETF (HHA), and the HealthShares Ophthalmology ETF (HHZ). They're expensive (0.75 percent a year) and, well, there's just no reason to hold these tiny market slivers, essentially market bets, in any portfolio. Will there be a cancer cure in the next several years? Perhaps. Will that make The HealthShares Emerging Cancer ETF soar? Not necessarily. One of the companies in the fund may see its stock shoot to the sky, but the others, the losers in the race for a cancer cure, would very likely tank at the same time. **Overall rating: D.**

Exploring the Outer Limits of Indexed Stock Investing

There is nothing wrong with your television set. Do not attempt to adjust the picture. We are controlling transmission. If we wish to make it louder, we will bring up the volume. If we wish to make it softer, we will tune it to a whisper. We will control the horizontal. We will control the vertical . . . Welcome to the Outer Limits of index stock investing.

This is where indexers of a decade or two ago couldn't even imagine we would be today . . . for better or worse. The categories I have in mind are screened index funds (such as socially conscious funds), high dividend funds, leveraged funds, inverse funds, and leveraged inverse funds.

Socially conscious stock index funds: Putting your money where your heart is

If you don't like the idea of investing in tobacco, nuclear weapons, or countries that have no child-labor laws, there are *screened indexes* (and index funds) that filter out such undesirable investments.

Some people argue that companies that do good tend to do well. Maybe that's true. None of these funds has been around long enough to know for sure. In most cases, socially responsible funds cost a little bit extra but not so much that you should be turned off to them.

A few good index options are available. I would urge you to use the same set of criteria you would for any other index investment: Look for overall low cost, a respectable management team, an index that makes sense, and tax efficiency.

With a socially conscious fund you also have one other consideration: Is the management team using its muscle to lobby companies to do better for the world? I hate to say it, but the management of any index fund will probably not be as active in this regard as would the management of an actively managed fund. For active management you want active management — duh.

Nonetheless, here are a few socially conscious index fund options to consider:

✔ If you want a mutual fund, choose the Vanguard FTSE Social Index Fund (VFTSX). This is a large cap U.S. fund with an expense ratio of 0.23 percent and a minimum investment of $3,000. The top five companies are Microsoft, AT&T, Procter & Gamble, Johnson & Johnson, and Cisco Systems. The funds filters out the corporate riff-raff.

✔ Among ETFs, you have several options:

- The iShares Select Social Index Fund (KLD) uses a popular index that overweights companies purportedly making money in ethical fashion and underweights companies that aren't. It is a large cap U.S. fund, mostly growth companies, with an expense ratio of 0.50 percent. The top five companies are Microsoft, AT&T, Procter & Gamble, Johnson & Johnson, and Cisco Systems.

- You may also choose the iShares KLD 400 Social ETF (DSI), which attempts to eliminate companies involved in the production of tobacco, firearms, gambling, or anything nuclear. The expense ratio is 0.50 percent, and the companies are large U.S., mostly growth. The top five companies are Johnson & Johnson, Wells Fargo, IBM, General Mills, and Kimberly-Clarke.

- A handful of other ETFs are based on indexes of companies working on clean energy or other environmentally beneficial projects. Options include the PowerShares WilderHill Clean Energy ETF (PWB), the Van Eck Market Vectors–Global Alternative Energy ETF (GEX), and the Van Eck Market Vectors–Solar Energy ETF (KWT). All these offerings are on the pricier side of ETFs, and I have to wonder if choosing a reasonably priced actively managed fund in this area may not make more sense.

High dividend funds: Wanting cash in hand

People love dividends. But is that love warranted? I don't think so. Whether a company's extra cash is issued directly to you (the investor) in the form of a dividend or funneled back into the company in which you are invested should not, in the long run, make a whole lot of difference. In fact, studies show that companies that pay high dividends, which tend to be value companies, don't necessarily provide any better returns to investors over time than any other value companies do.

So why have a gadzillion high dividend–paying ETFs hit the markets in the past years? It's because dividend-paying stocks performed exceptionally well for a few years, and investors made the eternally wrong decision that that would have to continue. Wall Street has been more than happy to cater to the market's whims.

As I discuss in Chapter 16, the best way to raise cash (should you need it) is not through dividends but through regular portfolio rebalancing.

So in the end, I don't really suggest dividend funds. If, however, you feel you must, an index fund makes enormous sense. As always, I urge you to choose one that is low-cost and well diversified. Two good options are the Vanguard High Dividend Yield ETF (VYM) with an annual expense ratio of 0.25 percent and the WisdomTree Total Dividend Fund (DTD) with an expense ratio of 0.28 percent.

Leveraged and inverse "indexing": Taking a gamble

Enter now into the twilight zone . . . beyond the outer limits of index investing. There are a few investments that I'm not sure whether to include in a book on index investing. So I'm going to compromise and mention them briefly.

Leveraged funds take a basic index (say the S&P 500) and, through a lot of financial hocus pocus, promise you a return double the index (more or less). They exist in mutual fund form, but most are ETFs.

Inverse funds promise you a return in direct inverse (more or less) from the index: If the index goes down 5 percent, your fund goes up 5 percent, minus expenses.

Some funds are *leveraged inverse funds,* meaning that if the index goes down 5 percent, you could stand to profit 10 percent.

Scores of these funds — nearly all of them ETFs — have been introduced in the past year or so. ProShares has a lineup of dozens. So does Rydex. Using one company's ETFs or the other's, you can leverage or short just about any kind of index imaginable, from U.S. stocks and foreign stocks to individual industry sectors to non-equities, like bonds and commodities.

Why would anyone wish to do such a thing? To make double the money, of course! But, believe me, there is a catch (actually three, including one whopper):

- ✔ **First catch:** The leveraged indexes include no dividends.

- ✔ **Second catch:** These funds are expensive, charging between 0.70 percent and 0.95 percent in operating fees . . . way more than most ETFs.

- ✔ **Third catch (the Big One):** These funds double (or triple) your money on a *daily* basis, but that often means falling considerably short of doubling your money in the long run. The math is a bit tricky, but here it goes. Pay attention!

    Imagine that you own $1,000 worth of shares in the Ultra Semiconductors ProShares ETF (USD), which charges you 0.95 percent for the honor of tracking the Dow Jones Semiconductors Index and doubling your money on a daily basis. Suppose that the Semiconductors Index goes up 10 percent tomorrow but then drops 10 percent the next day. Even Steven? Well, no. Tomorrow, your $1,000 invested in the index is suddenly worth $1,100. The next day it drops 10 percent and is worth $990. Overall, the fund lost 1 percent ($10) in two days. The ETF, meanwhile, gets double the punch both ways. Tomorrow, your $1,000 gains 20 percent and suddenly is worth $1,200. But the next day it drops 20 percent and is now worth $960. Uh-oh. You didn't lose 1 percent, as you would have in the index; you lost a total of 4 percent ($40). Ouch. Volatility, all things being equal, is not a good thing! You are getting double or triple the risk with leveraged indexes (perhaps more!), but not double or triple the return.

If you want to take more risk in your portfolio, you should get commensurate returns! Move from bonds to stocks or from large cap stocks to small cap or micro cap stocks before you consider a move to leveraged funds.

As for the inverse funds, these have existed for years in mutual fund form and recently have become all the rage in ETF form. But betting against the market is betting! The stock market goes up and down, but mostly it goes up. If you put your dollars on it going down, you are very likely to lose in the long run. If you want to hedge your long bets on stocks, do so with other asset classes — like bonds and commodities — that are likely to have positive long-term returns.

Not convinced? Here are the returns you would have earned investing in the ProFunds UltraShort NASDAQ-100 mutual fund (an inverse and leveraged fund that tracks the largest 100 stocks traded on the NASDAQ), according to the company's own Web site (`http://profunds.com/PricesPerformance/PerformanceData.fs`).

As of 5/2/2008:

- ✔ Average Annual One Year: –4.69%
- ✔ Average Annual Three Year: –10.05%
- ✔ Average Annual Five Year: –22.41%
- ✔ Average Annual Since Inception: –32.10%
- ✔ Cumulative Since Inception (June 2, 1998): –97.77%

Enough said?

Chapter 8

Investing in Bond Indexes: Protecting Your Principal

*W*hether driving on a calm spring day or a wicked winter night, for the sake of safety, you're well advised to wear your seat belt and shoulder strap. In fact, it's the law. Investing in the stock market in smooth times (do those exist anymore?) or rocky times, you are advised to invest in bonds, as well. It's for the sake of safety. It should be a law.

Bonds are not typically high-yielding investments, but bonds — particularly high-quality bonds, which is the kind I generally recommend — tend to be stable, which is their main purpose in life. They'll keep your portfolio afloat when everything else is sinking like stones. If your grandparents weren't reduced to selling apples in the street during the Great Depression, bonds were very likely the reason.

Just as the world of stocks offers many index funds in which to invest, so too does the world of bonds. And what makes sense in one world makes about just as much sense in the other . . . although, as I discuss shortly, not necessarily for all the same reasons.

In this chapter, I introduce you to bond index funds. I reveal why you want them in your portfolio, and I help you to figure out which are the very best choices for you.

Getting a Handle on What Bonds Are and Why You Want Them

Investment opportunities abound: stocks, bonds, real estate investment trusts, oil wells . . . But when all is said and done, despite all the fancy names and myriad money-making schemes, you can generally divide the entire world of investments into but two categories:

- **Equity:** Things you buy and own, and that you hope will appreciate in value. They may or may not pay dividends. Examples include stocks, commodities, real estate, and collectibles.

- **Debt:** Money you lend to someone else in return for that someone's promise to pay you interest, usually for a certain period of time, and, when that period of time has expired, to return your money in full. Examples include bonds and CDs, as well as IOUs from your brother-in-law.

Stocks (and stock funds) are the mostly popular form of equity investment. Bonds (and bond funds) are the most popular form of debt instrument. That's largely because everything else is, generally speaking, more problematic. The IOU from your brother-in-law will probably never be paid back, or only paid back in beer. The CD barely keeps up with inflation. The commodities are too volatile. The rental real estate is a pain in the neck, with the tenants calling you at all hours of the night. And making money in precious collectibles requires a lot of expertise, not to mention a safe and insurance.

In comparison with most other investments, stocks and bonds are easy . . . and often the most profitable.

Traveling into bondland

Bonds are not only the largest category of debt but also the largest investment of *any* kind — including stocks.

According to the Securities Industry and Financial Markets Association (SIFMA), the total value of all bonds issued around the world is now a little over $67 trillion. In contrast, the total value of all stocks issued around the world — the investment that gets the lion's share of media attention — is "only" about $54 trillion. To put both numbers into some kind of perspective, if you took the gross domestic product (the value of all goods and services produced in a year) of every single country on earth, and added them all up, you'd get a figure (according to the World Bank) of about $65 trillion.

So who issues all those bonds, and in what parts of the planet?

Here's what SIFMA says: Of all the bonds issued in 2006, 49 percent were issued in the United States, about 24 percent were issued in Europe, 13 percent were issued by Japan, and the remainder came from all the other countries of the world.

Most of the bonds on the planet — 64 percent, according to Bank of International Settlements — are issued by corporate concerns such as Toyota, Bayer, General Electric, Honda, and so on. The rest — 36 percent — are issued by governments. They may come from federal governments (obligations of central governments, such as U.S. Treasury bonds, are generically known as *sovereign* bonds), as well as state and local governments (these are often referred to as *municipal* bonds).

Recognizing the many different breeds of bond

Different kinds of bonds have different characteristics. But in general, most bonds are issued in denominations of $1,000, most make interest payments (often called *coupon payments*) twice a year, and most come with ratings — AA, A, BBB, and so on — that give you some idea of the creditworthiness of the issuer. The more creditworthy the government or corporation that issues the bond, the lower the interest rate will generally be. That's because lower-rated issuers must pay higher interest rates, or investors simply wouldn't want their (riskier) bonds.

Bonds can be categorized in different ways. Often, they are referred to by the nature of the issuer: They are government bonds, corporate bonds, or agency bonds.

But they may also be categorized by their quality. *Quality,* in bondtalk, means the financial muscle of the issuer. Those bonds that come from borrowers with lots of financial muscle (strong companies and governments) are commonly called *investment-grade* bonds. Those that come from weaker issuers are often referred to as *high-yield* (that's the positive spin) or *junk* bonds (the negative spin).

There are credit-rating agencies that (in addition to making a lot of money for themselves) help investors to better fine-tune the quality of a bond. Bond funds, index or other, generally lump their bond holdings by such quality distinctions. In Table 8-1, I outline these distinctions and what they mean according to three of the most popular credit-rating agencies: Moody's, Standard and Poor's, and Fitch. Note that the ratings shown in the table do not apply to municipal bonds. *Munis* (the vast majority of which tend to be high-quality bonds) have their own rating system.

Table 8-1	Corporate Bond Credit Quality Ratings		
Credit Risk	Moody's	Standard & Poor's	Fitch
Investment grade			
Tip-top quality	Aaa	AAA	AAA
Premium quality	Aa	AA	AA
Near-premium quality	A	A	A
Take-home-to-Mom quality	Baa	BBB	BBB
Not investment grade			
Borderline ugly	Ba	BB	BB
Ugly	B	B	B
Definitely don't-take-home-to-Mom quality	Caa	CCC	CCC
You'll be extremely lucky to get your money back	Ca	CC	CC
Interest payments have halted or bankruptcy is in process	C	D	C
Already in default	C	D	D

Bonds also come in taxable and tax-free form. The term *tax-free* usually means that a bond is issued by a municipality, and the interest payments are generally free from federal income tax and sometimes (particularly if you buy a bond in your home state) free of local taxes, as well. Bonds issued by the U.S. Treasury are never referred to as tax-free because you *do* pay federal income tax on the interest, but you won't pay state or local income tax.

Finally, bonds are also commonly categorized by their maturity dates. Those bonds with maturity dates of 12 years or more in the future are called *long-term* bonds or, for short, *long* bonds. Bonds with maturity dates of less than 12 years but more than 5 years are called *intermediate* bonds. And any bond with a maturity of less than 5 years away is called a *short-term* or simply a *short* bond. Long bonds usually pay higher interest rates than short bonds.

Since this is a book on indexing, I talk more about bond funds than I do about individual bonds. Whereas bond funds do not have maturity dates, per se, most funds, including index funds, are made up of bonds of somewhat similar maturities, be they short, intermediate, or long. Bond funds comprised of long bonds usually yield higher return but with greater volatility. Bond funds comprised of very short bonds often behave much as money-market funds do, with little volatility but modest return.

Keeping your expectations realistic

Even the longest of bonds (with 30 years maturity) and even the riskiest of bonds (the so-called high-yield or junk bonds) rarely yield the same kind of returns that stocks do. In the long run, most bonds yield considerably less than stocks. What is true of individual securities is equally true of funds: Bond funds tend to yield considerably less than stock funds over time.

According to figures from Morningstar, one dollar invested in long-term government bonds at year-end 1925, with all coupons reinvested, grew to $78.78 by year-end 2007. This represents a compound annual growth rate over the 82-year period of 5.5 percent. One dollar invested in long-term corporate bonds at year-end 1925, with all coupons reinvested, grew to $105.86 by year-end 2007. This represents a compound annual growth rate over the decades of 5.9 percent.

Adjusted for inflation, the real return on government bonds has historically been about 2.4 percent; corporate bonds have yielded about 2.7 percent. This compares to a real (post-inflation) return of about 7.1 percent for large-company stocks and 9.1 percent for small-company stocks.

As you can see, bonds over the past eight decades have returned considerably less than half what stocks have. When you factor in taxes, you're looking at even less than that. Moral of story: Don't expect to get rich off bonds. That isn't what they're for!

Buying bonds for the right reasons

If you aren't going to make a lot of money off your bonds, there must be another reason to buy them, or I wouldn't be devoting an entire chapter to bonds, right? Right! And the reason must be the steady stream of income that bonds provide, right? Wrong!

Yes, bonds do provide a steady stream of income (except for *zero-coupon bonds,* which pay all your interest in a lump sum upon maturity). If you choose bond funds (and as an index investor, that's exactly what you would do), you'll similarly get a steady stream of income.

But for most investors — even including retired people living off the fruits of their portfolios — I generally don't advocate using that steady stream of income to pay the bills. I explain more in Chapter 16, but in short, the best way to tap a portfolio is through regular rebalancing. You sell whatever has done the best and buy (or leave untouched) those assets that haven't done as well.

If bonds have produced more than stocks, you sell off your bonds (or index bond funds). If stocks have produced more than bonds, you sell off your stocks (or index stock funds.) By doing that, you are allowing that steady stream of income to be reinvested into your bond funds, preventing your principal from getting eaten up by inflation and tapping into the funds only when the going is good. This method of raising cash allows you a *rebalancing bonus*: By constantly selling high and buying low, you juice your total returns. (How much you juice your returns depends on the performance and volatility of your portfolio, but we're talking ballpark 0.50 percent a year.)

The reason that I want you to own bonds, if not for cash flow, is this: diversification.

Bonds offer the surest, most time-tested way of diversifying a portfolio of primarily stock. Bonds very often (but not always) provide zig when stocks zag. And *that* is why you want them.

In Figure 8-1, you can see the delicious lack of correlation: When stocks perform well, bonds (at least high-quality bonds) often don't, and vice versa. And that, dear reader, is what protecting a portfolio through diversification is all about.

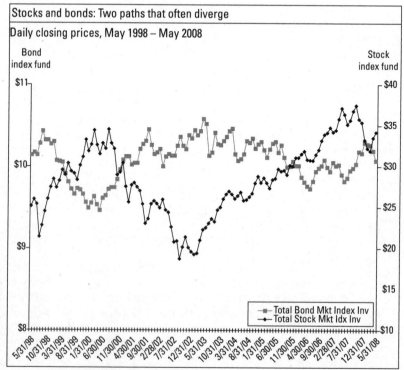

Figure 8-1:
Bonds are the best complement to stocks.

Source: Vanguard, with permission

Banking on predictability

Unlike stocks, bonds promise you a steady stream of income. Whether you decide to tap into that stream of income or not is your choice. But bonds also tend to have much more stable prices than do stocks. The prices of bonds can go up or down, but they usually go up when you need them to most — when stocks are tanking.

When the going is tough for the stock markets, money is often said to "rush to safety," which is really a euphemism for cash and bonds. When lots of people are scrambling to buy something — *anything*, be it bonds, bacon, or bananas — the price of that something will usually (if you remember from Economics 101) be driven up. Simple supply and demand is one reason that quality bonds are a good thing to have in bad economic times.

Another reason relates to interest rates. During a recession or depression, interest rates usually drop, which is partially a byproduct of low inflation and partially a result of government tinkering to try to get more steam into the engines of industry. As interest rates drop, bonds in existence (paying "old," higher interest rates) tend to rise in value. And that is the second reason that quality bonds tend to more than hold their own during the darkest of economic times.

In Figure 8-2, you can see that the worst years for stocks have generally been rollicking good times for bonds.

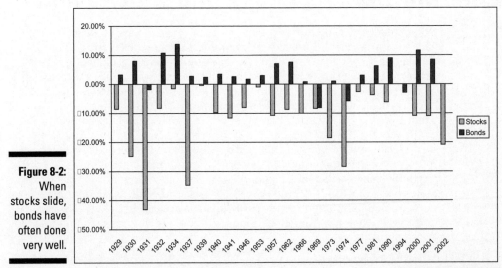

Figure 8-2: When stocks slide, bonds have often done very well.

Source: Vanguard, with permission

There are other means of diversifying a portfolio that is primarily stocks, for sure. But none is as powerful as bonds. Hedge funds? They're expensive and unpredictable. Gold? The gold metal is volatile as hell, and the price over the past 100 years has just kept even with inflation. Cash, CDs? Great, you need cash, but you won't get much of a return . . . you'll very likely lose money to inflation, even by shopping the best CD rates in town.

Consider how bonds would have protected your portfolio in the last bear market. Say you had a $100,000 portfolio before the market slide, on August 31, 2000. What would your portfolio have been worth on September 30, 2002, after 25 horrid months for the stock market? Consider three scenarios:

- **100 percent invested in stocks:** Ending value $55,880
- **60 percent in stocks, 40 percent in bonds:** Ending value $82,900
- **40 percent in stocks, 60 percent in bonds:** $96,410
- **100 percent in bonds:** $123,430

Note: For "stocks," I am using the Dow Jones Wilshire 5000 Composite Index; for "bonds," I am using the Lehman Brothers U.S. Aggregate Bond Index.

Bonds are the best hedge going. And there's no better way to hold bonds, generally speaking, than in the form of a bond index fund.

Entering the World of Bond Index Funds

Bond indexes are somewhat trickier to construct than are stock indexes. That's in large part because there are thousands of stocks but *millions* of bonds out there. One corporation or one government, for example, may issue many different series of bonds, each with its own coupon rate, maturity, and call features. How do you possibly corral such a large and diverse universe and create an index, never mind an *index fund* of a manageable number of securities that can accurately represent the entire kit and caboodle?

It isn't easy. And largely for that reason, bond indexing has lagged stock indexing by a large margin. In the world of traditional mutual funds, according to Morningstar, a mere 2.55 percent of fixed-income funds in the United States are index funds (29 out of 1,137). These index funds account for 8.9 percent of all bond-fund money ($107 billion out of $1.2 trillion). This figure does not include any municipal bonds, as there are no indexed municipal bond mutual funds.

But the recent advent of ETFs has rocked both Wall Street and fixed-income investing, and now, for the first time ever, bond indexing is coming into its own. Virtually all ETFs are index funds. The number of fixed-income ETFs — including a few municipal offerings — is now 55 and growing fast. Together these 55 bond ETFs total more than $45 billion in assets.

As you can see in Table 8-2, bond index funds have an impressive history, tending to clobber actively managed bond funds — just as stock index funds tend to clobber actively managed stock funds. The table shows the percentage of actively managed funds that underperformed appropriate indexes over the ten-year period ending December 31, 2006.

Table 8-2	% of Actively Managed Bond Funds That Underperformed the Indexes over a Recent Ten-Year Period	
Bond Category	*Government*	*Corporate*
Short term	79 percent	88 percent
Intermediate term	96 percent	94 percent
Long term	96 percent	96 percent

Source: Vanguard

The reason bond index funds do so well vis-à-vis actively managed bond funds is a wee bit different than the reason stock index funds do so well. Bond investing is potentially less *efficient* than stock investing. That is, because there are so many bonds issued (way more than stocks) and because bonds tend to be more complicated than stocks, a really smart manager can more easily find inefficiencies in the market — cases where he can actually beat the market by finding superior securities.

On the other hand, the operating fees when buying a bond fund are even more important than they are when buying a stock fund. This is so because the anticipated returns are so much less. If you expect to earn only 5 percent a year on a bond fund, paying a manager 1.5 percent means that you are dishing out 30 percent of your gains to the manager. A stock fund expected to earn 10 percent a year can charge 1.5 percent a year, and that requires that you fork over "only" 15 percent of your gains to the manager. Big difference.

Note that the bond index funds I recommend (coming in just a minute!) tend to charge waaaay less than 1.5 percent — and some actively managed bond funds charge waaaay more than that! (In the case of those very expensive bond funds, the long-term performance records are painfully predictable. Consider, for example, the Morgan Stanley High-Yield Security C Fund, with an annual expense ratio of 2.20 percent. The 10-year average annual return on this "gem" is –3.53 percent. Ugh.)

Finding a good bond mutual fund

With only 29 index bond mutual funds, the pickings aren't huge. I look for low costs, broad and solid indexes, and low costs (did I already mention low costs?). The particular kind of bond you choose, and how large an allotment to give to your portfolio, I address in Part III. Here, I simply present a few top-notch selections — index funds appropriate to most portfolios — along with some particulars you should know about each fund.

Vanguard Total Bond Market Index (VBMFX)

Indexed to: The Lehman U.S. Aggregate Bond Index. Although the index includes over 9,000 bonds, this fund uses a (very healthy) representative sampling of nearly 2,700 bonds. About 80 percent of those have a Moody's rating of Aaa, meaning the risk of defaults within the fund is negligible. (With 2,700 bonds, if one or two did default, it would amount to nothing more than a burp anyway.)

Expense ratio: 0.18 percent

Average maturity: 7.0 years

Quality of bonds: Very high

Minimum investment: $3,000

Minimum investment in IRA: $3,000

Notes: It's hard to go wrong with a bond fund that charges this little and gives you exposure to such a broad index (you won't find broader). If you qualify for the Admiral Share class of this fund ($100,000 invested immediately, or $50,000 invested in the fund over ten years), the expense ratio drops to an extremely friendly 0.10 percent.

T. Rowe Price U.S. Bond Index (PBDIX)

Indexed to: The Lehman Brothers U.S. Aggregate Index, which consists of about 9,000 investment-grade bonds, including Treasuries, agency bonds, and corporate bonds. This fund uses about 520 bonds to capture the performance of the index.

Expense ratio: 0.30 percent

Average maturity: 7.0 years

Quality of bonds: Very high

Minimum investment: $2,500

Minimum investment in IRA: $1,000

Notes: This fund is very similar to the Vanguard Total Bond Market Index, with a higher expense ratio but lower minimum. Use it if you are just getting started. Use it if you happen to have your money at T. Rowe Price and like their service. Note that the fund invests in fewer bonds than does Vanguard. These are mostly high-quality bonds, and yet, the lesser number of bonds will raise the risk of this fund just a bit. If one or two bonds should happen to default, it may make more than a burping sound.

Unit investment trusts (UITs): The pseudo-index of bonds

Some brokerage houses wrap up a bundle of bonds, usually 20 to 30 of them, and sell them to customers as a package deal. They call them *unit investment trusts.* There's a commission to buy the bundle (usually 1 to 3 percent) and a modest management fee (typically 0.20 to 0.30 percent) that you pay on a yearly basis. The UIT will have a maturity date of anywhere from a year to possibly 30 years down the road. When the UIT matures, just as is the case with an individual bond, you get back your principal. Before the UIT matures, the bonds just pay you interest collectively, and the managers don't play with the mix.

In other words, a UIT is like a mini-index of bonds . . . sort of. Some brokers may make a big deal about how their UITs are handpicked and likely to outperform the bond market. Other, more honest brokers present them for what they are: pseudo-indexes that offer you instant diversification in the bond market. A well put-together UIT can make as much sense as a comparable (similar bond quality and maturity) index mutual fund or ETF. But because you pay a commission, you want to make sure this is going to be a fairly long-term investment. I'm not sure, for example, that a one-year UIT, no matter how well constructed, would be a wise investment.

Most bond UITs require a minimum investment of $5,000.

Vanguard Short-term Bond Index (VBISX)

Indexed to: Lehman 1–5 Year U.S. Government/Credit Index. The fund holds approximately 900 bonds, two-thirds of which are Treasuries or U.S. agency bonds, and the rest are investment-grade corporate bonds. All are short term, meaning less return but less volatility.

Expense ratio: 0.18 percent

Average maturity: 2.4 years

Quality of bonds: Very high

Minimum investment: $3,000

Minimum investment in IRA: $3,000

Notes: Given that these are short-term, high-quality bonds, you aren't going to get rich off the interest payments from this fund. But your money will be safe. And you'll tweak out a little more than you would in an all-Treasury fund, such as the Fidelity option immediately following. If you qualify for the Admiral Share class of this fund ($100,000 invested immediately, or $50,000 invested in the fund over ten years), the expense ratio drops to a jolly 0.10 percent.

Fidelity Spartan Intermediate Treasury Bond Index Fund (FIBIX)

Indexed to: Lehman Brothers 5–10 Year U.S. Treasury Bond Index

Expense ratio: 0.20 percent

Average maturity: 6.3 years

Quality of bonds: Highest

Minimum investment: $10,000

Minimum investment in IRA: $10,000

Notes: Given the intermediate-term maturities and the iron-clad guarantee of the U.S. government, you aren't going to get a very high rate of interest with this bond fund, but you'll know your money is secure. The operating fee is certainly reasonable. This is a very good option for a place to park money that you feel you may need in a few years, or money that you want to make sure will be intact even in the worst of economic conditions. The Advantage Class of this fund (FIBAX) charges only 0.10 percent a year in expenses.

Buying a fixed-income exchange-traded fund

Bond ETFs have become an important part of the growth of the ETF market. From the time I finish writing this book to the time it appears in print, there could be a whole fresh crop of them out there! (Appendix C lets you know where to go on the Web for the latest fund updates.) Some of the bond ETFs are great, and others not-so-great. Here, I present some of the better choices.

Note: As with all ETFs, you'll pay a commission to buy and sell, which is usually modest. But remember that those commissions can add up if you are regularly depositing money or making withdrawals. If that's your game plan, you may be better off with a mutual fund.

Second note: ETFs have a reputation for being tax efficient, and that reputation is largely well-deserved. Keep in mind, however, that the vast majority of money produced by bond funds — whether ETFs or mutual funds, index funds or actively managed funds — will be interest, not capital gains. Interest, unless you get it from municipal tax-free bonds, is going to be taxable as regular income. The great tax efficiency of stock ETFs doesn't, by and large, translate to bonds.

Vanguard Total Bond Market ETF (BND)

Indexed to: The (very broad) Lehman U.S. Aggregate Bond Index. Although the index includes more than 9,000 bonds, this fund uses a (very healthy) representative sampling of nearly 2,700 bonds. About 80 percent of those have a Moody's rating of Aaa, meaning the risk of any defaults in the portfolio are small.

Expense ratio: 0.11 percent

Average maturity: 7.1 years

Quality of bonds: Very high

Notes: This is the ETF version of the Vanguard Total Bond Market Index mutual fund (VBMFX). It is essentially the very same beast but with a lower expense ratio (unless you should happen to qualify for the Admiral Shares class of the mutual fund) and no minimum investment.

iShares Lehman TIPS Bond Fund (TIP)

Indexed to: Lehman Brothers U.S. Treasury TIPS Index. *TIPS* stands for Treasury Inflation-Protected Securities. This fund adjusts with inflation, while giving you a very modest rate of return beyond that rate of inflation. This fund uses 24 bonds to match the index. Since these bonds have the full backing of the U.S. government, there is no need for greater diversification — 24 is fine.

Expense ratio: 0.20 percent

Average maturity: 9.6 years

Quality of bonds: Highest

Notes: In Chapter 12, I help you determine whether TIPS belong in your portfolio. For most folks, the answer is yes — roughly one-third of a typical bond portfolio should be in TIPS. Owning the iShares fund is a darned good way to achieve that goal.

iShares iBoxx $ Investment Grade Corporate Bond (LQD)

Indexed to: iBoxx $ Liquid Investment Grade Index, an index of 100 bonds (the fund also holds 100 bonds) that seek to capture the performance of the entire U.S. investment-grade corporate bond market. Despite the funny name, the iBoxx index makes sense!

Expense ratio: 0.20 percent

Average maturity: 11.6 years

Quality of bonds: Medium high

Notes: Quality corporate bonds, over the course of time, tend to return about 1 percent a year higher than Treasuries of similar maturity. (High-yield corporate bonds tend to return yet another point or two above.) If corporate bonds belong in your portfolio, this iShares offering is a very good way to get them there.

SPDR Lehman Municipal Bond ETF (TFI)

Indexed to: Lehman Brothers Municipal Managed Money Index, an index of long-term, tax-exempt bonds from municipalities across the nation. The fund uses approximately 130 bonds to mirror the performance of the index.

Expense ratio: 0.20 percent

Average maturity: 9.1 years

Quality of bonds: Very high

Notes: If tax-free is a priority (as it should be if you are in a high tax bracket and you are investing in a taxable account), this fund may be just the ticket for your bond portfolio — either part or all of it. An expense ratio of 0.20 percent is quite reasonable, especially considering the high markups involved in trading individual municipal bonds.

WARNING!

Inverse bond index funds: The worst investment idea of all time?

On May 1, 2008, ProShares introduced the first inverse bond index funds: the UltraShort Lehman 7–10 Year Treasury (PST) and the ProShares UltraShort Lehman 20+ Year Treasury (TBT). Here's the concept: If the bond index goes down, your fund goes up. More inverse bond funds are sure to follow. As you know if you read Chapter 7, I'm not a big fan of inverse stock index funds, but compared to inverse bond index funds, inverse stock index funds are pure gold!

Unlike stocks, which go up and down and up and down, bonds just aren't all that volatile. And when they do go down, they generally don't go down all that much. You're going to pay a gross expense ratio of 1.16 percent for a fund that will pay you the daily inverse of an index that usually goes up, and when it goes down, doesn't often go down by much? Um . . . Er . . .

The purveyors are selling these funds as "hedges" against potential losses in bonds. But . . . but . . . bonds themselves are hedges, and hedges don't need hedges! If you truly, truly have clairvoyant powers, yes, you can make money by bopping in and out of these funds in anticipation of the occasional sudden drop in the bond market. For most of us mere mortals, however, these funds are virtually *guaranteed* to lose money in the long run. Unless, of course, you happen to be the company selling one!

PowerShares Emerging Markets Sovereign Debt Portfolio (PCY)

Indexed to: The Deutsche Bank Emerging Market U.S. Dollar Balanced Liquid Index, an index that provides access to the sovereign debt of approximately 17 emerging market countries.

Expense ratio: 0.50 percent

Average maturity: 15.6 years

Quality of bonds: So-so

Notes: If you want high-yield (junk) bonds, it may make more sense to have international junk than U.S. junk. I explain why in a sidebar in Chapter 12. If you want to take an indexed approach, this fund is currently the only option you have. I'm not crazy about the 0.50 percent fee — on the high side for an ETF — but it's lower than you'll pay for any emerging-market debt mutual fund. Feel free to go with PowerShares for now, but keep your eyes open for a less expensive offering down the road.

Mixing and Matching Bonds and Stocks with an All-in-One Index Fund

For the ultimate in simplicity, you may want to choose a single fund that combines bonds with stocks. This may be a good choice if you have more than $3,000 but less than $30,000 to invest. Funds that combine stocks and bonds are known as *balanced* funds.

Choosing the static option

There is, as far as I'm concerned, only one choice for a combined stock-and-bond all-in-one-portfolio among index funds: the Vanguard Balanced Index mutual fund. It is low cost, broadly diversified, and could be just the ticket to an instant portfolio . . . for some.

Note that the Vanguard Balanced Index fund is static: It is basically 60 percent stock and 40 percent bonds. That's the way it is today and will be tomorrow. There are also variable options that change the ratio over time. These are called *lifecycle* funds, and I'm not crazy about them. I discuss why in a minute. First, allow me to introduce the Vanguard balanced offering.

Vanguard Balanced Index (VBINX)

Indexed to: 60 percent MSCI U.S. Broad Market Index and 40 percent Lehman U.S. Aggregate Bond Index. Together, we're talking 3,450 stocks and 1,885 bonds. The bonds are Treasuries, agency bonds, and investment-grade corporates.

Expense ratio: 0.19 percent

Average maturity (bond portion of portfolio): 7 years

Quality of bonds: High

Minimum investment: $3,000

Minimum investment in IRA: $3,000

Notes: If you belong in a 60/40 portfolio (60 percent stocks/40 percent bonds), you really can't lose with this simple all-in-one broad index fund. The question is, of course, whether you do belong in a 60/40 portfolio. That's something I can and do help you address in Chapter 11. If you qualify for the

Admiral Share class of this fund ($100,000 invested immediately, or $50,000 invested in the fund over ten years), the expense ratio drops to an extremely sweet and savory 0.10 percent.

Considering the variable options

Unlike the Vanguard (static) option for all-in-one investing, there are also variable options, otherwise known as *lifecycle* funds. In late 2007, a company called XShares Advisors teamed up with Amerivest Investment Management, a subsidiary of TD Ameritrade, to offer a bunch of lifecycle ETFs. These are index funds, and I know as an index investing advocate I'm supposed to like index funds, but I'm not too wild about these.

Currently, there are five lifecycle ETFs: The TDAX Independence 2010 ETF (TDD); the TDAX Independence 2020 ETF (TDH); the TDAX Independence 2030 ETF (TDN); the TDAX Independence 2040 ETF (TDV); and the TDAX Independence In-Target ETF (TDX).

All the funds have an expense ratio of 0.65 percent, and they track various lifecycle indices developed by Zacks Investment Research. A lifecycle index assumes that you want a more conservative portfolio as you get older. (Fair enough.) And so you pick a retirement date, such as 2020, 2030, or 2040, and the portfolio shifts over time from more aggressive (mostly stock) to more conservative (mostly bonds).

It sounds good in theory, but it's rather cookie-cutter, wouldn't you say? These funds assume that all people aiming to retire in the same year — rich and poor, healthy and unhealthy, with kids and without kids, good-looking and ugly — warrant the very same portfolio. Um . . . okay, maybe good-looking and ugly deserve the same portfolio. But all those others, too? No. Investing isn't that simple. And so I can't recommend these lifecycle index funds.

Your perfect portfolio "pie" should be determined by many factors. I review them in Part III.

Chapter 9

Diversifying Your Portfolio with Commodity, REIT, and Other Indexes

*I*n the not-so-distant past, if you wanted gold, you could either pan for it or go to a dealer and buy bricks or coins. Neither option was a particularly easy way to invest. Panning got your hands dirty. Buying bricks was perhaps easier, but you still had to make sure you were buying the real thing and not fool's gold. You'd need an assessment, and that would cost money.

You then had to store the gold somewhere, preferably under lock and key. You would also have been wise to insure it. If you were buying coins, you'd pay a very high markup to both purchase and sell.

Such practices are now unnecessary. You can own gold without ever touching the stuff. You want to invest in the precious metal? You can buy shares of an exchange-traded fund online in an instant. Each share of the ETF represents a piece of gold, and the price of the share goes up and down with the price of gold, tit for tat, minus the expenses of the fund.

The same is true of silver. And oil. The Hunt brothers (those famous silver speculators from a bygone era) never had it so easy. Nor did Jed Clampett or J.R. Ewing.

Whether these single-commodity funds qualify as true index funds, well, that's debatable — but let's not debate that here. I don't advocate that most folks invest in individual commodities. There's too much volatility without any way for you (or even the experts) to know which way that volatility will take you. But as for commodities as a whole — a mix of gold and silver, oil and platinum, pork bellies and wheat futures — yes, there is a rationale for investing in such a basket, and there are good index funds that make it easy to do.

Such commodity index funds are the first thing I discuss in this chapter. I then ask you to join me in a look at real estate — in the form of real estate investment trust (REIT) index funds — as another possible addition to your portfolio. And finally, I talk about a few index funds that are neither stocks nor bonds, commodities nor real estate. Such entities as a buy/write index and various currency indexes are truly on the fringes of index investing.

Panning for Gold with Commodity Investments

As I'm writing this chapter in mid-2008, gold, silver, and oil — the three most popular commodities for investment purposes (with the possible exception of Elvis dishware available on eBay) — have all seen a bull market like never before. In fact, the price of most commodities has gone through the ceiling, as evidenced in Table 9-1.

Table 9-1	Commodities Rock! (At Least in Mid-2008)	
Commodity Fund	*Average Annual Return, 1 Year*	*Average Annual Return, 3 Years*
Gold	28.15	25.48
Silver	21.39	NA
Oil	80.78	NA
Basket of commodities	24.05	NA
S&P 500	−4.68	8.23
Lehman Aggregate Bond Index	6.87	4.93

Note: Gold is measured by the performance of the SPDR Gold Shares ETF (GLD), silver by the iShares Silver Trust ETF (SLV), oil by the iPath S&P GSCI Crude Oil ETN (OIL), and the commodity basket by the iPath Dow Jones-AIG Commodity Index Total Return ETN (DJP).

Almost needless to say, investors have taken note, and there has been a huge influx of fresh capital into these commodity funds. Everyone is more than eager to join in the modern gold rush.

According to Morningstar figures, nearly $16 billion flowed into precious metal and natural resource ETFs in the past year (through April 2008). Compare that to the roughly $2 billion that flowed into technology ETFs! (Great money also poured into emerging-market stock ETFs, another category that has done well of late). Investors are forever chasing hot sectors, which is a huge mistake (even among index investors).

But back to commodities . . . Will all these recent investors in commodities make out in the next year or two or five as well as those who were fortunate enough to get into the commodity game in the recent past?

There is plenty of controversy at present as to whether the recent blastoff in commodity prices represents a bubble (just like the tech-stock bubble of the late 1990s or the Dutch tulip bulb bubble of centuries prior). Some people argue that it instead represents a fundamental shift in the world's demand for commodities (particularly due to the demands of resource-hungry nations like China and India) at a time when supply may be running short.

To be perfectly honest, I'm not sure. I expect there's at least a minor bubble. If the prices don't collapse, they are very unlikely to continue to climb at their present rate for too much longer. It may happen that commodities, if they do climb in price, will climb only about as fast as the general level of inflation. In fact, before this recent jump occurred, gold, over the past 100 years, had done more or less just that: It didn't reward investors in the long run at all; it merely kept up with inflation.

But investing in a commodity index fund, even if commodities rise in price only at the rate of inflation, may still make sense, in moderation. Let me explain why.

Protecting your portfolio from storms

I have a passion for diversification. That's why I like commodities. Commodity prices and performance tend to move on their own, with very little, if any, correlation to stocks, bonds, real estate, or Elvis dishware. If you're going to invest in something that holds its own in bad times for the major financial markets, commodities may be a good choice. Figure 9-1 demonstrates why.

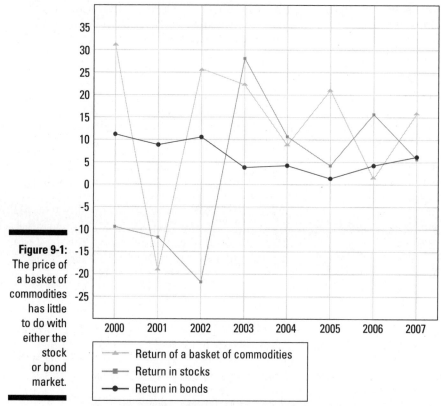

Figure 9-1:
The price of
a basket of
commodities
has little
to do with
either the
stock
or bond
market.

Return of a basket of commodities
Return in stocks
Return in bonds

Note: The basket of commodities is measured by the Dow Jones-AIG Commodity Index; stocks are measured by the S&P 500 Index; bonds are measured by the Lehman Aggregate Bond Index.

I must take a minute to concede that not all investment advisors agree with me that investing in a commodity index makes sense. John Bogle, the father of index investing (see his Q&A in Chapter 20), doesn't believe in commodity investing. Commodities, he points out, are not productive assets. Over the long run, he says, the growth in this index isn't likely to be much greater, if greater at all, than the general level of inflation. Bogle is right (as he usually is). We just have a minor difference of opinion as to whether, given this fact of nonproductivity, commodities still deserve a spot in your portfolio.

Bogle says no. I say yes, but only a minor position in your portfolio should be devoted to commodities — ballpark 5 percent. And I further suggest that you hold reasonable expectations for this allotment. I believe that through regular rebalancing (which I discuss in-depth in Chapter 16), you can eek out a return slightly better than inflation. *And,* just as importantly, you'll have a piece of your portfolio that very well may shoot up when everything else is sinking like, well, a brick of gold. I'm willing to accept only very modest long-term returns on 5 percent of my portfolio in return for that security.

But I'm also not telling you that commodities are an essential part of your investment plan. I like the exposure to gold, silver, and oil. It isn't necessary to hold them, however, to achieve a (ahem) well-oiled portfolio.

Assessing the commodity index options

Given the superlative performance of commodities — practically all commodities — in the months just prior to my writing this chapter, the number of exchange-traded products that track individual commodities or groupings of commodities hitting the markets has been staggering. I counted 32 total last, but the number will grow. Like the rest of the exchange-traded product market, the niches are now getting niched into nothingness. You can focus your investments not only on gold, silver, and oil, but also on grains, livestock, copper, or nickel.

I wouldn't advise nickel. Or copper. Or anything that goes moo. Commodities are volatile enough. Choose a fund that indexes a bunch of commodities — a fund such as the iPath Dow Jones-AIG Commodity Index Total Return ETN (DJP), which I describe momentarily.

In my description of this fund, please take special note of the section I call "Nature of the beast." (This particular fund moos a wee bit, but that's not what I'm talking about.) This fund is an exchange-traded *note,* which is quite different than the vast majority of index products.

iPath Dow Jones-AIG Commodity Index Total Return ETN (DJP)

Indexed to: The Dow Jones-AIG Commodity Index. The index currently is built of 34 percent energy (oil, natural gas), 7 percent livestock (moo), 10 percent precious metals (gold, silver, platinum), 21 percent industrial metals (copper, nickel), and 28 percent agriculture (wheat, corn).

Expense ratio: 0.75 percent

Issued by: Barclays Bank PLC

Rating of issuer: S&P: AA; Moody's: Aa1 (both indicate premium quality)

Nature of the beast (IMPORTANT!): This product looks like an ETF, but it is an ETN — an *exchange-traded note* — and there is a world of difference between the two. ETNs are unsecured debt obligations, sort of like bonds. You are actually lending Barclays your money, and the bank promises you a rate of return commensurate with the index, plus your principal back (adjusted to meet the index) when you ask for it. If Barclays were to go under, you'd stand to lose your money. (Not so with an ETF or index mutual fund.) I would recommend a product like this only if it were issued by a very solid company, which Barclays certainly is.

If you are going to invest in this note, know that at present commodity ETNs are taxed quite gingerly. (This is not true of all ETNs; with currency ETNs, you can get IRS-clobbered.) You generally won't pay any tax unless you sell at a profit and experience a capital gain. As such, this tax-efficient fund can find a home in your taxable account. But keep an eye on it. The IRS may change its initial ruling on commodity ETNs, making them less tax efficient. If that becomes the case, it may be time to reassess the wisdom of this fund.

Other financial instruments that allow for an indexed approach to commodity investing include the iPath GSCI Total Return Index ETN (GSP) and the Deutsche Bank Commodity Index Tracking Fund (DBC). Of the three funds, I prefer DJP because it offers the greatest diversification within commodities. At present, no other index fund tracks a similarly diversified portfolio. I use DJP in my own portfolio.

Holding Property in Your Portfolio with Real Estate Investment Trusts (REITs)

Real estate investment trusts, otherwise known as REITs (rhymes with *Keats,* the poet), are companies that hold property: shopping malls, office buildings, hotels, healthcare centers, storage facilities, or timberland. Alternatively, these companies may hold certain real estate–related assets, such as commercial mortgages. About 200 publicly held REITs exist in the United States. There are at least as many in Western Europe, Australia, and Japan.

Yes, there are various REIT indexes, and yes, you can find a good number of funds — both mutual funds and ETFs — that track those indexes.

REITs have caught on with investors in the past few years, mostly for the wrong reason. You can probably guess what that reason is: They are chasing high returns.

The so-called NAREIT All REIT Index has enjoyed an average annual return of 16.64 over the past five years. That outshines the S&P 500's annual return of 10.62 percent for the same time frame. Foreign REITs have similarly done great guns. European REITs have seen a five-year annual average return of 18.16, and Asian REITs, 20.88. (As is the case with most foreign investments over the past years, the weakening dollar and strengthening of other currencies has helped to propel returns for the Yankee investor.)

Will such phenomenal performance continue? Who knows? But the primary reason to invest in REITs (or anything else, for that matter) shouldn't be to chase recent performance. Rather, the reason should be to add to your portfolio diversification — to add a holding that is going to go up over the long run but not move in lockstep with the rest of your portfolio.

According to NAREIT, the National Association of Real Estate Investment Trusts, the correlation between the S&P 500 and the NAREIT index is less than 40 percent. In other words, your odds are at least 6 in 10 that if the broad stock market falls, your REIT holding may not . . . and vice versa. Figure 9-2 demonstrates this fact.

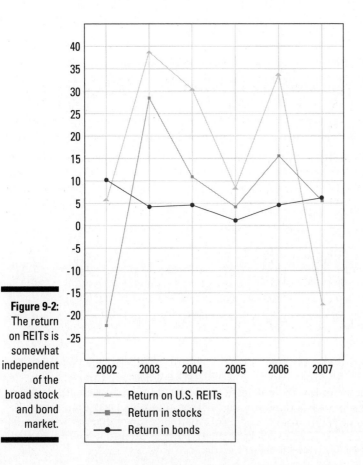

Figure 9-2:
The return on REITs is somewhat independent of the broad stock and bond market.

Note: REIT returns are measured by the NAREIT All REIT Index; stocks are measured by the S&P 500 Index; bonds are measured by the Lehman Aggregate Bond Index.

Understanding the true nature of REITs

For whatever reason, REITs are very often misunderstood. So before I introduce you to a few good REIT index funds, I'd like to talk about what makes REITs special and, in some cases, not so special:

- ✔ Ultimately, REITs are stocks. And to a certain extent, they behave as other stocks do. The price of REITs, and their return to investors, is subject to the same irrational exuberance and despair that other stocks are. We've seen some despair in the last year or so.

- ✔ REITs pay very high dividends. That's because REITs get special tax status, and in exchange for that status, they are required by law to pay out 90 percent of their income as dividends to shareholders. Over the past decade or two, REITs have tended to pay dividends in the 5 to 7 percent ballpark. In the months prior to my writing this chapter, with all the problems in the real estate market, those dividends have shrunk to about 4 to 5 percent. But that is still way higher than the 1.6 percent dividend being paid by a basket of S&P 500 stocks — even higher than the highest-paying dividend ETFs (which tend to be made up of mostly financial stocks), now yielding perhaps 3 percent.

- ✔ Any fund that pays high dividends is going to be not terribly tax efficient. That's especially true of REIT funds. Few, if any, REIT dividends qualify for the dandy 15 percent dividend tax rate. For that reason, REIT funds, even REIT index funds, belong in a tax-advantaged account, such as your IRA or 401(k).

- ✔ REITs mostly represent commercial real estate — not domestic real estate. But the value of REITs and the value of your home will tend to be somewhat related. If you have a whole lot of your personal wealth tied up in the value of your home (or rental properties you own), you may want to pass on REITs or choose to invest in foreign, not domestic, REIT funds. You don't want all your eggs tied up in the value of U.S. real estate. As we've all seen in 2007 and 2008, that value can go down as well as up.

- ✔ Speaking of international REITs . . . They have a delightful lack of correlation to all U.S. stocks, including U.S. REITs. When you think about it, real estate is the quintessential local economy. It involves very little international trade, which is the primary reason that, say, large Canadian and European growth stocks tend to move up and down in price very closely with large U.S. growth stocks.

✔ REITs comprise a sector of the stock market that tends to have limited correlation to the rest. That is, the market can go down, and REITs may hold their own. Or the market can go up, and REITs don't, or perhaps they tumble. But other sectors — most notably energy, utilities, and consumer staples — also can have minds of their own. REITs are not as special as some people (including many investment professionals) make them out to be. Yes, I do think they belong in your portfolio as a separate category. But if you don't want REITs, for whatever reason, you can still have a good portfolio. In fact, if you have room only in your taxable account, and you are in a high tax bracket, you may not want REITs. Ditto if you have lots of money tied up in real estate holdings.

Choosing REIT funds that will work best for you

As with all other index funds, you're looking for an index that makes sense, and you're looking for low costs. Remember that REITs pay mostly so-called *nonqualified* dividends, which means you'll likely pay a tax on them in the year they roll into your account, equal to your income tax rate. For that reason, REIT funds can sting you on April 15. You should try to store them in a tax-advantaged account, such as an IRA — yes, even though they are index funds, and you've heard that index funds are tax efficient!

Index mutual funds

Although there are several dozen REIT mutual funds, the REIT index mutual funds are scarce. In fact, only four of them exist. Of these, we can eliminate two: the Wells Dow Jones Wilshire U.S. REIT Index Fund (WDJAX) and the Wells Dow Jones Wilshire Global RESI Index Fund (WDGAX). These funds are from Wells Real Estate Funds, a company based in Norcross, Georgia (town motto: "Just like Wall Street, only more humid"). Both of the Wells funds bear *loads* (heavy commissions) and high expense ratios. They make no sense. You should never pay a load (4 percent in this case) or a high expense ratio (1.1 percent) for an index fund. Never!

I could easily recommend the two others funds, especially the Vanguard REIT Index Fund (VGSIX). The Northern Global Real Estate Index Fund (NGREX) offers REIT holdings in both the United States and abroad.

Vanguard REIT Index Fund (VGSIX)

Indexed to: The MSCI U.S. REIT Index, which is a free float–adjusted market capitalization–weighted index that represents approximately 85 percent of the U.S. REIT universe. Vanguard typically uses 100 REITs to replicate the MSCI index. (*Free float–adjusted* means that it includes shares held only by the general public and excludes those held by the controlling groups, which almost never trade. This is perhaps a bigger factor in REITs, which tend to be modest-size companies, than in most other stocks.)

Expense ratio: 0.20 percent

Average cap size: $5.8 billion

P/E ratio: 37.8

Current dividend yield: 5.6 percent

Minimum initial purchase: $3,000

Minimum initial purchase in IRA: $3,000

Top five holdings: Simon Property Group, Inc. REIT; ProLogis REIT; Vornado Realty Trust REIT; Boston Properties, Inc. REIT; Public Storage, Inc. REIT

Notes: With $100,000 you can move to the Admiral Class of this fund (VGSLX) — the very same animal as VGSIX but with a yearly fee of only 0.14 percent. Or, if you want the ETF version of the same fund, you can purchase the Vanguard REIT ETF (VNQ), which has an annual expense ratio of only 0.12 percent.

Northern Global Real Estate Fund (NGREX)

Indexed to: The FTSE EPRA/NAREIT Global Real Estate Index. (*EPRA* stands for the European Professional Realtors Association, and *NAREIT* stands for the National Association of Real Estate Investment Trusts.) The index reflects the stock performance of more than 300 REITs, as well as non-REIT real estate companies in North America, Europe, and Asia.

Expense ratio: 0.64 percent

Average cap size: $10.5 billion

P/E ratio: 14.97

Current dividend yield: 3.60 percent

Minimum initial purchase: $2,500

Minimum initial purchase in IRA: $500

Top five country holdings: United States, Japan, Hong Kong, Australia, United Kingdom

Notes: All things being equal, I'd like to see you split your REIT holdings into one U.S. REIT fund and one foreign. But I also don't want to see you slicing and dicing your portfolio so many ways that it becomes unwieldy. So here's a compromise: If you have a handsome enough portfolio — say, at least $75,000 — consider two REIT funds. If you have anything less than that, you're probably better off with a global REIT fund that combines U.S. holdings and international. Northern Global isn't a bad option. Another option: the First Trust FTSE EPRA/NAREIT Global Real Estate Index Fund (FFR), which I discuss shortly; it's an ETF, and it costs just a wee bit less than the Northern fund.

Exchange-traded funds

Unlike the world of mutual funds, the world of ETFs offers lots and lots of REIT funds. But as far as I'm concerned, it isn't hard to eliminate a whole bunch of them that focus on narrow niches of the REIT universe. (The REIT universe itself is narrow enough for me!)

So, unless you happen to have a huge portfolio, I'd just forget about the REIT ETFs that specifically shoot to tap into mortgage REITs, residential REITs, retail REITs, and industrial/office REITs.

Among those I do recommend are the Vanguard REIT ETF (VNQ) and the Dow Jones Wilshire REIT ETF (RWR) on the domestic side. And on the foreign side, I recommend the iShares FTSE EPRA/NAREIT Global Real Estate Ex-U.S. Index Fund (IFGL), as well as the SPDR DJ Wilshire International Real Estate ETF (RWX).

Vanguard REIT ETF (VNQ)

Indexed to: The MSCI U.S. REIT Index, which is a free float–adjusted market capitalization–weighted index that represents approximately 85 percent of the U.S. REIT universe. Vanguard typically uses 100 REITs to replicate the MSCI index.

Expense ratio: 0.12 percent

Average cap size: $5.8 billion

P/E ratio: 37.8

Current dividend yield: 5.6 percent

Top five holdings: Simon Property Group, Inc. REIT; ProLogis REIT; Vornado Realty Trust REIT; Boston Properties, Inc. REIT; Public Storage, Inc. REIT

Notes: This fund is the ETF share class of the Vanguard REIT Index Fund (VGSIX). They are identical funds, except for their structure, a minor point. Note that you'll save money on the expense ratio of the ETF, but you'll have to pay a small fee to buy and sell it. The tax efficiency of the ETF shouldn't differ much, if at all, from the index mutual fund.

Dow Jones Wilshire REIT ETF (RWR)

Indexed to: The Dow Jones Wilshire REIT Index. State Street Global Advisors, the purveyors of this fund, currently use 87 REITs to represent the index of all U.S. REITs.

Expense ratio: 0.25 percent

Average cap size: $5.2 billion

P/E ratio: 28.1

Current dividend yield: 4.7 percent

Top five holdings: Simon Property Group, Inc. REIT; Prologis REIT; Vornado Realty Trust REIT; Boston Properties, Inc. REIT; Equity Residential REIT

Notes: This fund is similar enough to the Vanguard offering that the higher price tag makes it, in my book, an obvious second choice. It's a good fund, and worthy of investing in, but only if you have some reason that I don't know about to pass on the Vanguard REIT fund.

iShares FTSE EPRA/NAREIT Global Real Estate Ex-U.S. Index Fund (IFGL)

Indexed to: FTSE EPRA/NAREIT Global Real Estate Ex-U.S. Index. (*EPRA* stands for the European Professional Realtors Association, and *NAREIT* stands for the National Association of Real Estate Investment Trusts.) Barclays is using 172 REITs to capture this broad index of the international global REIT market, which exempts all United States–based REITs.

Expense ratio: 0.48 percent

Average cap size: $7.6 billion

P/E ratio: 14.7

Current yield: 2.25 percent

Top five country holdings: Japan, Australia, Hong Kong, United Kingdom, France

Notes: This fund, which entered the market a year after the SPDR DJ Wilshire International Real Estate ETF (RWX), is a little bit more economical while offering largely the same kind of diversification.

SPDR DJ Wilshire International Real Estate ETF (RWX)

Indexed to: The Dow Jones Wilshire ex-U.S. Real Estate Securities Index. State Street Global Advisors, the producers of this ETF, use 132 REITs to mirror the performance of this global index that includes exposure to 19 different countries, the United States not included among them.

Expense ratio: 0.60 percent

Average cap size: $6.0 billion

P/E ratio: 15.6

Current yield: 3.4 percent

Top five country holdings: Japan, Australia, United Kingdom, Hong Kong, France

Notes: Not a bad fund, by any means, but the iShares version costs less for very similar exposure.

First Trust FTSE EPRA/NAREIT Global Real Estate Index Fund (FFR)

Indexed to: The FTSE EPRA/NAREIT Global Real Estate Index. (*EPRA* stands for the European Professional Realtors Association, and *NAREIT* stands for the National Association of Real Estate Investment Trusts.) The index reflects the stock performance of more than 300 REITs, as well as non-REIT real estate companies in North America, Europe, and Asia. First Trust uses almost all 300 REITs to replicate the index.

Expense ratio: 0.60 percent

Average cap size: $10.5 billion

P/E ratio: 14.97

Current dividend yield: 3.60 percent

Top five country holdings: United States, Japan, Hong Kong, Australia, United Kingdom

Notes: All things being equal, I'd like to see you split your REIT holdings into one U.S. REIT fund and one foreign. But I also don't want to see you slicing and dicing your portfolio so many ways that it becomes hard to manage. So here's a compromise: If you have a chunky enough portfolio — say, at least $75,000 — consider two separate REIT funds. If you have anything less than that magic number, go with a global REIT fund that combines U.S. holdings and international. This First Trust fund is a good option.

Knowing how much to invest in REITs

I can't give you an exact percentage. The optimal allocation of REITs in your portfolio depends on a number of factors, including how much of your personal wealth is tied up in non-portfolio real estate (your home, rental properties, and so on) and how much space you have in your tax-advantaged accounts. (You need room in there for other tax-inefficient funds, like most bond funds.) I'll get personal in Part III and try to address these questions specifically. For now, let me throw out just a few rough guidelines:

- ✔ For most folks, 10 to 20 percent of your total equity holdings might be in REITs. Let's split the numerical baby and say 15 percent would be a good starting point.

- ✔ I would divide that up so that roughly 15 percent of your domestic stock holdings are in domestic REITs, and 15 percent of your foreign holdings are in foreign REITs. (Thus, if you have a portfolio of 75 percent stocks, and 60 percent of that is domestic, your U.S. REIT allocation may be 6.75 percent [$75 \times 60 \times 15$ percent] of your total portfolio. Your foreign REIT allocation may be 4.5 percent [$75 \times 40 \times 15$ percent] of your total portfolio.)

A lot of people assume that their U.S. REITs and their foreign REITs will show similar patterns of performance. Uh-uh. Largely because of exchange rates, your foreign REITs are more likely to perform similarly to your other foreign stocks than they are to your U.S. REITs.

Go with those REIT funds, both U.S. and foreign, based on the broadest indexes (such the funds I introduce in this chapter). Avoid the niche areas, such as mortgage REITs and retail REITs, unless you have a fat portfolio (more than, say, half a million) and could really stand to benefit from huge diversification. I generally prefer traditional cap-weighted indexes to the newfangled fundamental indexes. Avoid like the plague the Ultra Real Estate ProShares fund (URE) and the UltraShort Real Estate ProShares fund (SRS) — such leveraged and inverse ETFs are more tools of speculation than investments.

Investing — or Not — in Some Truly Unorthodox Indexes

The explosion of exchange-traded products in the past several years has not only led to a great number of new ways for index investors to tap into the stock, bond, commodity, and REIT markets; it has also stretched into areas where few investors — index or otherwise — have ever ventured. There's no compelling reason that I've found to venture into these areas, and the fact that they are now indexed doesn't in itself create a compelling reason. Hold onto your seat — whoooeeee! — while I take you on a quick tour of currency indexes, as well as indexes of preferred stock, covered calls, and private equity.

Cashing in on currency quackery

As every international traveler knows (as well as buyers of French cheeses, Italian wines, and BMWs), the U.S. dollar has plummeted vis-à-vis most foreign currencies. On October 26, 2000, the U.S. dollar was at a high water mark, and it could buy you 1.21 Euros. By April 22, 2008, a greenback would get you only 0.62 Euros. On January 18, 2002, the U.S. dollar could get you 1.61 in Canadian dollars. By November 7, 2007, cashing in that same U.S. dollar would get you only a lousy 92 Canadian cents.

And *that,* dear reader, is why there are now dozens and dozens of currency ETFs, each linked to an index of various sorts. People are thinking, "Hey, if the dollar keeps falling, and if I index my investments to some other currency, I'll get rich!" But that isn't going to happen. If the U.S. dollar keeps falling at the rate it has been, in another few years, an average Canadian plumber would be able to work an extra weekend, saunter across his southern border, and buy the state of Vermont. Look again. Currency fluctuations work both ways! They always have.

I'm not even sure that these currency ETFs qualify as index investing. But they're being advertised as index funds, and most people think (rightfully so) that ETFs are index funds, so I suppose I need to comment both on the funds and the advertisements. (Note to advertisers: You aren't going to like what follows.)

One such advertisement, for WisdomTree Dreyfus Currency Income ETFs, reads, "Your stocks and bonds have gone international. Why not your cash?" I'll tell you why not: *Because cash should be kept as cash!* Cash is meant to be spent in the present or in the near future. It isn't supposed to be gambled with. Stocks and bonds are where you expect to see return (and deal with risk) — not cash! The price you pay for the WisdomTree ETFs — 0.45 percent a year — is going to drain whatever meager interest you make on the cash. And the currency fluctuation is just as likely to work against you as for you. *That's* why your cash should not go international.

Oh, one more reason: If you have foreign stocks and bonds (which you should) then you already have exposure to foreign currencies — probably too much!

The WisdomTree Dreyfus Currency Income ETFs — such as the WisdomTree Dreyfus Brazilian Real Fund (BZF), the WisdomTree Dreyfus Chinese Yuan Fund (CYB), and the WisdomTree Dreyfus Indian Rupee Fund (ICN) — are very short-term debt funds (sort of like foreign-denominated money markets). Some of the other currency index ETFs, such as the CurrencyShares (Rydex) lineup of ETFs, are a bit different in structure but offer the same promise. Funds like the CurrencyShares Mexican Peso Trust (FXM) and the CurrencyShares British Pound Sterling Trust (FXB) charge 0.40 percent a year and promise to make you money only if the U.S. dollar continues to drop vis-à-vis the currency you choose.

PowerShares has also jumped onto the currency bandwagon with its PowerShares DB U.S. Dollar Index Bullish Fund (UUP) and — for real contrarian index investors — the PowerShares DB U.S. Dollar Index Bearish Fund (UDN), each with an expense ratio of 0.55 percent. Barclays is in the game, too. You can buy exchange-traded notes the likes of the iPath EUR/USD Exchange Rate ETN (ERO) or the iPath GBP/USD Exchange Rate ETN (GBB), each with a yearly expense of 0.40 percent. Unlike the commodity-based ETNs I discuss earlier in this chapter, these babies are not tax efficient at all. And you take the same (minor, but real) default risk that you do with bonds but not ETFs. I like Barclays. A lot. I dislike these particular funds. A lot.

I'm not saying that the currency funds don't make any sense in any circumstance for any person. They make a lot of sense for the people selling them! They may also make sense for certain institutional buyers and very sophisticated financial types (exporters, importers, international bankers) who need currency hedges for various reasons. For a typical buy-and-hold individual investor, especially a smart index investor who demands rhyme and reason to his investments, they make no sense. They'll make you no cents. Or pesos. Or yen. Or whatever. Over the long run, these currency plays will only bite you on the derriere. Stay away.

Doing like the rich: Investing in private equity (sort of)

The term *private equity* brings to mind caviar, yacht clubs, and toy poodles with pedicures. Private equity means just what it sounds like: ownership in a business interest that is not publicly traded, most typically very small start-up companies. There's often great risk but potentially great return. Some legendary hedge fund managers have made billions with their private equity deals. (Clarification: They've made billions for themselves, and typically much less for their investors.) How do you turn private equity into an investment for the unwashed masses? And, even trickier, how do you index such a thing? The folks from PowerShares say they've found a way with the PowerShares Listed Private Equity ETF (PSP).

Note the word "Listed." That's the alleged trick. "The PowerShares Listed Private Equity Portfolio seeks to replicate the Red Rocks Listed Private Equity Index, which includes over 30 U.S. publicly listed companies with direct investments in more than 1,000 private businesses," says the PowerShares brochure. (The Red Rocks literature says "30 to 50" companies. Who knows?) In other words, you're getting in through the back door. Or maybe the side door. I'm not sure. You're investing in mud flaps by buying a truck, investing in toothpicks by buying a lumber company. Hmmm . . .

It's a novel idea, and it promises great return. In fact, the Red Rocks index has a reported ten-year return of 14.64, which clobbers the return of the S&P 500 (5.9 percent), as the PowerShares literature makes abundantly clear. But is that a fair comparison? The companies that make up the Red Rocks Listed Private Equity Index are, by and large, small and mid cap value companies. The return on small value over the past ten years: 13.80. The cost of the PowerShares ETF: 0.60 percent a year. So even if the future is as kind to these companies as was the past (and that's a huge question), the cost of this fund, considerably more than you'd pay for a typical small or mid cap value ETF, may be enough to wash out any advantage.

This is a novel idea, and I give PowerShares lots of credit for creativity, but I don't see PSP as a terribly good choice for your portfolio.

Making a preference for preferred stock

Preferred stock is often described (accurately enough) as something of a cross between a stock and a bond. Preferred stocks pay high dividends (usually taxed more delicately than bond interest). And some preferred stock (*convertible* preferred) offers an opportunity for considerable price appreciation, like a common stock, sort of. Generally speaking, preferred stock offers a return potential higher than bonds but lower than common stock. It is riskier than bonds but less risky than stocks.

Does preferred stock make sense? I'm not a huge fan. Why not instead invest in stocks and bonds, and create a hybrid portfolio? To me, that makes more sense. But some people (those with a dividend fetish, mostly) really like preferred stock. They could do worse, I suppose. Until recently there was no way for an index investor to touch preferred stock, but all that has changed with the advent of exchange-traded products. Two ETFs now attempt to mirror the performance of indexes created to track the market performance of preferred stock:

✔ The iShares S&P U.S. Preferred Stock Index Fund (PFF) has an expense ratio of 0.48 percent and a current yield of 6.6 percent. (Don't confuse yield with return! This fund, as I'm typing this paragraph in May 2008, is showing a three-year annualized return of only 0.5 percent; that's because the price of the shares had tumbled.)

✔ The PowerShares Preferred Fund (PGX) tracks the Merrill Lynch Fixed Rate Preferred Securities Index Fund. It has an expense ratio of 0.50 percent and a current yield (for what that's worth) of 7.3 percent.

There you have it. They are available. But I'm not urging you to buy.

Covering calls with the buy/write index

Perhaps the most innovative, unusual, and exotic of all ETFs uses something called a *covered call* strategy in hopes of capturing good returns with minimal risk. I am intrigued with this strategy, for sure, but I don't think it's quite ready for primetime just yet.

In a covered call strategy, you, the investor, buy a certain stock, and then you write call options (which are "covered" because you actually own the stock), allowing someone else the option to buy the stock at a set price at a certain time. That someone else pays you a premium for that right. In most cases, especially when the markets are relatively flat, the options expire, and the writers of the options make good money off the premiums. When the markets are shooting up, however, writers of call options don't fare as well, as they tend to lose their appreciating shares.

So far, so good? The folks from Barclays and PowerShares have created a way to index covered calls, in which you buy shares of the S&P 500 and then write calls on a regular, systematic basis.

In theory, the process works well. The index, when backtested, shows average annual returns of five and ten years only a tad less than the S&P 500, with only about two-thirds the volatility. Who knows if that's the way it will work in the next five to ten years. But even if the strategy does work, is it such a great thing? You can accomplish pretty much the same objective, I feel, by adding 20 percent or so bonds to your stock portfolio. And you can do it for less money than the two buy/write exchange-traded products, both of which charge a fairly hefty annual fee of 0.75 percent.

The PowerShares product is called the PowerShares S&P 500 Buy/Write fund (PBP), and the Barclays product is called the iPath CBOE S&P 500 BuyWrite ETN. I encourage you to wait a few years before investing in either of these products to see if the performance in the real world matches that of the backtested index returns. You may be surprised. I may be surprised! If you absolutely must go for one or the other sooner, I'd choose the PowerShares option — the ETF rather than the ETN — and I'd stick it into a tax-advantaged account.

Part III

Drawing a Blueprint for Your Index Portfolio

The 5th Wave   By Rich Tennant

Being Dracula's slave didn't pay much, but Renfield always found extra money to invest.

In this part . . .

To your left (the first two parts of this book), you find the tools and the building blocks with which an index investor works. It all starts with good, low-cost index funds based on reasonable indexes. To your right (this part of the book), you find out how to use those tools and building blocks to construct the optimal portfolio.

In Chapter 10, for example, you discover the best brokerage houses where index funds may be purchased. I then guide you through the all-important allocation questions: How much should you have in stocks? In bonds? In cash? I help you understand that the right allocation for you and the best index funds for you are very individual matters. Finally, in Chapter 15, I present you with sample portfolios. Use them as starting points for drawing up your personal portfolio blueprint.

Chapter 10

Finding a Happy Home for Your Money

*W*hen you shop for food, you can go to the farmer's market and buy directly from the source. That would be akin to buying an index mutual fund directly from a mutual fund company. Or, you can do like the masses and buy your food at the supermarket. That would be similar to buying an index mutual fund or exchange-traded fund through a retail brokerage house (such as a Charles Schwab, Fidelity, or T. Rowe Price), which is sometimes called, aptly enough, a *financial supermarket*.

Going to the farmer's market (or the mutual fund company) directly may have a few advantages, but supermarkets can be awfully convenient.

In this chapter, I compare and contrast the two ways for you to buy an index fund: either directly from a mutual fund company, or through a financial supermarket. (With mutual funds, you have a choice. But with exchange-traded funds, you must go through the intermediary; you generally cannot buy an ETF directly from the source.) Some mutual fund companies and financial supermarkets are friendlier to small investors than others. Some offer special sweet deals on new accounts. Some are better suited to meet the specific needs of index investors.

I can't say I've had intimate relationships with every mutual fund company and brokerage house in America, but I do have enough experience to pass on a few words of wisdom to make your shopping easier. These shopping pointers, along with a few tips about negotiating the best deals with brokerage houses, form the bulk of this informative chapter.

Knowing What's Important and What's Not

As an index investor, you have special needs and desires, hopes and dreams. (Oh, you weren't aware?) For example, it hardly makes sense to own low-cost index funds if you're going to pay a small fortune to buy and sell them. You don't need stock-picking or market-timing advice, thank you, and you certainly don't want to pay for it. Perhaps most of all, you need access to the best selection of index funds available.

Additional considerations:

- ✔ How knowledgeable and friendly is the staff?

- ✔ Do you get to a staffer by second or third ring, or are you put through voicemail hell and connected intercontinentally to someone on a fuzzy phone line who seems half asleep?

- ✔ What kind of return do you get in your cash (money market) account?

- ✔ Does the financial supermarket help you to keep track of your capital gains, or are you on your own to do that onerous task?

- ✔ Can you reinvest your dividends and interest payments automatically, at no cost?

- ✔ How user-friendly or tech-scratchy is the Web site interface?

So many questions . . . It's hard to pick the best brokerage house. But I will say right off the bat that as an index investor, you want a discount brokerage house such as Fidelity, Vanguard, Charles Schwab, T. Rowe Price, TD Ameritrade, Zecco, or ShareBuilder (run by ING Direct).

As an index investor, you do *not* need a full-service brokerage house with full-service prices and hungry salespeople in expensive suits who call themselves "advisors" and try to convince you to trade often. You don't need a Morgan Stanley, a Smith Barney, a Merrill Lynch, or a UBS. Their prices are high, their advice is unnecessary, their 50-page colorful performance reports are ridiculously devoid of any important information, and if they have their own index funds, those funds generally stink. (Sorry if I sound a bit opinionated, but I really am speaking the truth here!)

Sorting through apples and oranges

Among the discount brokerage houses, you'll find considerable differences in everything from service to price. Unfortunately, just as when you buy tires or mattresses, it can sometimes be difficult to compare and contrast.

Fidelity and Schwab, for example, charge you different prices for purchasing an ETF online versus on the phone. They may charge you different prices depending on how much money you have in your account and how often you trade. Zecco, in many cases, will charge you nothing to place a trade for an ETF, but you're going to have to pay to buy a mutual fund. Vanguard issues different phone numbers to different customers . . . the richer customers get somewhat richer service. T. Rowe Price, which has excellent service all around, charges slightly higher fees for its index funds than do other major discount brokers, but the minimum balances tend to be considerably less.

The largest of the brokerage houses — Vanguard, Fidelity, Schwab, T. Rowe Price — issue their own index mutual funds, and they all make it easier, naturally, for you to buy their own brand rather than one of their competitor's products. Buying and selling from the home team is usually free.

Despite all these many considerations, there is a brokerage house (or a combination of brokerage houses) best for you. Don't despair — I'll help you to find it!

Allowing your specific investments to guide you

If you're new to index investing, you need to determine whether you are going to build an indexed portfolio out of mutual funds, exchange-traded funds, or a combination of the two.

If you are going the pure mutual fund route, I don't think you can do better than to open an account with Vanguard. Vanguard started index investing. Vanguard has the largest selection and the lowest-cost mutual funds of any brokerage house. Of course, you can buy Vanguard funds at just about any financial supermarket, but you often have to pay to do so. Fidelity, for example, typically charges $75 to buy a Vanguard fund. (Vanguard and Fidelity, like the Army and Navy teams, don't tend to like each other very much.)

If you're going with a pure or predominantly ETF portfolio, your considerations change. Unlike a mutual fund, an ETF — *any* ETF (Vanguard, Barclays, ProShares, State Street) — can be purchased and held at any brokerage house. There is generally no advantage to holding an ETF with the home team.

Because ETFs trade just like stocks, you pay the usual commission to trade stocks. That commission, provided you make the trade online, should run you no more than $20 or so. If you are a buy-and-hold investor with lots of bucks, the fee will obviously matter less than if you are a frequent trader or if your portfolio is still in the four figures.

Is it safe to put all your money into one brokerage house?

After the chaos surrounding Bear Stearns and Lehman Brothers (once two of America's most prestigious brokerage houses) and the sub-prime mortgage crisis, you may wonder if storing all your index funds under one roof is a good idea. Know that U.S.-based brokerage houses are required by Congress to be insured by the Securities Investor Protection Corporation (SIPC). The SIPC, in turn, regulates the broker-age houses, making sure that your funds are kept separate from the brokers' own funds and securities (including all those subprime mortgage contracts). If the broker should go belly up, as brokers do from time to time, your stock or bond funds should remain intact. They remain yours to transfer to another institution. In a worst-case scenario, the SIPC will protect you up to $500,000.

Since the SIPC was founded in 1970, a number of brokerage bankruptcies have occurred. The SIPC estimates that "no fewer than 99 percent of persons who are eligible have been made whole" in such cases.

Most large brokerage houses carry supple-mental insurance that will protect you well beyond that half-million covered by the SIPC. (TD Ameritrade carries enough insurance through Lloyd's of London to insure each client account up to $150 million; Zecco carries insur-ance to protect each client up to $35 million.) For more information, check out the SIPC Web site: www.sipc.org. If you have more than $500,000 in your portfolio, you may want to ask a prospective broker about supplemental insur-ance it carries.

Choosing the Financial Supermarket That Best Meets Your Needs

In this section, I help you choose among the discount brokerage firms by highlighting some of the personality quirks that make each one distinct.

The Vanguard Group

One can only speculate where index investing would be, or if it would even exist, if it weren't for Vanguard. Vanguard was founded by John Bogle (who participates in a Q&A session with me in Chapter 20). It was founded specifi-cally as an index shop, and today that remains its main focus. In addition to Vanguard's 29 index mutual funds (and many more ETFs), it also offers actively managed funds, but the actively managed funds are very index-like (meaning low cost, low turnover).

If you are going to invest in index mutual funds, you'll find none better than Vanguard's. If you house them at Vanguard, you will save yourself the transaction costs that just about any other firm will charge you. (That could be $10 at Zecco or $75 at Fidelity.) It makes sense. To buy and sell ETFs, Vanguard tends to charge more than some of the other discount brokers — $20 per online trade, for most folks.

Founded: 1975

Assets under management: $1.5 trillion

Number of proprietary index mutual funds: 29

Best features: Way more index funds, and better index funds, than most other major brokerage houses. Also, the customer service people are index-oriented. You will never be encouraged to make quick trades or time the market. None of Vanguard's funds — index and active — charges a *load* (a sales fee). If you're going to mix and match active and index investing (as I discuss in Chapter 13), Vanguard active funds are among the best you'll find anywhere. Yields on Vanguard cash and near-cash (short-term bond) funds tend to be the highest available.

The Vanguard conversion gig

The Vanguard Growth Index Fund (VIGRX) and the Vanguard Growth ETF (VUG) are, technically speaking, different classes of the same fund. Same thing for the Vanguard European Stock Index Fund (VEURX) and the Vanguard Europe Stock ETF (VGK). Why should you, technically speaking, give half a hoot? Because Vanguard, like no other purveyor of either mutual funds or ETFs, allows you to switch from the mutual fund to the ETF. It will cost you $50 to make the conversion. Again, you can only do this with Vanguard funds; the firm actually has a patent that gives it a monopoly on this kind of swap-out deal.

Doing the conversion can save you from having to pay capital gains tax on a mutual fund that you may have held for years. And by moving from, say, the Vanguard Growth Index Fund to the Vanguard Growth ETF, you'll be saving money in the long run: The mutual fund charges 0.22 percent a year in operating fees, and the ETF charges only 0.11 percent. So if your balance is $20,000, you'll save (0.22 – 0.11 = 0.11 percent) $22 per year. You'll have your payoff in a little over two years.

Caveat: If you have $100,000 or more in the Vanguard Growth Index Fund, you can qualify for the Vanguard Growth Admiral share class of the mutual fund and pay only 0.10 percent a year. As a rule, therefore, I'd say you should consider conversion of any individual Vanguard mutual fund in which you have more than $20,000 but less than $80,000. (The $80,000, in a good market, could become $100,000 in little time.) Be aware that the conversion process works only one way; you can't convert back from an ETF to a Vanguard mutual fund, except by cashing out of the ETF, which could result in a tax hit.

Worst features: If you go the ETF route, the trading costs will tend to be several dollars higher than with most other brokerage houses. Vanguard is also second rate where it comes to tax reporting on capital gains; I find myself having to call them every April, which I never have to do with Fidelity. And, if you have mutual funds and ETFs, your Vanguard statements will come broken in two, which is a bit of a pain to keep straight.

Address:
The Vanguard Group
P.O. Box 1110
Valley Forge, PA 19482-1110

Telephone: 800-992-8327

Web site: www.vanguard.com

Fidelity Investments

Fidelity is huge, but the company has been able to keep its commitment to decent service. Although it boasts less than half the number of index funds as its top competitor, Vanguard, the index funds that Fidelity does offer are pretty good. Lately (in an effort to steal away clients from Vanguard, I'm sure), Fidelity has been lowering the fees on its index funds. It now boasts some of the lowest-cost index funds to be found.

I use Fidelity quite a bit. I like the Web site interface. The statements are readable. The tax reporting is excellent. The price of trades (for ETFs, for example) is fair but varies depending on how much you have invested. For most folks, it's $10.95 per online trade, although Fidelity can be very generous (especially if prompted to be) in awarding free trades to new account holders. The company also runs specials from time to time, whereby you can get goodies, like free airline miles, for every trade you make.

Founded: 1946

Assets under management: $1.5 trillion

Number of proprietary index mutual funds: 11

Best features: Fidelity's funds network is among the largest in the business. There's no problem building an entire portfolio at Fidelity. Its own index funds are extremely low cost and sensible. And its money-market funds are among the highest paying in the industry. Customer service is available 24/7, even on Christmas Day, which few, if any, other brokerage houses offer.

Worst features: Only some of the non-Fidelity funds in the company's fund network can be purchased without a transaction fee. If you buy a mutual fund outside of the Fidelity universe, you're going to pay a pretty penny: $75 to purchase most Vanguard mutual funds, for example.

Special deals: The cost of Fidelity trades is based on the amount of money you have in your *household* account. I have found some, but not all, Fidelity reps to be quite liberal when it comes to defining "household." Argue, for example, that you and your parents, or you and your brother, are very close and share many financial matters. You may just luck out.

Address:
Fidelity Investments
P.O. Box 770001
Cincinnati, OH 45277-0001

(Or check the Web site for the location closest to you.)

Telephone: 800-343-3548

Web site: www.fidelity.com

Charles Schwab

As the original discount brokerage house, Schwab ("Talk to Chuck") had lost its way for a while, charging too much. Lately, however, prices have dropped, and most folks will now spend $12.95 for an online trade of a stock or ETF.

Founded: 1971

Assets under management: $1.4 trillion

Number of proprietary index mutual funds: 15

Best features: If you have a minor child who has job income and wants to open a Roth IRA (a *great* idea!), Schwab is the only major brokerage I've found that will allow you to do so.

Worst features: Others may disagree, but I find Schwab's Web site extremely clunky. "Chuck" also took a big black eye in 2008 when its YieldPlus fund, sold to the public as a cash-like investment, tumbled by more than a third. Schwab is currently being sued by angry investors, many of whom, if they could get Chuck on the phone, might have some rather ugly words to share with the guy.

Address:
Charles Schwab Bank
5190 Neil Road, Suite 100
Reno, NV 89502-8532

(Or check the Web site for a location near you.)

Telephone: 866-232-9890

Web site: www.schwab.com

T. Rowe Price

The Baltimore-based financial supermarket clearly positions itself as an ally to the small investor. Reps tend to be very friendly (they seem almost lonely at times) and well trained at avoiding jargon. The index mutual funds have lower minimum investments ($2,500 for taxable accounts; $1,000 for IRAs) than most brokerage houses require.

Founded: 1937

Assets under management: $400 billion

Opening an account and placing trades

Opening a mutual fund account is usually done by sending a check or wiring money to an institution, and filling out a bunch of forms. After the institution gets your money, you're sent confirmation that you are now the proud owner of X shares of the ABC Mutual Fund. Nothing could be simpler.

When buying an exchange-traded fund, you have to first set up your account by filling out all the necessary forms. Then you transfer money to the brokerage house. Finally, you place an order to buy — either by phone or online. Do it online! It will always be cheaper.

There are two basic ways to place an order for an ETF: You can place a *market* order or a *limit* order. A market order places your bid on the market, and you get the best available price at the moment you place the bid. A limit order is a more conservative way to go: You place an order to buy, say, 100 shares of an ETF at $30.10 a share. If someone, somewhere is willing to sell you 100 shares at that price, you'll have your purchase. If no one is willing to sell at that price, you won't get your purchase.

Which is better? In most cases, for a buy-and-hold investor purchasing an ETF for a long-term investment, I'd say that you should simply place a market order. I would recommend that you do so after the market has been open for at least half an hour (after 10 a.m. Wall Street time). Don't place your market order after 3:30 p.m. (The market closes at 4:00 p.m.) The markets can be jumpy at the beginning and end of the trading day. You're more likely to get a fair price at some point in between.

Number of proprietary index mutual funds: 5

Best features: If you happen to be self-employed and you would like to open an individual Roth 401(k), T. Rowe Price is the only major brokerage house that will allow you to do so.

Worst features: This financial supermarket's proprietary index funds cost a bit more than the competitors' — between 0.40 percent and 0.50 percent, versus many of Vanguard and Fidelity's index funds, which tend to run 0.20 percent or less.

Address:
T. Rowe Price
P.O. Box 17630
Baltimore, MD 21297-1630

Telephone: 800-225-5132

Web site: www.troweprice.com

TD Ameritrade

Ameritrade and TD Waterhouse, for years known as the two bargain-basement brokerage houses, merged in 2006. The resulting company, TD Ameritrade, charges a flat $9.99 for online trades. Not bad.

Founded: 1971

Assets under management: $300 billion

Number of proprietary index mutual funds: 0

Best features: Nice, clean Web site. Low prices.

Worst features: The culture of the place isn't exactly what it is at Vanguard. Frequent trading is promoted, and you may be made to feel like something of a schlump if you "settle" for an index portfolio.

Address:
TD Ameritrade
P.O. Box 2760
Omaha, NE 68103-2760

Telephone: 800-669-3900

Web site: www.amtd.com

Zecco

Zecco — which stands for "Zero Commission Cost" — allows you ten free ETF (or stock) trades a month, provided you maintain a total account balance of $2,500 or more. If your balance falls under that amount or you exceed ten trades in a month, the price per trade is $4.50. A buy-and-hold index investor with a fair-sized portfolio isn't going to save a fortune, percentage-wise, going with Zecco over another discount broker. But the smaller investor with total assets of $2,500 to $25,000 may do well with Zecco.

Founded: 2006

Assets under management: Small, but apparently growing

Number of proprietary index mutual funds: 0

Best features: Free trades! Free trades!

Worst features: Given the price you pay, you shouldn't expect great service. Some users complain of long waits on the phone and a Web site that leaves something to be desired.

Address:
Zecco Trading
P.O. Box 60126
Pasadena, CA 91116

Telephone: 877-700-7862

Web site: www.zecco.com

Dimensional Fund Advisors (DFA)

Arguably, Dimensional discovered "fundamental" indexing that is now suddenly so popular. Using scads of historical data, the founders of Dimensional reckoned a long time ago that leaning a portfolio toward value and small cap may bring better long-term performance, and they structured their index funds accordingly, using their own proprietary indexes rather than the S&P 500 and such. So far, Dimensional funds' real-world performance has been quite extraordinary.

Founded: 1981

Assets under management: $160 billion

Number of proprietary index mutual funds: 54 (Morningstar categorizes most of these as active funds, not index funds; I disagree.)

Best features: Very smart indexes, packaged in funds by very smart people.

Worst features: Dimensional funds are mid-priced when compared with other index funds. And you can't buy them unless you're an institution or you go through a fee-only registered investment advisor. As such, Dimensional funds make sense only to people with fair amounts of money (at least $300,000) who can find a really good investment advisor willing to work for a reasonable fee. I discuss where you may find such a bird in Chapter 17.

Address:
Dimensional Fund Advisors
1299 Ocean Avenue
Santa Monica, CA 90401

Telephone: 310-395-8005

Web site: www.dfaus.com

Other discount brokers

If you want still more options for where to park your money, you may wish to consider the following:

- ✔ ShareBuilder (part of ING Direct): www.sharebuilder.com
- ✔ E-trade Financial: www.etrade.com
- ✔ Scottrade: www.scottrade.com

What, No Index Funds in Your 401(k)?

Most company retirement plans are chosen by the human resources department. Most human resources people know no more about investments than I know about the ancient artists of Uzbekistan.

I've seen 401(k) plans so bad, with such pitiful choices of investments, that it would be a miracle if any of the participants in the plan will ever be able to retire. (Hey, maybe that's what the boss wants!) If your 401(k) plan has no index funds — only expensive actively run funds with horrible track records — you may want to cry, and I couldn't blame you. Do know, however, that human resource people are amenable to being educated.

Hand the folks in your personnel department a copy of this book, and let them know that good retirement plans that offer low-cost index funds — both mutual funds and ETFs — are available!

Your HR people can contact Vanguard, Fidelity, or T. Rowe Price — all three companies can set up 401(k) plans with index options. (Contact information can be found earlier in this chapter.) Another good bet is to contact Invest n Retire by checking out www.investnretire.com or calling 503-419-2894.

Rolling Over Your Retirement Plan

If you leave your present job to take another job, you will have the option, in most cases, of rolling your existing 401(k) into either your new company 401(k) or an IRA. In most cases, you'll be better off rolling the entire bundle into an IRA. When the money is in an IRA, you can invest in index funds, and nothing but — the investment decisions will be all yours.

The rules for a 401(k) and a traditional IRA are the same: You can't touch the money until you are 59$\frac{1}{2}$, unless you care to pay taxes and a penalty; and you must start taking the money out when you turn 70$\frac{1}{2}$. Roth IRAs (which get you no tax deduction when you put the money in, but incur no taxes when you take the money out) do not obligate you to ever take distributions.

Here's a handful of things to be careful of before you transfer your retirement hoard:

✔ Transfer the money directly into your IRA so the IRS doesn't get the impression that you are cashing out of your retirement plan, at which point they may want to tax and fine you.

✔ If you think you ever may want to roll the money back into a company 401(k), keep the transferred money in a separate IRA and don't mingle it with any other funds. I'm not sure why you would want to do this, but perhaps keeping the option open isn't a bad idea.

✔ If you believe that someone may someday sue your pants off for any reason, know that 401(k) plans are federally protected from lawsuits. IRAs may or may not be; it depends on the state in which you live.

✔ If you have company stock in your current 401(k), know that you may be giving up some very positive tax benefits by liquidating that stock. You may want to speak with a financial professional before disinvesting.

Chapter 11

Developing Your Broad Investment Goals

*O*ne of the great unsung virtues of index investing is its predictability, at least compared to active investing. Mind you, I'm not saying that index investing is entirely predictable — only that it is, especially in the long term, much more predictable than some other kinds of investing. By putting together a mix of largely index funds, you can fine-tune your portfolio (as much as a portfolio can ever be fine-tuned) to just the right degree of aggressiveness or conservatism.

Do you want a high-rolling, risk-be-damned, poised-for-prosperity portfolio? (Hint: You may want to buy some stock index funds.) Or do you want a tried-and-true, tortoise-paced, can't-lose-too-much-but-probably-won't-gain-too-much portfolio? (Hint: Think bond index funds and money-market funds.)

Unsure which kind of portfolio you want? This chapter helps you to determine just that.

Understanding Asset Allocation

The single largest determinant in whether you can expect stomach-churning volatility in your portfolio (but potentially very sweet returns) is the percent of the portfolio you have in stocks and the percent you have in bonds.

Stocks, which represent ownership in companies, rock when it comes to long-term returns. But the ups and downs can be extreme, and sometimes, if not handled with care, the volatility can be devastating. Bonds, which represent money you lend to either companies or the government, tend to provide modest returns but limited volatility.

Over the past 80 or so years, the *nominal* (preinflation) return on bonds has been about half that of stocks (roughly 5 percent average annual return for bonds versus 10 percent for stocks). After inflation, bonds have yielded more like one-third the return of stocks. After inflation and taxes (bonds are generally taxed more harshly than stocks), bonds have yielded about one-quarter as much as stocks.

But the nominal value of bonds rarely goes down, and if it does, not by much. Stocks, on the other hand, have seen periods in which they've lost half their value in a bear market; see Table 11-1. The value of cash — money-market accounts, savings accounts, CDs — doesn't change at all on paper, but over time, it can be eaten away severely by inflation.

Table 11-1	Major Stock Market Hits	
Beginning of Bear Market	*% Decline in Stock Portfolio*	*Number of Months Before Market Started to Climb*
August 1956	–21.6 percent	15
November 1968	–36.1 percent	18
January 1973	–48.2 percent	21
September 1976	–19.4 percent	17
January 1981	–25.8 percent	19
August 1987	–33.5 percent	3
March 2000	–47.4 percent	31

In general, money invested that you aren't going to need to touch for the very long run — at least several years (I get more specific later in the chapter) — should be invested mostly in stock index funds. Shorter-term money needs are best invested in less volatile investments, like bond index funds and money-market funds.

Setting basic parameters for a sensible portfolio

There are, alas, no simple formulas to tell you what percent of your portfolio is best put in stocks and what percent in bonds and cash. You will, of course, hear talk of all sorts of simple formulas. A popular one tells you to subtract your age from 100, or your age from 110, and that's what you should have in stocks. Pay (almost) no attention to such formulas! Age is but one of many determinants you should use to get to your optimal asset allocation — and by far not the most important one.

Before I delve into the nitty-gritty, however, know that I am a strong advocate of diversification, and I can foresee almost no circumstances where an investor would want all stock or all bonds (or all of *any* one investment of any kind, for that matter).

The most aggressive of aggressive portfolios should still have some bonds; the most conservative of conservative portfolios should still have some stocks. For most folks, I would use 60/40 (60 percent equity, 40 percent bonds) as a good default position.

Studies — lots of them — show that a 60/40 portfolio, more than perhaps any other kind of portfolio, is apt to persevere in both good times and bad, to hold its own against both inflation and market turbulence. It is a very good default position from which to begin tweaking your portfolio to the left or to the right.

Viewing asset teamwork in action

A portfolio that contains different kinds of assets (stocks, bonds, cash, possibly real estate and commodities) is the strongest of portfolios. That's because stocks and bonds (and commodities and real estate) tend to zig and zag and sometimes zog: When one goes down, the others (not always, but much of the time) may go up or at least hold their own. This lack of correlation is what good diversification is all about.

Diversification among asset classes keeps your portfolio on a more even keel. It also allows for effective regular *rebalancing*. Every year or so, you can sell off whatever asset is up and buy whatever is down. By so doing, you'll be continually buying low and selling high, which over the course of many years will likely juice your total average annual returns by 0.5 to 1.5 percentage points. The *rebalancing bonus* will depend on how often you rebalance and how good your diversification is.

Beyond these diversification basics, stocks, bonds, and cash play different essential roles in a diversified nest egg.

Stocks: Your primary engine for growth

Over the past 80 years, stocks have gained about 10 percent a year, on average. But they lose money almost one in every three years. Stocks are your best investment for the long run . . . almost sure to beat bonds, and almost sure to keep you ahead of inflation, which has run at an average of about 3 percent a year.

If you have a timeframe of, say, 15 years, stocks are sure to be your best bet, at least if history is our guide. (No guarantees.) Generally speaking, however, because of their volatility, you don't want to invest in stocks any money you may need in the next two to three years.

Also, because the future may not be as kind as the past, don't put all of your money in stocks. More aggressive portfolios may warrant as much as 85 percent stocks — a variety of stock index funds, preferably. A more conservative portfolio may contain only 40 percent stocks.

Bonds: Your stabilizer in a storm

Over the past 80 years, bonds have gained between 5 and 6 percent a year, on average. But there have been a good number of years in which bonds have failed to keep up with inflation.

High-quality bonds are probably your best hedge against a serious bear market, so make sure you have enough money in bonds to keep you covered for any funds you may need in the next couple of years. If you are living off your portfolio, I'd like you to have at least five (and preferably ten) years' living expenses in intermediate- and long-term high-quality bonds.

Conservative portfolios may include as much as 60 percent bonds. I generally wouldn't recommend more than that, except perhaps for some people in high tax brackets who don't need much return, and for whom tax-free municipal bonds may make up almost an entire portfolio. Just about everyone should have at the very least 15 percent of his or her portfolio in bonds.

Cash: Your lick of liquidity

Although bonds aren't as jumpy as stocks, sometimes (especially when interest rates are rising) bond prices can sink, and you don't want to have to cash them out at that point. As a general rule, try to keep six months' living expenses in cash. That means money-market accounts, short-term CDs, very short-term bond funds, or online savings accounts.

Real estate: Net worth you can live in and possibly live on

I suggest that you *not* tally up the value of your home as part of your nest egg. After all, you will always need a place to live, so cashing out completely isn't in your stars. The exception is if you plan to downsize, in which case part of the net worth you have tied up in your home will be available for other expenses. In that case, your home equity can be counted as part of your portfolio. Ditto for a rental property or other real estate that you can opt to turn into cash.

Real estate tends to be a nice diversifier to stocks and bonds. If you don't want the hassles of direct ownership, consider a position in real estate investment trusts (REITs), which I discuss in Chapter 9.

Commodities: As good as gold

Gold, silver, oil, and such provide the promise of return independent of the ups and downs of stocks and bonds. Unfortunately, their long-term return is very uncertain. Commodities are not, in themselves, productive assets. Gold, for example, has shot up in the past few years, but prior to that, for decades and decades, its price rose at just about the level of inflation.

Commodities are an optional investment. For added diversification, you may want about 5 percent of your portfolio — no more — devoted to a diversified commodity index fund, such as I discuss in Chapter 9.

Annuities: Steady streams of income

Especially for healthy older folks with no dependents and no fears of dying broke, a fixed-income annuity can make a lot of sense. Here's how it works: You fork part of your portfolio over to an insurance company, surrendering the capital and your right to it, in exchange for a steady stream of income. That stream of income would likely be much greater than anything you could pull from a diversified index portfolio.

If you fit the bill, I suggest a good, hard look at annuities after you reach the age of 70 or so. I'm talking about an *immediate fixed annuity,* and I suggest you start your shopping by looking at the offerings at Vanguard and Fidelity, which work with top-rated insurance companies.

Other annuity products (such as variable annuities, which offer a stream of income that varies based on the return of a hypothetical portfolio) may make sense for some other folks, under certain other conditions. But be careful out there! No area of the investment world is rifer with fraud, deceit, and consumer manipulation!

Alternative investments: Nothing is too wild

Hedge funds and hedge fund–like mutual funds can be expensive and unpredictable. They can also, if chosen carefully, offer good diversification and a reasonable expectation of favorable returns. Ditto for collectibles and expensive art . . . if you have the education. You need to be very picky about which alternative investments you choose. I discuss a few in Chapter 9 and offer some examples of how they may work into your portfolio in Chapter 15. In only very rare circumstances would I suggest that alternative investments make up more than 10 percent of your portfolio.

Zeroing in on your optimal percentages

I'm going to disregard the more exotic investments for the moment and focus on where the lion's share of your wealth should be invested: diversified stock index funds and diversified bond index funds. Using 60/40 (stocks/bonds) as our default, which way might you want to tweak your portfolio to best suit your personal financial needs? Following are a few guidelines. I also invite you to visit Chapter 15, where I provide sample portfolios. Perhaps you'll see yourself in one of my case studies, and you can model your own portfolio accordingly.

✔ **Get a handle on your time frame.** Simply put, the more time you have, the greater the chances that your stock investments will outshine your bond investments. When you invest in stocks, you stand to lose a good chunk of your capital tomorrow. That's not so serious if you have the time to allow the market to (we hope) recoup. It's also not so serious if you are making regular, sizeable deposits that allow your balance to float upwards. But losing a good chunk can be very serious if you are recently retired, with no more money going into your account, and selling your depressed stock index funds becomes a necessity.

If you are fairly certain that you aren't going to need to tap your funds in the next 15 years, consider putting perhaps 85 percent into diversified stock index funds. If your investment time frame is 10 years, perhaps 80 percent . . . 5 years, maybe aim for 75 percent.

✔ **Know your own tolerance level for risk.** It's easy to say, "Oh, sure, I'm tough. I can handle ups and downs in my portfolio." It's another thing to actually do it.

One of the most common, and more painful, mistakes that even a smart index investor can make is to pull out of the stock market just as the market falls. (For a full list of such morbid mistakes, see Chapter 19.) An aggressive portfolio of, say, 85 percent stocks, no matter how well indexed and diversified, is going to take a few tumbles in your lifetime. Using history as our gauge, you'll probably lose money in one out of every three years.

I would say the odds are very small that you would lose more than 25 percent in one year — that has happened only once in most readers' lifetimes, in 1973–74. However, it's certainly possible. Be realistic with yourself. Could you handle that loss without panic? (A personal note: If you Google "Hitchhiker's Guide to the Galaxy — Don't Panic," and hit *Search Images*, you'll see the wallpaper image I use on my office computer.)

✔ **Assess your personal financial situation carefully.** You may think you aren't going to need any cash infusions in the next two or three years, but how secure is your income, really? If you needed money in a hurry, do you have any family members who could help you out? How strong are your home, auto, and health insurance policies? Very importantly, what are your sources of income? A 70-year-old retiree who is comfortably living off Social Security and a pension can take much more risk with her portfolio than a person of similar age who is directly dependent on her portfolio income to pay the bills.

✔ **Take no more risk than is necessary.** In the following section, I help you to determine how much you're going to need to be financially independent. The more you need, generally speaking, the more reason you have to push for higher portfolio returns by upping the percentage of your pie that you have in stocks. Anything beyond financial independence, and you're looking at pure gravy. Is it worth losing sleep at night so you can have that gravy?

I generally recommend that as you get within arm's length of your reasonable financial goals, you start to temper the risk. There comes a point in our lives where protecting against loss becomes more important than securing gains.

Determining How Much You Need to Have . . . and Save

I can imagine all sorts of financial goals. You may, for example, want to leave tens of millions of dollars to your already spoiled kids. You may want to save enough to start your own foundation, *à la* Bill and Melinda Gates, and start issuing grants to worthy causes. You may be aiming to fork over a pile of cash to your alma mater in exchange for their naming the new sports center in your honor. But such goals are rare.

For the rest of us simple folk, our financial goals tend to be similar: We want to get out of debt and then build up a reserve large enough so that we have enough money to meet our anticipated spending needs at some point in the future. Those needs may include a college education for the kids, a new home, or a few weeks at the beach next summer. Ultimately, people without fixed pensions (that is, the vast majority of under-65 Americans who aren't public school teachers or members of Congress) will need a nest egg to live off if they're ever going to stop gassing up the car and showing up at work every morning.

But how much do you need in dollar terms? And what will it take to get there? In this section, I give you a rough idea and refer to resources that can offer a more specific picture.

Employing the 20x rule

To get you in the ballpark of what you're going to need in your portfolio to call yourself financially independent, start with the amount of money you need to live on comfortably for a year. Throw in all of your expenses, including not only the biggies — food, shelter, and medical care — but also transportation, clothing, movie money, and taxes. What's your figure?

Let's suppose it's $60,000. Now subtract from that amount whatever you expect to get in income from sources other than your nest egg. Let's suppose you plan to collect $20,000 a year from Social Security. You are left with $40,000 a year that you'll need from your savings.

Okay, take that $40,000 and multiply it by 20. That gives you $800,000. That is *roughly* the size of the portfolio you're going to need to stop working at normal retirement age (mid-60s) and live comfortably for the rest of your life. (We can shave that 20 number down if you're willing to be flexible in your spending; see the last section of this chapter.)

If you plan to give up the paycheck at a younger age, you should multiply your yearly expenditure need by 25. (Again, this can possibly be shaved down a bit; see the last section of this chapter.)

How much will you need to save to achieve that goal? For many of us, the answer is, very roughly, about 10 to 12 percent of our paychecks throughout our working years. That amount, invested wisely, should give us the nest egg we'll need to be financially independent. But the amount you should be saving will vary greatly depending on how much you have right now, how well you invest, luck, inheritances, and other factors. To get more specific, both on the ultimate number and how much you have to save, I would refer you to a number of fairly good online retirement calculators, which I discuss next.

Using retirement calculators

The goal here is to plug your personal numbers into a *good* retirement calculator. Many retirement calculators will do you more harm than good!

You've undoubtedly seen the kinds of retirement calculators I'm talking about, because they are all over the Internet. You input your current age, your retirement age, your presumed lifespan, the amount of money you think you'll need a year, and — presto! — out pops a number, telling you the lump sum you need to save in order to retire without resorting to eating cardboard. You may get another number, as well, telling you how much you should be saving right now in order to get your requisite lump sum.

Um . . . I hate to tell you this, but the amounts being recommended by most online calculators are probably too small. Most of these calculators figure that you'll be getting returns year in and year out that approximate the historical average returns of the markets (10 percent for stocks, 5 to 6 percent for bonds) and that the average inflation rate will continue to be 3 percent. In the real world, even if these averages end up being correct, you're bound to experience huge fluctuations along the way. The only way to account for such fluctuations is to use a retirement calculator that employs something called *Monte Carlo simulations.*

Understanding Monte Carlo simulations

If you were to stop collecting a paycheck tomorrow, and if you were to start drawing money from your nest egg, a few lousy market years at the start of the game could just about kill the entire plan. On the other hand, if you experience a few up market years at the start of the game, you'll wonder why you didn't retire years ago. Monte Carlo simulations look at all possible permutations of the stock and bond markets, and they show you the range of possibilities.

Figure 11-1 shows a typical Monte Carlo retirement analysis model. Note that some retirement calculators that use Monte Carlo actually show this analysis, while others use it behind the scenes and then just spit out the numbers you need to know.

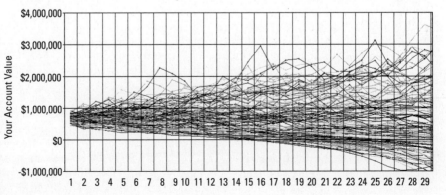

Figure 11-1: Monte Carlo simulations show you how well your portfolio will do in good times and bad.

This analysis reveals that a portfolio of $800,000, from which you are taking $40,000 a year, has a fairly good chance of lasting 30 years.

Calculators that use Monte Carlo analysis aren't perfect, but they are a whole lot better than calculators that use just straight-line analysis.

Here are three online calculators that I recommend:

- ✔ www.firecalc.com: *FIRE* is short for Financial Independence/Retire Early, and this free Web site (feel free to contribute!) is one of the best you'll find. There's lots more here than a calculator, including some pretty good general investment advice, and even a forum where you can chat with others about retiring young, if that's your thing.

- ✔ www.moneychimp.com/articles/volatility/retirement.htm: Moneychimp is a funny name, but it's a great Web site full of all kinds of financial calculators. For some funny reason, there's a ridiculously simple and simple-minded retirement calculator featured on the home page. The better calculator is buried deeper within. Make sure you use the long link provided here.

- ✔ www3.troweprice.com/ric/RIC/: Many of the financial supermarkets offer silly retirement calculators, but T. Rowe Price's uses Monte Carlo simulations and is presented in an easy-to-read fashion. *RIC* stands for Retirement Income Calculator.

Knowing the limitations of even the best retirement calculators

The problem with the straight-line retirement calculators that don't use Monte Carlo analysis is that they tend to greatly underestimate what you'll need to be financially independent. But, alas, the Monte Carlo calculators tend to overestimate.

For example, suppose I have $500,000 in my portfolio and I'm a year off from retirement. If I assume an average 7 percent growth rate in my portfolio, and I plan on living off my money for 30 years, I can withdraw $40,300 a year and my money will last, according to the simple straight-line calculator on the homepage of www.moneychimp.com.

But if I run the same numbers though the Monte Carlo retirement calculator that appears elsewhere on the same Web site, I'm told that, given the volatility of markets, my $500,000 portfolio has only a 46 percent chance of lasting 30 years if I withdraw $40,300 a year. To have a 96 percent chance of my money lasting as long as I do, I'd have to have $800,000 in the bank, according to this calculator!

So which is it? If I need $40,300 a year, am I shooting for a $500,000 nest egg or $800,000? The answer: Something in between. Yes, you need to account for the volatility that exists in the real world, and that is reflected in the Monte Carlo analysis. On the other hand, Monte Carlo analysis is looking at worst-case scenarios, and do you really want to scrimp your entire life on the chance that you'll encounter a worst-case scenario?

If I wanted to enjoy a 30-year retirement, and I needed $40,300 a year (inflation-adjusted) from my portfolio to have that retirement, I'd feel great if I had $800,000 in the bank. If I didn't have that kind of money, but I dreaded going into the office every day, I'd make a deal with myself: To retire and withdraw $40,300 a year (adjusted upward slightly each year for inflation), but to be willing to tighten my belt and reduce that spending amount considerably if the market didn't do well, especially in the early years of my retirement.

My asset mix would likely be somewhere in the 60/40 (60 percent stocks/40 percent bonds) range. The vast majority of that money would be in low-cost index funds, of course. And I'd have diversification not only between stocks and bonds, but *within* the stock and bond sides of my portfolio, as well. What kind of diversification? Glad you asked! That's the subject of the very next chapter.

Chapter 12

Fine-Tuning Your Index Selections

- -

In This Chapter

▶ Applauding diversification

▶ Dividing your stock portfolio into domestic and foreign

▶ Appreciating that size matters

▶ Understanding the difference between value and growth

▶ Differentiating among your bond index holdings

- -

*I*f you've read Chapter 11, you should have step one of your index portfolio blueprint complete. (If you haven't done so, I encourage you to back up one chapter!) You know where your risk–return sweet spot is generally located, and you have determined your proper mix of stocks and bonds.

Now comes step two.

There are *thousands* of stock indexes, and nearly as many bond indexes. They come in every size, nationality, industry sector, maturity, and quality. Which ones do you choose (and in which proportions?), and which ones do you ignore?

Whereas the split between stocks and bonds is fairly easy to grasp, this second stage of portfolio diversification usually leaves hapless investors tearing out their hair by the roots. Those who decide to become index investors must still decide which indexes to follow. INDEX INVESTING DOES NOT MEAN PLUNKING ALL OF YOUR MONEY INTO THE S&P 500! (Sorry to shout, but some obnoxious proponents of active investing sometimes throw this assumption out as a straw-man argument against indexing, and it ticks me off!) Proper index investing calls for a diversity of index funds.

But do you want primarily U.S. stocks or foreign stocks? Value companies or growth companies? Large caps or small caps? Index funds exist for all of them. On the bond side, do you want Treasuries or corporate bonds? Long-term bonds or short-term bonds? Investment-grade bonds or high-yield bonds? Index funds exist for all of those, too.

The answer, in a nut: You want them all, provided that your portfolio is large enough and that you don't wind up slicing and dicing yourself into too complicated a portfolio to properly manage.

Achieving excellent diversification through index funds isn't really that hard. All you need is a bit of background information, which I give you on the following pages. Please note that I mention plenty of individual index funds in Part II (stock funds in Chapter 7, bond funds in Chapter 8, others in Chapter 9). In Chapter 15, I present model portfolios with specific funds. This chapter isn't so specific . . . It's more about the *kinds* of indexes you want your funds to mirror. To put it another way, this chapter is about *asset allocation* — what kinds of assets do you want to invest in?

Expanding Your Geographic Horizons

The world is a big place, and yet U.S. investors seem to have only recently discovered that. Thanks to the high returns in international stocks over the past decade, Mr. and Mrs. Smith have finally been diversifying. Still, the world stock market is now about 60 percent non-U.S. (see Figure 12-1), and few U.S. investors have anywhere near that percentage of foreign stock in their portfolios. That's okay . . . 60 percent isn't necessary. I would, however, like to see you with *at least* 40 percent international holdings on the equity side of your portfolio.

Of that minimum 40 percent in non-U.S. stocks, you want a division between developed (rich) markets and emerging (not-so-rich) markets, because the two kinds of markets tend to move in different cycles. (Emerging market economies tend to be tied very much to the prices of the commodities they produce.)

There's no magic formula for deciding what percent of your stock portfolio should be invested in General Electric, Microsoft, and Wal-Mart versus Nestle, British Petroleum, and Toyota Motor Corporation. But for maximum diversification, you want to spread your bets out as much as possible. The most highly diversified (and therefore, in some ways, safest) portfolio would give you a share of every stock on the planet, in every country.

In the real world, however, foreign stocks, even big ones in stable countries, bring somewhat more volatility. That's because of currency swings. Emerging-market stocks, as you would expect, are considerably more volatile in their own right, given that poor countries are more susceptible to economic upheavals, government coups, and such. In addition, the index funds that invest in foreign stocks, especially emerging-market stocks, tend to carry heavier expenses.

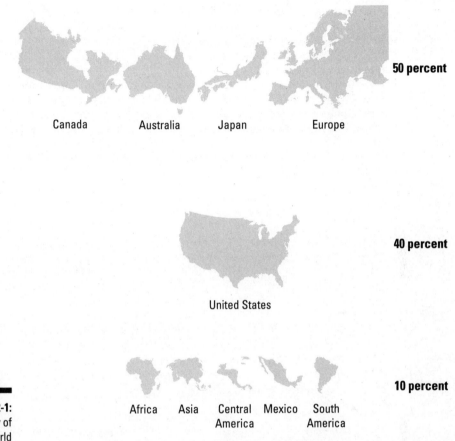

50 percent

Canada   Australia   Japan   Europe

40 percent

United States

10 percent

Africa   Asia   Central   Mexico   South
                    America   America

Figure 12-1:
A view of
the world
stock
markets.

For those reasons, and not for any jingoistic inclinations, I assure you, I feel that an optimal portfolio is justified in overweighting the United States a bit. That's why I don't insist that you invest 60 percent of your stock portfolio abroad — 40 percent is just fine. A range of 35 to 50 would work.

Considering correlation

You hear lots of people these days talk about how it's a small world. They speak of globalization and the greater correlation among national stock markets caused by that globalization.

Yes, oui, si, ja. There is truth to that indeed.

In 1998, about 30 percent of all the revenues of U.S. corporations were derived from business activities outside of the United States — the sale of McDonald's hamburgers in France and John Deere tractors in Argentina. That figure is now higher than 40 percent. So even if you hold nothing but U.S. stocks, your portfolio returns will be closely linked to foreign economies. And the reverse is very much (even more) true, as well: Most foreign stocks and all foreign stock markets are at least somewhat linked to the humongous U.S. economy.

But that doesn't eliminate the need for global diversification in your stock portfolio.

While stocks in different countries have become largely correlated in the same direction, there is still *plenty* of diversification, at least in the degree of change.

Even the stock markets of Canada and Mexico — two countries whose economies and stock markets are very, very closely tied to the U.S. economy — still offer good diversification power. In the first seven months of 2008, for example, the Dow was down 16 percent, while the Canadian market had dropped only 1.6 percent and the Mexican market barely 5 percent.

Also, keep in mind that while large company stock indexes tend to move more in synch, small company stock indexes still very much go up and down somewhat independently. Small companies generally cater to local markets much more than they export. That's why I suggest that a full half of your foreign stock investments be linked to foreign small company indexes. (I discuss this topic more in a few pages.)

Just a few years ago, foreign small company indexes were hard to invest in. That has changed. Several foreign small company ETFs now allow you to index this important part of your portfolio.

Going regional, not national

I do feel a need to issue one strong suggestion where it comes to international investing: Go regional, please. Think Europe, Asia, and emerging markets as your asset classes — not Belgium, Singapore, and Brazil.

Many ETFs, in particular, track foreign single-country indexes. With the exception perhaps of the Japanese and British stock markets — the second and third largest in the world — I would avoid buying such ETFs. The Japanese and British markets are large enough to qualify as regional investments. Other countries' stock markets are generally smaller than you'd think, offering lots in the way of volatility and little in the way of diversification. The entire *market capitalization* (all public stocks of all companies based in a country) of certain nations is only a fraction of the total market capitalization of certain single corporations! (See Figure 12-2 for examples of this point.)

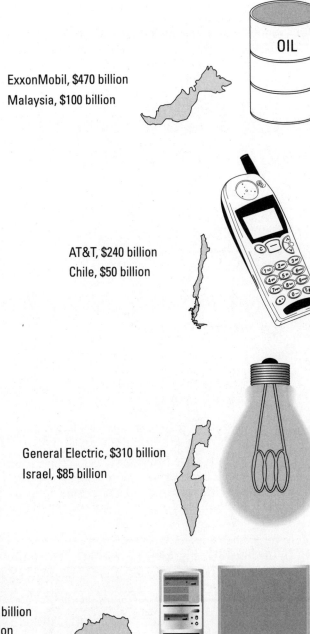

ExxonMobil, $470 billion

Malaysia, $100 billion

AT&T, $240 billion

Chile, $50 billion

General Electric, $310 billion

Israel, $85 billion

Figure 12-2:
Sizing up
single-
country
bets.

Microsoft, $270 billion

Austria, $90 billion

You can slice and dice a portfolio only so many ways. It is impractical to own ETFs representing 50 individual countries, and it is overly hopeful to think that you are smart enough to pick the one or two countries that will do better than all the rest. Choose ETFs or index mutual funds that represent good-sized areas of the planet, not pin-points.

Choosing Large and Small, Value and Growth Stocks

In the often Alice-in-Wonderland world of investing, where little makes sense, people seemingly can't get enough in the way of big company stocks and, in particular, growth stocks. But if you're going to pick any kind of company to invest in, small value companies, rather than large growth companies, make the most sense.

Sizing up the difference between large and small

Ready to witness a big, fat paradox? According to Morningstar figures, the amount of money invested in U.S. large cap stock funds is now $2.7 trillion. That compares to only $315 billion invested in small cap stock funds. The ratio is 8.6 to 1.

Yikes!

Consider now, again from Morningstar, the standard deviation (a classic measure of volatility), total return, and Sharpe Ratio (which measures return per unit of risk) for large cap stocks versus small cap stocks over the past 15 years. Table 12-1 shows all the details.

Table 12-1	Large Cap versus Small Cap: Risk and Return		
	Standard Deviation	*Total Annualized Return*	*Sharpe Ratio*
U.S. large cap funds	14.77	8.55	0.37
U.S. small cap funds	18.68	9.29	0.40

If we go back even farther in time, the difference in long-term return on small company versus large company stocks becomes even starker. The average annual return for all U.S. large company stocks from 1925 to the present is estimated to be 10.4 percent. For all U.S. small company stocks, the average annual growth rate has been 12.5 percent. That's a difference in return of 20 percent a year between the two.

General moral of story: Small cap stocks are a bit more volatile than large cap stocks, but they provide greater long-term return. On balance, per unit of risk, small cap stocks are the winners.

Specific moral of story: As much (or almost as much) as you invest in large cap, you should also invest in small cap stocks, both on the U.S. side of the portfolio and the international. This is not only because of the numbers in Table 12-1; it's also because there's less correlation between U.S. and international small cap stocks than between U.S. and international large caps.

Will a portfolio of 50 percent (or almost 50 percent) small cap stocks be more volatile than an S&P 500 portfolio? A bit, yes. If you feel uncomfortable with that risk, tone it down by adding to your bond and cash positions.

Tallying up the difference between value and growth

A much stronger paradox — an almost *unbelievable* paradox — exists where it comes to comparing growth company stocks to value stocks. People just love growth stocks. But value stocks truly kick butt.

As I discuss in Chapter 7, value stocks are bargain-basement stocks, usually in "turtle" industries like utilities, natural resources, and banking. Growth stocks are often popular and may be expensive, but they belong to hot, fast-growing companies usually in "hare" industries, like microtechnology, genetic medicine, and solar energy panels.

According to Morningstar figures, the amount of money invested in U.S. growth stock funds is now $1.26 trillion. That compares to only $880 billion invested in value stock funds. Double yikes!

According to figures from Ibbotson Associates, a Morningstar company, consider the difference between the historical return of value stocks and growth stocks. As Table 12-2 shows, the difference in return per unit of risk is rather dramatic. These figures are for the period 1969 through 2007.

Table 12-2	Growth versus Value: Risk and Return	
	Standard Deviation	*Total Annualized Return*
All U.S. growth funds	19.5	9.2
All U.S. value funds	16.3	11.4

How can it be that value stocks have such a superior long-term track record — higher returns with lesser volatility? No one knows for sure, but it's probably due to people's perpetual confusion that good companies make for good stocks.

Growth companies, undoubtedly the best companies to work for, do not always make for the best investments. Everyone expects them to grow, and the lofty price of their stocks (often a great multiple of actual earnings) reflects that. If the company grows as everyone expects, the stock may do well. If the company doesn't do as well as everyone expects — even if it does well! — ker-pow!, the stock gets hammered.

Value companies, on the other hand, aren't expected to take off, and therefore their stocks sell cheap. If the company does better than expected — even if it doesn't make money! — the stock may take off. Value companies also pay much higher dividends than do growth companies, which typically funnel most of their profits back into R&D, advertising, and fuel for the CEO's yacht.

Moral of story: In the large cap arena, given the long-term track record of value versus growth, I would lean toward value. You don't want to put everything in value, should we have another decade like the 1990s, when growth ruled. But I would suggest that if you have, say, 20 percent of your stock portfolio devoted to large cap U.S. stocks, and you divide that into value and growth, you might have 11 percent in a large cap value index fund and 9 percent in a large cap growth fund.

On the small cap side, the value "premium" is much stronger . . . or at least, it has been. There are no guarantees that the value premium will continue. But I do doubt that it will disappear entirely, and it is hard for me to imagine a growth premium lasting for too long. If you have, say, 20 percent of your portfolio allocated to U.S. small cap stocks, and you are splitting that up between a small cap value and a small cap growth fund, I might devote 12 percent to the value fund and 8 percent to the growth fund.

Yes, the value premium is just as strong in other countries as it is in the United States. Your international holdings also deserve a good solid value lean.

Putting the Stock Side of Your Portfolio Together

When you factor in the divisions between U.S./foreign, large/small, and value/growth, you get a portfolio that looks something like the one I present in Table 12-3. This is a very general guideline to what an optimal portfolio (at least the stock side of the portfolio) may look like for an average investor.

Table 12-3	Rounding Out the Stock Side of Your Portfolio		
Asset Class	Good Allocation	Acceptable Range	Note
Large U.S. stocks	20	15–30	Light lean toward value
Small U.S. stocks	20	15–25	Heavy lean toward value
Large foreign stocks (developed world)	12	5–15	Light lean toward value
Small foreign stocks (developed world)	12	5–15	Heavy lean toward value
Emerging markets	10	5–15	
U.S. REITs	10	5–15	
Foreign REITs	6	0–10	
Alternative investments*	10	0–20	

* Alternative investments may include hedge fund–like stock holdings that do not march in tune with the larger market. These may include long–short funds, merger funds, and so on.

Factoring in your personal connection to the markets

I need to talk to you very personally for a moment. You are, after all, an individual. Unique . . . even if you're a twin. Your optimal portfolio is not your brother's or your best friend's. I want you to think about several things before choosing your optimal asset allocation. That optimal asset allocation may look a lot like the one I present in Table 12-3 — or it may not.

Recognizing industry sector funds

Some people choose to divide their stock portfolios up entirely by industry sector: energy, consumer staples, consumer discretionary, utilities, natural resources, and so on. There are many ETFs, as well as index mutual funds, that allow for this kind of portfolio diversification.

There's nothing wrong with this approach, but I find it more cumbersome than dividing up a portfolio by style (large/small/value/growth).

It also tends to be more expensive. The style funds, for whatever reason, tend to be cheaper than the sector funds.

The main beef I have against the industry-sector approach is that it doesn't allow you to take advantage of the value or small cap premiums I discuss in this chapter. And those are premiums well worth taking advantage of!

Do you, for starters, own real estate other than your primary home? If so, and if the value of your combined properties equals a good percentage (more than 40 percent or so) of your net worth, you may want to lighten up on your U.S. REIT exposure, applying more of your portfolio money to either non-U.S. REITs or the rest of your stock portfolio. Housing prices, including the price of your home and the performance of REITs, go somewhat hand-in-hand.

Adding up your options

Next personal question: Do you own company stock? If your 401(k) is filled with company stock, or if you are given stock options as a bonus of the job, you may want to factor that into your portfolio mix.

If, for example, you work for a large, foreign value company, and the value of your stock options with that company is equal to half your net worth, you certainly would want to lighten up on the large foreign allocation that I suggest for the average portfolio, or at the very least lean that allocation heavily toward growth stocks.

See how it works?

Fixing Your Fixed-Income Side of the Portfolio

Just as on the stock side of your portfolio, it makes perfect sense to diversify the fixed-income side of your portfolio by choosing various index funds that mirror different indexes. It may not be as crucial, because bond indexes aren't as volatile as stock indexes, but diversification is still important.

Stocks tend to be broken up by geography, cap size, and style, and sometimes by industry sector. Bonds, on the other hand, tend to be broken up most often by maturity and credit quality, both of which I discuss in Chapter 8.

Reframing the reason for bonds

The purpose of bonds is to provide ballast to a portfolio. The high returns (*we hope* the high returns!) in your portfolio will come from stocks. So the first question I ask myself in constructing the bond side of a portfolio is, naturally enough, how to get the most ballast.

You obviously want your bonds to zig if the stock market should zag. For that reason, I'm not a big fan of high-yield (junk) bonds, which tend to sink in value, just like stocks do, in hard economic times. Rather, I prefer top-quality bonds issued by institutions that are unlikely to go belly-up. I'm also wary of holding too much in very long-term bonds, which offer less price stability than shorter-term bonds. Long-term bonds, although they tend to be less volatile than stocks, can be volatile all the same.

Do you need international bonds?

Having a global bond portfolio adds diversification but also, because you are most likely adding in foreign currency, adds possible volatility. I don't mind volatility on the equity side of a portfolio, but I don't like it in fixed income. For that reason, if you buy my advice and already have roughly half your stock allocation abroad, I'd say you can pass on international bonds.

If you really want them, there are currently a handful of indexing options, including the SPDR Lehman International Treasury Bond ETF (BWX) and the SPDR DB International Government Inflation-Protected Bond ETF (WIP). Both offer high-quality international bond exposure; both charge 0.50 a year in operating expenses.

You can also find two international high-yield options: the PowerShares Emerging Markets Sovereign Debt Portfolio ETF (PCY) and the iShares JPMorgan USD Emerging Markets Bond Fund (EMB). Although I'm not a big fan of junk bonds or international bonds, when you combine them, they actually make for an okay investment. I would suggest considering one of these funds if your portfolio is more than $100,000 or so. I have a slight preference for the PCY, which has a lower expense ratio than EMB: 0.50 percent versus 0.60 percent.

International junk bonds promise high returns without the correlation to the U.S. stock market that you'll find with U.S. junk. I would not, however, include this as part of the fixed-income side of your portfolio. Even though it is technically fixed income, you'll be seeing possible stock-like returns and stock-like volatility; include this fund as part (a small part — less than 10 percent) of the equity side of your portfolio.

Zeroing in on safety first, returns second

U.S. Treasuries, backed by the full credit of the federal government, represent the gold standard of high-quality bonds — just what you want if the stock market starts to tank. Investment-grade corporate bonds, issued by solid companies, also tend to hold their own in bad economic times, and they provide a little added juice, generally a percentage point higher than Treasuries.

Treasury Inflation-Protected Securities (TIPS) are issued by the federal government. They pay you a very modest rate of interest, but the principal is adjusted upwards twice a year to meet inflation. TIPS tend to move in somewhat different cycles from traditional bonds.

For most folks, I recommend a bond allocation that looks something like what I present in Table 12-4. There are plenty of index funds to represent each of the bond asset classes.

Table 12-4	Building the Bond Side of Your Portfolio		
Asset Class	*Good Allocation*	*Acceptable Range*	*Note*
Short-term high-quality bonds*	20	10–30	Treasuries or high-grade corporate
Intermediate-term Treasuries*	25	15–50	
Intermediate-term corporate*	25	15–50	
TIPS	30	20–50	

* May be replaced by tax-free municipal bonds if you are in a high tax bracket. (Yes, there are indexed muni-bond ETFs.)

Chapter 13

Mixing and Matching Passive and Active Investing

· ·

In This Chapter

▶ Examining index-like active mutual funds

▶ Ferreting out the best fund companies

▶ Seeking out irrational despondency

▶ Tilting your portfolio to (maybe, just maybe) beat the market

· ·

*T*his is the chapter, dear reader, where I, your friendly well-meaning author, risk getting tarred and feathered, and possibly hanged, drawn, and quartered, by the most diehard proponents of index investing. If you *are* such a diehard proponent, please give me a chance to explain why I think all active investing isn't all bad all the time! I have my reasons. *Good reasons.* I promise!

Before you read this chapter, please know that nothing I say within contradicts what I say in this book's other chapters. Index investing is far and away a superior kind of investing, and if you do nothing but index invest (provided you do it with intelligence), you're going to beat the pants off the vast majority of investors. There is no *need* to delve into active investing. This chapter is optional. You can do just fine without it. Honest.

If, however, you're willing to do a bit of extra legwork and take on perhaps a smidgeon of added risk, I believe that mixing and matching index investing with active investing may make for a truly optimal portfolio. It's the portfolio I built for myself years ago (yes, that portfolio has done very well, thank you) and the portfolio I recommend to my clients (they've done very well, too). The portfolio is mostly an index portfolio . . . with a few carefully chosen exceptions, which are all made for solid reasons.

On the pages that follow, I describe those exceptions. They come in two large, general categories, which I call *Buy-and-Hold Index Investing Exception Type A* and *Buy-and-Hold Index Investing Exception Type B*. Here is how I define them:

> ✔ *Buy-and-Hold Index Investing Exception Type A:* Incorporating some funds — mutual funds or ETFs — into your portfolio that use active management, but *only* certain funds from certain well-trusted companies that pay deep respect to the important lessons of indexing, such as low costs, tax efficiency, and strategic clarity. Even then, I look for one more thing in an actively managed fund: a tendency to zig when my stock index funds zag.
>
> ✔ *Buy-and-Hold Index Investing Exception Type B:* Tweaking — preferably mildly! — your index fund holdings to overweight sectors of the market that are perhaps undervalued and poised for a return from oblivion. In essence, this is the exact opposite of what most investors do, which is to chase hot sectors. You (oh-so-cautiously) chase *cold* sectors! If you want a fancy word for this strategy, some investor types call it *tactical asset allocation.*

I'll now explore each of these exceptions in turn. Hold the tar and feathers at least until the end of the chapter!

Using Active Strategies That Borrow from the Wisdom of Indexing

As you know if you've read the first few chapters of this book, the reasons that index investing works, and works so well, are numerous. But tops on anyone's list is the low cost of indexing. You can easily build an entire indexed portfolio that'll run you about 0.30 percent or less in operating fees a year — a full percentage point less than what most actively managed portfolios would cost you. That difference, over the course of time, gives indexers an almost unbeatable advantage.

Following right behind the difference in operating fees, we find differences in miscellaneous expenses (namely, the costs involved with the frequent trading of stocks that often occurs in actively managed portfolios) and big differences in tax efficiency. Actively managed portfolios, by virtue of their constant turnover, often send you very depressing tax bills.

But what if you could find an actively managed fund, or two, or three, that offer you low costs and tax efficiency? Or what if you were to build your portfolio in a tax-advantaged account, such as an IRA, where the tax efficiency of individual funds isn't really an issue? Might an actively managed approach make possible sense in such circumstances?

Yes, it might. *Might.* You will still likely lose if you start picking actively managed funds willy-nilly. But if you follow a few rules, you may just do okay for yourself.

Seven rules for investing in actively managed funds

If you want to add an actively managed component to a primarily indexed portfolio, I would ask you to start your shopping by going through the rules below, step by step.

Rule 1: Look for index-like qualities in any fund you pick

The link between long-term fund performance and operating expenses (sometimes called the *net expense ratio* or *management fees*) is as tight as the link between green grass and rain. Low-cost funds are best. Don't even consider any funds with *loads* (up-front commissions); choose only no-load funds. From the universe of no-load funds, look most strongly at funds that charge less than other funds in their category. For domestic stock and bond funds, for example, you shouldn't need to go over 1 percentage point a year in expenses. For international funds, perhaps 1.5 percent should be the maximum you're willing to spend.

Rule 2: Avoid closet index funds

If you're going to choose an actively managed fund to slip into your predominantly indexed portfolio, make sure that you are actually getting an actively managed fund. Some "active" fund managers, knowing full well the power of indexing, sneakily hug the indexes but charge you much higher fees than you would have to pay for an index fund. These are called *closet index funds.*

How do you identify one? If you have access to certain fund analysis programs (such as Morningstar Premium), you can check the fund's *coefficient of determination,* otherwise referred to as *R-squared* or *R2.* Any fund with an R-squared of more than 85 or so may qualify as an index fund. An R-squared of, say, 85 in a large cap U.S. blend fund would mean that 85 percent of the fund's holdings are the same as the holdings of the S&P 500 index. If that's the case, why not just hold the index?!

The other, perhaps easier, thing you can do is go to `http://finance.yahoo.com`, look up the fund in question, find the chart for one-, three-, and five-year performance, and compare the ups and downs to those of the index. If they move in unison, you may as well just hold the index.

Rule 3: Show a bias for small cap

This isn't a biggie, but if you are going to go active anywhere on the style chart (large growth/large value/small growth/small value), you probably up your chances of beating the market in the small cap arena. I suppose it is logical that an active manager who focuses on small cap stocks has a better chance of discovering a hidden gem than some manager focusing on large cap companies, which tend to be much more in the public (and analyst) eye. What seems true and what is true are often not always the same, but in this case, some research shows that small cap actively run funds do have a better chance than large cap funds of beating their respective indexes. Keep in mind, however, that in *both* categories — large cap and small cap — the odds are in the favor of index funds.

Rule 4: Search for yin and yang

This is the corollary to the point I make above about avoiding a closet index fund. You want something different than the indexes you already own . . . something that will add to the diversification of your entire portfolio . . . something that may do well when everything else in tanking. One of the very first things I look at in choosing an actively managed fund is that fund's performance record during the bear market of 2000–2002. And look again at how the fund did in the more dismal days of 2008. Any fund that held its own during these terrible times for the stock market just may hold its own the next time the market starts to bleed.

Rule 5: Pick a fund company that you can trust

Too many actively managed funds have been involved in scandals of one sort or another, with investors losing money in the process. (As I'm writing this chapter, the business pages are full of news about Bear Stearns executives allegedly stealing money from investors in certain of its hedge funds.) That sort of thing never happens with index funds, and likely never will.

Do a Google search of any fund companies you are considering, and check out the ten clean fund companies I list in the next section. I list one possible fund to consider from each company, but in most cases, you can find other funds worth investigating. This is especially true for Vanguard, T. Rowe Price, and Dodge & Cox — these are all scandal-free companies with a diverse selection of actively managed funds that tend to be among the best in the industry. Vanguard and T. Rowe Price also serve as discount, diverse brokerage houses (sometimes known as *financial supermarkets*) where you can invest in index mutual funds, ETFs, or just about whatever you like. Fidelity Investments, although involved in at least one minor scandal involving certain traders and certain strippers, is also an overall reputable mutual fund company and brokerage house.

Rule 6: Check the long-term performance history

I put performance history almost last on my list, even though it is first — and often the only thing! — on most people's lists. Don't buy a fund because it scored big in the past 12 months and is now featured on the cover of *Wise Money* magazine! That's just plain dumb. The fund manager may have been lucky. More often than that, the fund is simply investing in a certain kind of investment (such as commodities or Latin American stocks) that happens to have done exceptionally well last year. Performance figures don't mean squat unless you are looking at long-term performance figures! Check the figures for 10 years, 15 years, or longer if possible. Performance figures are especially important when you are looking into funds that use highly unconventional investment strategies, such as merger arbitration or long–short tactics.

Rule 7: Don't go overboard! Remember that index investing is likely to be superior in the long run!

Keep the majority of your money in index funds. Consider the active funds section of your portfolio the ancillary part of your nest egg. Limit it to no more than 25 percent of your portfolio. Some call this strategy a *core–satellite* approach to portfolio construction: Use index funds as the core of your portfolio and actively managed funds as your satellites. Alternatively, limit the overall average expense ratio on your entire portfolio to no more than 0.50 percent, and you'll force yourself to keep an index or largely index-like approach.

Ten actively managed funds that fit the bill

To get you started in the possible (strictly optional!) mixing and matching of active with passive investing, I'm going to share some of the actively managed funds that I've used either in my own portfolio, the portfolios of clients, or both. I give you some basic information, such as the operating expenses, the long-term performance record, and the fund's bear-market performance track record. And I share with you my rationale for considering that a particular fund be added to a primarily indexed portfolio. Please research these funds carefully before buying, however. You always incur somewhat more risk when buying an actively managed fund than when buying an index fund. (The manager could go on an African safari tomorrow and be trampled by an angry hippopotamus, for example.)

You may note that all of the funds below are mutual funds, and none are ETFs. Actively managed ETFs are new, and they lack the track record that gives me any great confidence. Some of the *fundamental indexed* ETFs that I discuss in Chapter 14 may qualify as actively or quasi-actively managed in some people's books, I realize. But I'll leave those to Chapter 14 and restrict the conversation here to the self-acknowledged and universally agreed-upon active management mutual funds.

I present these funds in alphabetical order, so you can't assume the top one is my favorite. These funds are all over the map in terms of what they invest in. In choosing a particular fund, you want its asset class to fit into your entire portfolio, as I discuss in all the other chapters of Part III. (*Asset class* means a category of investment that tends to move somewhat independently of others. Some examples are large cap value stocks, long-term municipal bonds, and gold.) Your choice of asset classes will tend to have a greater bearing on your portfolio performance than the choice of individual funds.

CGM Focus (CGMFX)

This fund doesn't have the longest of track records, but what it does have has been beyond spectacular. Could it be luck? Yes, it certainly could be. If you're itching to test a bit of your portfolio with active management, a small percentage of your portfolio in the CGM Focus fund may just pay off — but be sure you're willing to take the added risk. *Caveat:* The turnover on this fund is HUGE (around 400 percent a year). Do not put this terribly tax-inefficient fund into a taxable account! This fund belongs only in your IRA. And limit your exposure to a small percentage of your portfolio — no more than 5 percent, and preferably 4. This fund can be very volatile! Note, too, that the CGM Focus fund, unlike the vast majority of mutual funds, is not available at most financial supermarkets. You must go directly to the Boston-based fund company. Filling out the application form isn't too onerous, but keeping this fund will require a bit of extra paperwork year in and year out.

What the fund invests in: About 25 company stocks, roughly half of them U.S.-based and the other half from Canada and farther away. The companies are fairly large, with a bias toward growth.

The fund's birth date: September, 1997

Minimum purchase, IRA: $1,000

Your yearly fees to the mutual fund company: 0.99 percent

10-year average annual return (5/31/08): 25.72 percent

10-year average annual return of relevant index (S&P 500): 4.1 percent (Note that since half of the fund's stocks are non-U.S., this benchmark is not terribly relevant, but I don't know of any that are.)

Performance during the three-year bear market (2000, 2001, 2002): 53.9 percent, 47.6 percent, –17.8 percent

Other quality actively managed funds from the same purveyor: CGM Realty (CGMRX)

For more information: www.cgmfunds.com

Dodge & Cox Stock (DODGX)

This Boston-based company has been around for a very long time, and they quite obviously get it. With an index-like approach to active investing, Dodge & Cox's five mutual funds rather consistently match the markets or sometimes do a little better. The fund management is done by teams, and they clearly take a long-term, sensible approach to what they do, eking out enough alpha to earn their management fee and have a bit left over for investors. (*Alpha* is a bit of industry jargon; it means return due to active management.) If you are inclined to step a little bit into active management, the flagship Dodge & Cox Stock fund is without question one of the best choices you could make. The other Dodge & Cox funds aren't bad, either.

What the fund invests in: Stocks of largish U.S. companies with a lean toward value.

The fund's birth date: January, 1965

Minimum purchase, non-retirement account: $2,500

Your yearly fees to the mutual fund company: 0.52 percent

15-year average annual return (5/31/08): 13.26 percent

15-year average annual return of a relevant index (S&P 500): 9.88 percent

Performance during the three-year bear market (2000, 2001, 2002): 16.3 percent, 9.33 percent, –10.54 percent

Other quality actively managed funds from the same purveyor: Dodge & Cox International Stock (DODFX); Dodge & Cox Income (DODIX)

For more information: www.dodgeandcox.com

Fairholme Fund (FAIRX)

Fairholme is a one-fund shop, and even though this fund charges a teeny bit more — 0.01 percent more! — than I would normally advocate for any domestic stock fund, I find it enticing enough to bend my rule. Whatever it takes to pick stocks, the people behind Fairholme seem to have the stuff. Still, the fund doesn't have a very long track record. It is also subject to style drift, making crisp portfolio allocation difficult. So even though I am impressed and intrigued with Fairholme's performance — especially during the bear market years — I wouldn't recommend that you put more than a few percentage points of your portfolio into Fairholme . . . certainly no more than 5 percent. You are taking something of a gamble.

What the fund invests in: Stocks in mostly large companies, generally with a value lean, largely U.S.-based but with some international exposure

The fund's birth date: December, 1999

Minimum purchase, non-retirement account: $2,500

Your yearly fees to the mutual fund company: 1.01 percent

5-year average annual return (5/31/08): 18.21 percent

5-year average annual return of a relevant index (S&P 500): 9.77 percent

Performance during the three-year bear market (2000, 2001, 2002): 46.5 percent, 6.2 percent, −1.58 percent

Other quality actively managed funds from the same purveyor: N/A

For more information: www.fairholmefunds.com

Fidelity Low-Priced Stock (FLPSX)

Fidelity is a humongous company, and sometimes the right arm doesn't know what the left arm is doing. (As a financial journalist, several times asking for permission to reprint Fidelity charts, I've run into more bureaucratic red tape than existed in the former Soviet Union. In fact, I'm certain that Fidelity has hired former Soviet KGB agents to run its legal department.) Nonetheless, the company does seem to get it right where it comes to running some of its many, many actively managed funds. Take Fidelity Low-Priced Stock, for example. It's been around for a good while and has a rather impressive track record.

What the fund invests in: Stocks of small and middle-sized companies, mainly in the United States but also abroad, all with a strong lean toward value

The fund's birth date: December, 1989

Minimum purchase, non-retirement account: $2,500

Your yearly fees to the mutual fund company: 0.97 percent

15-year average annual return (5/31/08): 15.0 percent

15-year average annual return of a relevant index (S&P Midcap 400): 13.23 percent

Performance during the three-year bear market (2000, 2001, 2002): 18.8 percent, 26.7 percent, −6.2 percent

Other quality actively managed funds from the same purveyor: Fidelity Leveraged Company Stock (FLVCX)

For more information: www.fidelity.com

Hussman Strategic Growth Fund (HSGFX)

This is what's known as a *long–short fund.* Technically, it's a stock fund. But the manager, John Hussman, picks both stocks he sees poised for growth, which he buys *long* (outright) and, at the same time, picks stocks poised for death, which he buys *short.* In the end, you get a fund that should, in theory, perform with very little if any correlation to the stock market. On the other hand, you probably aren't going to see the long-term performance that you would see by investing in stock index funds. Use Hussman, if you wish, for a hedge against your stock holdings. Although it's technically a stock fund, I would treat it more like a bond fund: Have bond fund–like expectations for this holding (about 5 percent growth a year), and you probably won't be too disappointed. If you see it as a stock fund, you likely will be disappointed. Use this fund only in a retirement account — the tax ramifications could be nasty.

What the fund invests in: Stocks of large companies, mostly U.S.-based and mostly growth. But, unlike most stock funds, Hussman buys some stocks long and others (banking on a downfall) short.

The fund's birth date: July, 2000

Minimum purchase, IRA: $500.

Your yearly fees to the mutual fund company: 1.17 percent

Five-year average annual return (5/31/08): 6.29 percent

Five-year average annual return of relevant index: There really is no relevant index, but I would tend to compare it to the Lehman Aggregate Bond Index, which in the past five years has returned an annual 3.83 percent. (The Hussman fund would tend to be a bit more volatile.)

Performance during the three-year bear market (2000, 2001, 2002): N/A, 14.7 percent, 14.0 percent

Other quality actively managed funds from the same purveyor: Hussman Strategic Total Return Fund (HSTRX)

For more information: www.hussmanfunds.com

Longleaf Partners Fund (LLPFX)

If all actively managed funds were this good, I may not have written this book! Longleaf uses an index-like approach (modest costs, little turnover) to choose stocks the managers see poised for growth. They've been at it for over two decades, and they are doing better than the vast majority of actively managed funds. Like Dodge & Cox, Longleaf offers an alternative approach to wise core investing. This fund, and the Dodge & Cox fund, are just about the only actively managed funds to which I would even consider allocating more than 5 percent of your portfolio. The flagship Longleaf Partners Fund could, if you want it to, give you much of your U.S. large cap exposure. Unfortunately, because it isn't a pure U.S. large cap stock fund, it will make your total portfolio construction difficult.

What the fund invests in: About 80 percent large U.S. company stocks, 20 percent large non-U.S. company stocks

The fund's birth date: April, 1987

Minimum purchase, non-retirement account: $10,000

Your yearly fees to the mutual fund company: 0.89 percent

15-year average annual return (5/31/08): 12.95 percent

15-year average annual return of relevant index (S&P 500): 9.88 percent

Performance during the three-year bear market (2000, 2001, 2002): 20.6 percent, 10.4 percent, –8.3 percent

Other quality actively managed funds from the same purveyor: Longleaf Partners International (LLINX)

For more information: www.longleafpartners.com

Loomis Sayles Bond Fund (LSBRX/LSBDX)

Honestly, I don't know how they do it. I also wrote *Bond Investing For Dummies,* so I do know something about bonds. And the rules of bond investing tell us that the bond markets are very efficient, so it's extremely hard to beat the market. Yet Dan Fuss and his team at Loomis seem to do it with great consistency. The long-term returns of the Loomis Sayles Bond Fund are eye-popping, far superior to the relevant indexes. As I said, I'm not entirely sure how they do it, but they do, and they've done it for a very long time. I must question, of course, whether the next 15 years will be as kind to Loomis investors as the past 15 years, but I think it may be worth a small gamble. You may consider as much as one-third of your long-term bond holdings in the Loomis Sayles Bond Fund, *especially* if you have a fat portfolio and can afford to allocate $100,000. That qualifies you for the Loomis Sayles Bond Institutional class (LSBDX), which comes with a much smaller expense ratio than does the retail class of the fund (LSBRX).

What the fund invests in: Bonds, bonds, bonds of all sorts, but mostly investment grade, mostly U.S., and mostly long term .

The fund's birth date: May, 1991

Minimum purchase, non-retirement account: $2,500 for LSBRX; $100,000 for LSBDX

Your yearly fees to the mutual fund company: 0.95 percent for LSBRX; 0.67 percent for LSBDX

15-year average annual return (5/31/08): 9.76 for LSBRX; 10.04 percent for LSBDX

15-year average annual return of relevant index (Lehman Brothers Aggregate Bond): 6.2 percent

Performance during the three-year bear market (2000, 2001, 2002): 4.1, 2.3, 13.2 (Note: These were not bear market years for investment-grade bonds, so most of the funds in the same category as Loomis did okay or better.)

Other quality actively managed funds from the same purveyor: Unfortunately, most other Loomis Sayles funds are load funds, although the loads may be waived if you are working with a financial advisor.

For more information: www.loomissayles.com

Merger Fund (MERFX)

The five managers of this fund look for news of corporate mergers and take-overs. Taking advantage of their many years of experience with such deals, they've figured out the likely trajectories of the stock prices in both the fish about to be eaten and the soon-to-be-fattened fish. It sounds a bit crazy, but these guys have been doing it for nearly two decades, with fairly consistent results. In the past ten years, they lost money in only one year (2002, when the fund dropped 5.7 percent). Overall, like the Hussman Fund, this fund can be seen as a potential hedge against the stock market, because it tends to have little correlation to the stock market. On the other hand, you shouldn't expect long-term performance on a par with the stock market. Keep your expectations for this fund modest, and you'll do okay! I wouldn't allocate more than 5 percent of my portfolio to the Merger Fund, and I would do so only within a tax-advantaged retirement account. The turnover is very heavy, which could result in your getting slammed at tax time.

What the fund invests in: Stocks of companies involved in publicly announced mergers, takeovers, tender offers, leveraged buyouts, spinoffs, liquidations, and other corporate reorganizations.

The fund's birth date: January, 1989

Minimum purchase: $2,000

Your yearly fees to the mutual fund company: 1.47 percent

15-year average annual return (5/31/08): 7.8 percent

15-year average annual return of relevant index: There is no relevant index.

Performance during the three-year bear market (2000, 2001, 2002): 17.6 percent, 2.0 percent, –5.7 percent.

Other quality actively managed funds from the same purveyor: N/A

For more information: This may be the last fund in America that has no Web site of its own! The Merger Fund can be purchased at any financial supermarket, and the supermarket should be able to provide you with a prospectus and other information.

T. Rowe Price Capital Appreciation Fund (PRWCX)

The Baltimore-based fund company and financial supermarket takes a reasonable approach to active investing, with low costs and a long-term strategic approach to investing. The Capital Appreciation Fund has been around for many years and has proven itself a winner on a number of counts: performance, limited volatility, and lack of correlation to the stock market. Whether the future will be as sweet as the past is unknowable, but if you are tempted to invest in an actively run, balanced fund, you could do a lot worse than the Capital Appreciation Fund. The turnover on this fund in 2007 was 53 percent, so I would strongly recommend that you use this fund only in a tax-advantaged account, such as your IRA.

What the fund invests in: About two-thirds of the fund is invested in the stocks of large, U.S. companies, mostly value companies. About one-third of the fund is invested in a combination of bonds and cash.

The fund's birth date: June, 1986

Minimum purchase, IRA: $1,000

Your yearly fees to the mutual fund company: 0.71 percent

15-year average annual return (5/31/08): 11.88 percent

15-year average annual return of relevant index (S&P 500): 9.88

Performance during the three-year bear market (2000, 2001, 2002): 22.2 percent, 10.3 percent, 0.5 percent

Other quality actively managed funds from the same purveyor: T. Rowe Price Equity Income (PRFDX); T. Rowe Price Growth Stock (PRGFX)

For more information: www.troweprice.com

Vanguard PRIMECAP Core Fund (VPCCX)

You would expect Vanguard, the world's largest purveyor of index mutual funds, to produce actively managed funds that somewhat resemble index funds. You'd be right. Vanguard's managed funds are low priced (compared to most other actively managed funds) with reasonable turnover and generally good tax efficiency. And, yes, they tend to perform very well — in the case of the Vanguard PRIMECAP fund, very well indeed. Note, however, that the fund doesn't have a very long track record. I would therefore probably not recommend this fund, except that it is a Vanguard product, which gives me the confidence to invest.

What the fund invests in: Stocks in U.S. large growth companies

The fund's birth date: December 2004

Minimum purchase, non-retirement account: $10,000

Your yearly fees to the mutual fund company: 0.55 percent

Three-year return (5/31/08): 10.31 percent

Three-year return of relevant index (S&P 500): 2.74 percent

Performance during the three-year bear market (2000, 2001, 2002): N/A

Other quality actively managed funds from the same purveyor: Vanguard STAR Fund (VGSTX); Vanguard Windsor Fund (VWNDX)

For more information: www.vanguard.com

For further research into mutual funds, I recommend Morningstar (www.morningstar.com). When you see four- and five-star funds, consider the ratings a good sign but not an outright license to buy. And think long and hard before choosing any fund without four or five stars. Another very helpful site is www.finra.org/fundanalyzer. FINRA is the Financial Industry Regulatory Authority, and the handy dandy Web site allows you see the cumulative fees involved in investing in any particular mutual fund. Fees are crucial to your long-term performance!

Spotting Irrational Despondency, and Tilting Your Portfolio Accordingly

In December 1996, with the stock market, and especially tech stocks, on a multi-year rage, then–Federal Reserve Board Chairman Alan Greenspan first used the phrase *irrational exuberance*. It seemed to Greenspan that the stock market, and particularly the tech sector, might be getting overheated. Investors, of course, paid little heed and continued to pour their money into dot-coms. Some of those same investors are still waiting to recoup their losses from what followed in 2000–2002.

Of course, it's easy to say in retrospect that the tech bubble seemed certain to pop.

It wasn't the first time, and it won't be the last, that investors sink the lion's share of their portfolios into whatever is hot hot hot. John Bogle, the founder of Vanguard and a great proponent of indexing and buy-and-hold investing, writes the following in *The Little Book of Common Sense Investing* (Wiley): "[D]uring the past 25 while the stock market index fund was providing an annual return of 12.3 percent and the average equity fund was earning an annual return of 10.0 percent, the average fund investor was earning only 7.3 percent a year." Why? As Bogle explains, "Fund investors have been chasing past performance since time eternal, allowing their emotions — perhaps even their greed — to overwhelm their reason."

I contend — with some caution — that if investors by and large chase past performance (buying the hottest funds in the hottest sectors) and lose heavily as a result, it may be possible to do just the opposite, using index funds to occasionally buy low and sell high, to wind up ahead of the game. Such a strategy is sometimes known as *tactical asset allocation*. I call it searching for *irrational despondency*. The strategy is hard to use and very easy to misuse, so I hesitate to bring it up. But because I do employ it myself, to a small degree, I feel the obligation to discuss it.

Here's the strategy in a nutshell: After you have your optimal portfolio allocation (see Chapters 11 and 12), consider *mild* tilts and *gentle* tweaks if you see a particular industry sector (technology, energy, consumer staples), style (growth, value, large cap, small cap), or geographical area or country (Europe, Japan) dragging for some time seriously below its historical return rate, dragging seriously below other kinds of investments, or (preferably) both. You are banking on a rule called *reversion to the mean:* If a particular asset class returned, say, an average of 10 percent a year for the past 80 years, and has seen a negative return over the past several years, a bounceback may be likely.

Discovering the secrets of tactical asset allocation

Mind you, picking market sectors likely to outperform the market isn't easy, cannot be done mechanically, and will increase your portfolio risk. That being said, I do believe that you can juice your returns without too much added risk if you can keep your enthusiasm in check.

A good number of my colleagues, even those who, like me, are strong proponents of indexing, similarly see value in tactical asset allocation. "Markets with low price/earnings ratios tend to do better than markets with high price/earnings ratios. Tilting your portfolio toward low price/earnings markets can boost performance," says Harindra de Silva, Ph.D., CFA, portfolio manager with Analytic Investors, a Los Angeles–based investment management firm. The price/earning ratio (P/E), a standard measure of an index's valuation, can readily be found on the fact sheet on any index mutual fund or ETF. The P/E ratio is something of a measure of the public's exuberance or despondency for a stock or sector.

De Silva recommends that 70 to 80 percent of your portfolio remain static, invested in broad indexes at all times, at set allocations. The remaining 20 to 30 percent may be invested specifically in indexes that seem beaten down. Your best bets, he says, will be asset classes that have been beaten down for a few years but have shown recent signs (in the past 12 months) of a turnaround and appear to be on their way back up.

He cautions that such a strategy is not market timing, and it is not going to make you rich quick. "Done right, I believe that tactical asset allocation using index funds can add 1, perhaps 1.5 percent to your annual returns over time," he says. But even the best tactical allocation strategists won't always get it right. "Expect that you're going to beat the broad indexes perhaps 55 to 60 percent of the time," he says. "Tactical asset allocation may not improve your bottom line until you've done it for a few years."

Fine-tuning your portfolio tilting skills

Michael Kitces, CFP, is director of financial planning with the Pinnacle Advisory Group in Columbia, Maryland, and publisher of *The Kitces Report* (www.kitces.com). He agrees that tactical asset allocation can beat owning the entire market, but it must be done with care and finesse. "We have plenty of evidence that asset classes that have done poorly tend to do better moving forward," he says. Part of the reason is that people get "overly gloomy" when an asset class tanks, and the valuations (P/E ratio) may become dirt cheap.

Still, says Kitces, identifying an overvalued asset class is difficult, and you are sure to sometimes get it wrong. He recommends that you lean your portfolio toward underperformers but set strict parameters for how much you'll lean so that you don't fall over backwards. "If you normally would want a portfolio that is, say, 60 percent stock and 40 percent bonds, and you decide to overweight stocks, you might want to commit to staying within 10 percentage points of your neutral allocation," he says. He recommends having similar parameters for U.S. versus foreign stocks and how much you may be willing to plunk into any one specific industry sector.

Like de Silva, Kitces also advises extreme patience. "I'm not suggesting market timing, and I'm not suggesting you're going to get instant rewards. As with basic index investing, you are focusing on the long term. The rewards of portfolio tilting will come, but it may take considerable time."

Searching the current landscape for opportunity

Let me offer an example of how tactical asset allocation can work. As I'm writing this chapter, the two industry sectors most beaten down are the financial and banking industry and the housing-construction industry. Several ETFs allow you to tap into these industry sectors, and I've got my eye especially on the iShares Dow Jones U.S. Home Construction ETF (ITB), a fund that tracks an index of companies such as Pulte Homes and Toll Brothers. At the start of 2007, shares of ITB were selling for more than $40. As I'm writing this chapter, they are going for around $14.50 — a drop of about two-thirds in value.

Granted, there are many reasons — good reasons — that the housing industry is in the doldrums. But could there be just a bit of irrational despondency in the air? I think there just may be.

I wouldn't take a huge bet on this ETF, but a small allocation may make sense. I have no idea what is going to happen to the housing industry in the next year or two. But I do know that as long as houses aren't being built, demand will slowly build. When the economy turns around — and chances are pretty good that it will (no guarantees) — housing should turn around as well.

If I were to expect the stock market at large to return, say, 8 percent in the next four to five years, I would expect housing to do a wee bit better, maybe 9 or 10 percent. But I wouldn't bank my house on that! If I want to lean my stock portfolio slightly toward this one sector, I'd invest maybe 5 percent of my stock allocation into ITB — it could tweak my returns upward.

Chapter 14

Making Your Final Investment Decisions

*O*kay, Mr. or Ms. Primarily Index Investor, the time has come to choose. Which of the two major kinds of index investments — index mutual funds or exchange-traded funds — will get the bulk of your money?

And a much trickier and stickier question: Are you going to choose funds that are tracking traditional, older indexes, such as the S&P 500 and the Wilshire 4500? Or are you going to pick funds that mirror the many newfangled *fundamental* indexes and, by so doing, shoot for potentially better performance than plain-vanilla indexing?

In this chapter, I aim to assist you in making both decisions, so you can be the strongest index investor possible. Ready or not, here we go . . .

But wait! I also explain in this chapter the timing of when to best launch your new index portfolio. Should it be today, regardless of where the markets were yesterday? Or should you wait for the stars over Wall Street to find just the right alignment? Answers are coming right up.

Making the Choice between Mutual Funds and ETFs

Don't sweat the small stuff. For the buy-and-hold investor (which I hope, hope, hope you are), the difference between an index mutual fund and an exchange-traded fund (assuming that both track the same index and carry the same expense ratio) is akin to the difference in flavor between two brands of bottled water — not all that great.

At first, keep your eyes on the big picture, please. What *kinds* of investments are you choosing? (Stocks? Bonds? U.S.? Foreign?) What are the funds' expense ratios? (Lower is better!) What sorts of indexes are being tracked? (I'll get to that momentarily.) After you've tackled these bigger issues, you can spend a bit of energy deciding on whether you want a mutual fund or an ETF.

Tallying up your costs

The easiest guide to follow is that if you are investing in drips and drabs, or if you are taking out money at regular intervals, you want mutual funds, not ETFs. The costs of buying and selling ETFs, if you are doing so wholesale, will amount to too much. This is pretty straightforward math. If you have $1,000 in an ETF, and you pay $10 per trade, making ten trades a year will add up to $100, or 10 percent of your investment. That would be an extremely costly way to invest.

What do you do for a living?

If you have strong economic ties to a certain industry (such as you work in the technology sector), and you have lots of company stock in your 401(k), you may want a portfolio that goes light on technology. If you have sizeable real estate holdings, you may want to avoid investing in REITs. If you work for a Swiss pharmaceutical company, and the company is loading you up with stock options, you may want to go easy on any investment in European stock index funds, and lean a little more than you normally would on U.S. and Asian indexes. The name of the game in successful investing is diversification. And the best diversified portfolios — index or other — take into consideration your job or other personal links to the economy.

If you have $1 million to invest, however, the $10 trade cost becomes marginal. In this situation, any reduction in yearly fees (which you may be able to achieve with ETFs) may easily become more substantial. For example, if a mutual fund will cost you 3/10 of 1 percent a year, and an ETF will cost you 2/10 of 1 percent, that's 1/10 of 1 percent you have to play with. If making the trade to buy the ETF is going to cost you 1/10 of 1 percent, you'll need only a year to make up the difference.

Adding up your total numbers

Generally speaking, for most folks, a diversified ETF portfolio will make the most sense for buy-and-hold investors with $50,000 portfolios or greater. Anything less than that, and you may want to consider index mutual funds or a mix of index mutual funds and ETFs.

If you have a substantial portfolio (several hundreds of thousands), look seriously at Vanguard Admiral shares. Available with most Vanguard index funds, they can wind up costing you even less than most ETFs (only about 8/100 of 1 percent) if held in an account at Vanguard. (Holding Vanguard mutual funds at another brokerage house will mean added costs.)

If you're just starting off as an investor, with several thousand or even just several hundred dollars, you may not have the minimum required to invest in most index mutual funds. In that case, you're better off with one or two broad-based index ETFs. (See the examples I provide in Chapter 15.)

Avoiding the itch to rapid trade

One of the prime reasons that ETFs have exploded in popularity is that they, unlike mutual funds, can be traded throughout the day. Most people see this as a great benefit. If the market falls, you can sell! If the market rises, you can buy! Of course, as you know from reading the rest of this book, I'm not in favor of such impulsive moves. More often than not, they lead to investors shooting themselves in the financial foot.

If you have any gambling tendencies whatsoever, perhaps you are better off avoiding ETFs and using index mutual funds, just so you aren't tempted to give in to panic at the worst times. Since index mutual funds can be bought and sold only at the end of the trading day, they can force impulsive investors to sit a few hours before making a rash decision.

Planning to pay less in taxes

Both index mutual funds and ETFs tend to be very tax efficient. In a retirement account, where all your money is taxed as income when you withdraw it, the tax efficiency of a fund doesn't really matter. But in a taxable account, it can matter greatly. I would therefore suggest that if all else is equal between two funds, one mutual fund and one ETF, and you are investing it in a taxable account, you may want to favor the ETF. That's especially true if you are in a high tax bracket or live in a state, like Connecticut or New York, with a significant income tax.

"There is a slight tax advantage to ETFs over index mutual funds," says Jeffrey Ptak, an ETF analyst at Morningstar, "so if you are choosing between the two for a taxable account, that could give the ETF an edge." The real tax differences, says Ptak, exist between actively run mutual funds and index funds. Actively run funds, which often rely on frequent trading, can be very tax inefficient. If you invest in them, placing them in a tax-advantaged account, such as your IRA, should be a priority.

Most index portfolios are, by their very nature, tax efficient, although some may be much more tax efficient than others. Taxable bonds are not tax efficient, even if indexed. Neither are real estate investment trusts (REITs). And growth funds are generally more tax efficient than value funds because they pay fewer dividends.

Deciding between Traditional Indexes and Fundamental Ones

You may be aware that a raging controversy is brewing among investment professionals. Are the newer fundamental indexes, upon which many of the newer ETFs and several index mutual funds are based, superior to the traditional (cap-weighted) indexes we've been using for decades?

The answer: We'll know for sure in about 20 years! In the meantime, I recommend that you take a skeptical approach to any full-page advertisements claiming the raw superiority of one type of index over another.

Favoring a newer approach

On one side of the argument are such financial gurus as Robert Arnott and Jeremy Siegel. They admit that traditional index investing has done a great job but insist that traditional cap-weighted indexes are flawed, and that newer indexes based on other criteria can do better. The problem with traditional, cap-weighted indexes, they say, is that the most heavily weighted securities are those with the largest cap value, and that they get that huge cap value as a result of being overpriced. (That's what they say . . . I'm not necessarily agreeing.)

So instead of weighting an index by cap size, Arnott and Siegel recommend other ways to weight companies. Siegel likes dividends. Siegel-inspired indexes are at the heart of most WisdomTree brand ETFs.

Arnott's formula looks at revenue, book value (the company's raw asset value), cash flow, and gross dividends. If you think Arnott is on to something, pick an ETF from PowerShares, or the new Charles Schwab or PIMCO mutual funds based on RAFI indexes.

There is also a whole lineup of ETFs — RevenueShares — based on indexes that weight companies according to their (you guessed it!) revenues.

Proponents of fundamental indexing "prove" that their way is better by *backtesting*: creating charts showing theoretical returns as if their indexes existed 5, 10, 20 years ago. This backtesting shows that the fundamental indexes yield bigger returns than the traditional S&P 500 or the Wilshire 4500.

The results of backtesting, and the results of forward-testing, however, have been known to diverge greatly.

Hugging onto the tried and true

Of course, traditional indexing doesn't mean you have to invest in a single fund that mirrors the S&P 500 (against which the fundamental indexes are frequently compared). All sorts of traditional, cap-weighted indexes allow you to lean toward, say, small cap stocks or value stocks.

And that is one of the arguments being trumpeted against fundamental indexes. Financial gurus such as John Bogle (founder of Vanguard) and Burton G. Malkiel (author of *A Random Walk Down Wall Street*) argue that much of the backtesting that shows the alleged superiority of fundamental indexes is due to the fact that fundamental indexes tend to favor value stocks and small cap stocks.

But a larger part of their argument is that even if fundamental indexes bring extra juice to a portfolio, will they bring enough extra juice to compensate for certain drawbacks? The drawbacks they cite are higher management costs (cap-weighted indexes are very simple to maintain), higher portfolio turnover (there's rarely a reason to change anything in a cap-weighted index), and a potentially higher tax burden (turnover can result in capital gains tax).

Equal-weighted indexes: Somewhat in-between traditional and fundamental

Equal-weighted index funds don't necessarily aim to beat the market, as do fundamentally based index funds. Instead, they aim to more fairly represent the market, and give you more equal exposure and better diversification. In reality, because you get more small cap exposure than you would with a cap-weighted, traditional index, equal-weighted indexes will tend to bring more volatility but potentially higher return. Nothing wrong with that, except that equal-weighted indexes must be regularly rebalanced to make sure that the components do have equal weight. That's one reason perhaps why the Rydex S&P Equal Weight Index ETF (RSP) has an expense ratio of 0.40, but the SPDR Trust Series 1 ETF (SPY), which tracks the same 500 stocks but cap-weights them, carries an expense ratio of 0.09 percent. All that trading brings other, largely unseen costs as well. I'm not a big fan of equal-weighted indexes.

Who do you believe?

My take on fundamental indexing? It is promising. Some kinds of fundamental indexing may possibly prove superior to traditional indexing. But while we're waiting for that proof, you're probably better off with traditional, cap-weighted indexes.

If, however, you have a hankering to "beat the markets," using ETFs or index mutual funds linked to fundamental indexes may allow you a better chance than would an actively managed fund portfolio. It's a way to quasi-index your money and still get off relatively cheaply, with limited managerial risk. Unlike active mutual funds, you know what you're getting. I have no huge objections to building a portfolio of funds that mirror these indexes.

If I had to choose, I'd say Robert Arnott's formulas make the most sense, at least on paper, of the newer fundamental indexes. Look for any funds that track a RAFI index. RAFI stands for *Research Affiliates Fundamental Index.* Arnott is the chair of Research Affiliates.

Should You Time Your Entry into the Markets?

A lot has been written about dollar-cost-averaging, and a lot of what's been written is wrong. Yes, it makes sense to *dollar-cost-average* — to buy into the market over time — if you are socking away $X a week out of your paycheck. The beauty of dollar-cost-averaging is that your $X a week will tend to buy the most shares during those weeks when shares are selling for cheap. Over the long run, you come out slightly ahead of where you would be if you purchased the same shares willy-nilly.

So by all means, if you want to take a certain amount out of your paycheck each week and invest, do it! (Just be careful of the trading costs, as I discuss earlier in this chapter.) But what if you are sitting on a pile of cash? In that case, I contend, it doesn't make sense to dole out your dollars slowly. If you're ready to invest, just do it!

Taking the plunge

It isn't just my opinion to take the plunge, of course. A good number of studies have shown that, if you have the cash, moving it into a balanced portfolio tomorrow, rather than waiting to do it over months or years, is usually — but not always — going to result in more money in your pocket. That's largely because the market tends to go up more than it goes down. (Over the course of history, the market climbs about two out of every three days . . . pretty good odds, if you ask me!)

Of course, by taking the plunge, you are taking some risk that the stock market could tank tomorrow. But by having a well-diversified index portfolio, that risk is something you can mollify . . . to whatever degree you wish to mollify it.

Living with your decision

In my book — hey, this *is* my book! — index investing and buy-and-hold investing go hand-in-hand. Rather than trying to time the market, you buy the market . . . and today is the best day to do that.

In the next chapter, I pull together actual sample portfolios, culled from the real-life world of index investing. You may want to choose one based on the client descriptions, finding one that resembles you, and use the suggestions I provide to start your own index portfolio.

Counting the Number of Funds You'll Be Buying

Two people may have everything in common to indicate that they should have similar portfolios, but someone with $10,000 will want to invest differently than someone with $1 million.

Trading off diversification for ease and economy

There is a tradeoff between optimal diversification (which may warrant a dozen or more index funds) and the costs and hassle involved with owning a whole bunch of holdings. Every time you rebalance (which I discuss in Chapter 16), you could face trading costs, either in the form of commissions (with ETFs), spreads (with either ETFs or mutual funds), or possibly other expenses. (You'll incur fees, for example, if you buy or sell a Vanguard index fund that's held at Fidelity or Charles Schwab.)

The size of your portfolio is an important consideration in deciding whether to own one index fund or (in the case of very large portfolios) a dozen or more.

Deciding between one index and many

As a rough rule, if you have $5,000 or less, you're probably better off with perhaps one or two index funds. With a portfolio of $500,000, you should be looking at about a dozen, and as you reach $1 million (if you're lucky enough to ever get there), you may want to think about 20 to 25 funds. Of course, for amounts in between, you should adjust accordingly.

In the next chapter, you find actual index portfolios, arranged by portfolio size. I start with smaller portfolios — those with less than $5,000 or so — and proceed to the $1 million and plus kitties. Somewhere in the selection of portfolios I provide, you may find one that fits you fairly well.

Chapter 15

A Bevy of Sample Index Portfolios

This text doesn't come with a workbook; the closest you're going to get is this chapter.

I ask you to follow me now through the construction of actual portfolios. In this chapter, you find some pie charts and the ingredients to bake them . . . various index funds, carefully measured. Most importantly, I share with you my logic for choosing a particular pie recipe for a particular individual.

It's tricky business coming up with a perfect portfolio. In fact, there is no such thing as a perfect portfolio! But I do the best I can to develop optimal index portfolios based on all the things that make an individual an individual.

At the end of this chapter, I ask you to take everything you've learned in this book and create a portfolio for yourself.

Investing with Small Change: Choosing an All-in-One ETF

I often get the question "How do I start investing?" It happened just the other day. I was having a bit of hip trouble, and as Roberto, my 29-year-old physical therapist, was yanking my leg back as far as it would go, he asked me how to get started in investing.

I told Roberto that the best way to get started in investing is to find out if his employer has a 401(k) plan and, if so, whether the employer provides matching funds. You simply can't beat a guaranteed 50 percent immediate return anywhere on the planet.

In this case, Roberto told me that he had been on the job only for several months and wasn't yet eligible for the 401(k). But, he explained, he had $500 to invest. His question was, "What could I do with it?"

As I explained to Roberto, if we're talking about several hundred dollars, and you're just trying to get your feet wet, that's a different ball of wax than building a serious portfolio.

If you have a bit of money that you won't need in order to pay bills, then what the heck — go ahead and put it all into stocks. *But,* be sure you put it in a very well diversified stock portfolio. There is a single ETF that will do the trick: the Vanguard Total World Stock ETF. The fund offers exposure to nearly 2,000 stocks from around the entire globe — roughly 40 percent U.S. and 60 percent everywhere else. VT (that's called the fund's *ticker*) is an ETF, which means you need to pay a commission to buy it. Do so online, and don't pay more than $20 for the purchase. The fund then costs you only 0.25 percent a year in operating expenses. Not a bad way to get started!

Because it is all stock, this fund will be fairly volatile. But if you want diversification in a flash, there's perhaps no better way to get it. (The Barclay's iShares MSCI ACWI Index Fund [ACWI] is similar to the Vanguard fund. It costs 0.35 percent a year.)

Want to add bonds? The simplest stock-and-bond portfolio imaginable would be a combination of VT and the Vanguard Total Bond Market ETF (BND). That fund, which is exactly what the name implies, has an expense ratio of 0.11 percent.

Sticking to the Simple and Easy

And now I'd like to continue this portfolio-building exercise by giving you two very sleek, elegant, yet adjustable portfolios, useful especially to those who don't want to be bothered with a more complicated portfolio. Both are most appropriate for people with less than $100,000 to invest. If you have more than that amount, you can afford greater diversification, although these simple portfolios would certainly be adequate.

The following two index portfolios — each with just seven holdings — can be adjusted to meet the needs of a conservative investor, a very aggressive investor, or anyone in between. The first portfolio is built of ETFs, and the second is built of index mutual funds. Favor the ETF portfolio if you intend to buy and hold, leaving your money untouched except for perhaps a yearly rebalance. Use the mutual fund portfolio if you will make regular deposits or frequent withdrawals.

Note: The mutual fund portfolio contains one ETF: the iShares MSCI EAFE Small Cap Index Fund (SCZ). The acronym EAFE stands for Europe, Australia, Far East (including Japan), and this particular ETF gives you exposure to smaller foreign companies. I believe it adds very important diversification to a portfolio, and there simply are no index mutual funds right now that do the same job.

A sleek and sexy ETF portfolio

Table 15-1 shows how to tailor a conservative, moderate, or aggressive portfolio using the same seven ETF components.

Table 15-1	A Simple ETF Portfolio		
	Conservative	*Moderate*	*Aggressive*
Vanguard Large Cap ETF (VV)	15 percent	20 percent	25 percent
Vanguard Small Cap ETF (VB)	7.5 percent	7.5 percent	10 percent
Vanguard Small Cap Value ETF (VBR)	7.5 percent	7.5 percent	10 percent
Vanguard Europe Pacific ETF (VEA)	10 percent	12.5 percent	15 percent
iShares MSCI EAFE Small Cap Index Fund (SCZ)	7.5 percent	10 percent	15 percent
Vanguard Emerging Markets ETF (VWO)	7.5 percent	7.5 percent	10 percent
Vanguard Total Bond Market ETF (BND)	50 percent	35 percent	15 percent

A sleek and sexy (mostly) index mutual fund portfolio

Table 15-2 shows how to tailor a conservative, moderate, or aggressive portfolio using the same six index mutual funds, plus one ETF.

Table 15-2	A Simple Index Mutual Fund Portfolio		
	Conservative	*Moderate*	*Aggressive*
Vanguard Large Cap Index (VLACX)	15 percent	20 percent	25 percent
Vanguard Small Cap Index (NAESX)	7.5 percent	7.5 percent	10 percent
Vanguard Small Cap Value Index (VISVX)	7.5 percent	7.5 percent	10 percent
Vanguard Developed Markets Index (VDMIX)	10 percent	12.5 percent	15 percent
iShares MSCI EAFE Small Cap Index Fund (SCZ)	7.5 percent	10 percent	15 percent
Vanguard Emerging Markets Stock Index (VEIEX)	7.5 percent	7.5 percent	10 percent
Vanguard Total Bond Market Index (VBMFX)	50 percent	35 percent	15 percent

Formulating a More Complex Index Strategy

If you have $100,000 or more to invest, I believe that adding several funds to the ones I suggest in the previous section provides diversification. Given the amounts of money involved, the increased hassle and the costs of holding the extra funds are worth it. In this section, I show you how to add index funds that allow you to build a portfolio that is aggressive, moderate, or conservative.

Going for glory: Building an aggressive index portfolio

Generally speaking, the two kinds of people who warrant the most aggressive portfolios are the very young and the very rich. It's something of a cruel paradox, but people who least need the potential return of a high-risk portfolio are just about the only ones who can afford to take that risk.

Take Mark and Elaine. They are, financially speaking (and by just about anyone's definition), quite fortunate. Mark (58) works as a senior manager for a pharmaceutical company. He not only pulls in very big bucks but actually has a fixed pension, like many people had years ago but few do today. That pension will kick in when he retires in about five years. (If he retires before that time, he'll get 80 percent of his salary.) Elaine (57) worked in real estate sales for a number of years and is no longer employed. Contrary to public wisdom that would put a couple in their mid- to late-50s into a conservative portfolio, Mark and Elaine actually warrant a quite aggressive portfolio.

The couple doesn't mind the risk that comes with a predominantly stock portfolio. Chances are very small that they will ever need, in their entire lifetimes, any of the $1.5 million currently in their portfolio. As Mark explained to me, this savings is earmarked as a legacy — something to leave behind for the two kids, both currently in high school. (Mark's $750,000 salary with guaranteed pension will more than pay for college, including textbooks and milkshakes, and any other expenses that come up in the next decade.)

The couple's portfolio is divided mostly between the two spouse's tax-advantaged IRAs, to which they have been contributing since their late 20s. In Figure 15-1, I show the investments I made on Mark and Elaine's behalf. I put the U.S. growth index funds and the commodity fund (both very tax efficient) into Mark and Elaine's taxable account, and everything else into the retirement accounts.

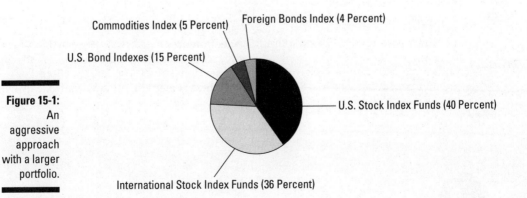

Figure 15-1: An aggressive approach with a larger portfolio.

Commodities Index (5 Percent)

Foreign Bonds Index (4 Percent)

U.S. Bond Indexes (15 Percent)

U.S. Stock Index Funds (40 Percent)

International Stock Index Funds (36 Percent)

Here are the specific funds I invested in:

- ✔ **U.S. stock index funds: 40 percent**
  - Vanguard Value ETF (VTV): 10 percent
  - Vanguard Growth ETF (VUG): 8 percent
  - Vanguard Small Cap Value ETF (VBR): 8 percent
  - Vanguard Small Cap Growth ETF (VBK): 6 percent
  - Vanguard REIT ETF (VNQ): 8 percent

- ✔ **International stock index funds: 36 percent**
  - iShares MSCI EAFE Value Index (EFV): 8 percent
  - iShares MSCI EAFE Growth Index (EFG): 6 percent
  - iShares MSCI EAFE Small Cap Index Fund (SCZ): 6 percent
  - Vanguard Emerging Markets ETF (VWO): 6 percent
  - SPDR S&P Emerging Markets Small Cap (EWX): 4 percent
  - SPDR Dow Jones Wilshire International Real Estate (RWX): 6 percent

- ✔ **U.S. bond indexes: 15 percent**
  - iShares Lehman Aggregate Bond Fund (AGG): 10 percent
  - iShares Lehman TIPS Bond Fund (TIP): 5 percent

- ✔ **Commodities index: 5 percent**
  - iPath Dow Jones-AIG Commodity Index Total Return ETN (DJP): 5 percent

- ✔ **Foreign bonds index: 4 percent**
  - PowerShares Emerging Markets Sovereign Debt Portfolio (PCY): 4 percent

Here are two important stats about this portfolio:

- ✔ The total expense ratio is only 0.29 percent.
- ✔ The standard deviation is 8.0, which means it's slightly less volatile than the S&P 500.

A very similar aggressive portfolio may be appropriate for a 30-year-old with no children, no debt, a fair salary, and many years until retirement.

Aiming for growth: Creating an aspiring but not too aggressive portfolio

Tom and Helene are by far more typical than Mark and Elaine. Tom (48) is a self-employed land surveyor. Helene (45) does freelance commercial writing. Together, they have cobbled together a portfolio of $445,000. They both enjoy what they do and have no dreams of early retirement. Still, their goal is to be economically self-sufficient within 12 years.

Given their yearly expenses of $70,000, I provided them with a ballpark figure of $1.4 million: When their portfolio gets to that size, more or less, they can work or not work. At the rate they are contributing to savings (roughly $30,000 a year), they will need to see an average annual return of about 8.0 percent in order to get to the magic $1.4 number within 10 years. (I discover this fact with the help of my handy dandy HP12C financial calculator.)

Given that they are both self-employed with fairly predictable incomes, and their only debt is a mortgage, Tom and Helene are unlikely to need to touch their nest egg in the next dozen years. If they tap into it at that point, it should initially be for only a modest amount. This couple warrants a more middle-of-the-road portfolio than do Mark and Elaine. There's no need to set the world afire with stratospheric returns. And unlike Mark and Elaine, a serious crash in the stock markets could most certainly adversely affect Tom and Helene.

Figure 15-2 shows how I divided up the moderate-growth portfolio I built for Tom and Helene.

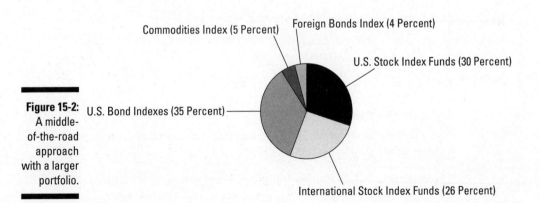

Figure 15-2: A middle-of-the-road approach with a larger portfolio.

Commodities Index (5 Percent)

Foreign Bonds Index (4 Percent)

U.S. Stock Index Funds (30 Percent)

U.S. Bond Indexes (35 Percent)

International Stock Index Funds (26 Percent)

Here are the funds that they're invested in:

- **U.S. stock index funds: 30 percent**
  - Vanguard Value ETF (VTV): 8 percent
  - Vanguard Growth ETF (VUG): 6 percent
  - Vanguard Small Cap Value ETF (VBR): 6 percent
  - Vanguard Small Cap Growth ETF (VBK): 4 percent
  - Vanguard REIT ETF (VNQ): 6 percent

- **International stock index funds: 26 percent**
  - iShares MSCI EAFE Value Index (EFV): 6 percent
  - iShares MSCI EAFE Growth Index (EFG): 4 percent
  - iShares MSCI EAFE Small Cap Index Fund (SCZ): 6 percent
  - Vanguard Emerging Markets ETF (VWO): 4 percent
  - SPDR S&P Emerging Markets Small Cap (EWX): 2 percent
  - SPDR Dow Jones Wilshire International Real Estate (RWX): 4 percent

- **U.S. bond indexes: 35 percent**
  - iShares Lehman Aggregate Bond Fund (AGG): 20 percent
  - iShares Lehman TIPS Bond Fund (TIP): 15 percent

- **Commodities index: 5 percent**
  - iPath Dow Jones-AIG Commodity Index Total Return ETN (DJP): 5 percent

- **Foreign bonds index: 4 percent**
  - PowerShares Emerging Markets Sovereign Debt Portfolio (PCY): 4 percent

Two important stats about this portfolio:

- The total expense ratio is only 0.28 percent.
- The standard deviation is 5.4, meaning it's about two-thirds as volatile as the S&P 500.

Taking few chances: Erecting a (mostly indexed) portfolio with limited volatility

Richard just turned 62, isn't too keen on working for any longer than he needs to, lives on $65,000 a year, and will not get any kind of pension when he retires from his job in newspaper production. Did I say retire? His job situation is anything but secure. Although Richard plans to work another three to four years, the future is anything but clear. If he loses his spot at the paper, Richard is uncertain that he'll be able to find employment elsewhere, and it's very unlikely that he'll be able to match his $80,000 salary. His $600,000 portfolio may have to support him for the rest of his life. If he can hang in there till age 65, his portfolio, along with Social Security, should be enough to comfortably get by. But there isn't a lot of room for error.

Richard is conservative by nature and would lose sleep if the markets took a serious dive. I am therefore limiting his stock market exposure. Because he lives in a state with high income tax (New York) and a part of Richard's portfolio is in a taxable retirement account, I have given him a position in a New York municipal index fund, which will yield tax-free income and provide some stability to the nest egg. Not eager to take on too much in the way of bonds, however, I have also put some of Richard's money into a couple of non-indexed, hedge fund–like "market-neutral" funds. I'd like to see a slightly greater return from them than the bonds will provide, yet they'll still provide ballast to the portfolio.

I've also given Richard a position in the Consumer Staples Select Sector SPDR ETF, a sector of the economy (toilet paper and such) that tends to hold its own fairly well, even in rough times.

Figure 15-3 shows what Richard's overall portfolio allocation looks like.

Figure 15-3:
A conservative approach to a larger portfolio.

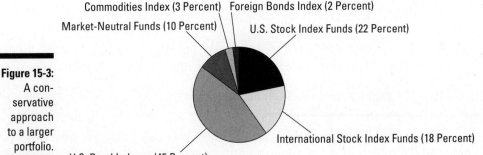

Commodities Index (3 Percent) Foreign Bonds Index (2 Percent)

Market-Neutral Funds (10 Percent) U.S. Stock Index Funds (22 Percent)

International Stock Index Funds (18 Percent)

U.S. Bond Indexes (45 Percent)

Here are the specific investments in the portfolio:

- ✔ **U.S. stock index funds: 22 percent**
  - Vanguard Large Cap ETF (VV): 7 percent
  - Vanguard Small Cap Value ETF (VBR): 4 percent
  - Vanguard Small Cap Growth ETF (VBK): 3 percent
  - Vanguard REIT ETF (VNQ): 4 percent
  - Consumer Staples Select Sector SPDR (XLP): 4 percent
- ✔ **International stock index funds: 18 percent**
  - Vanguard FTSE All World Ex-U.S. (VEU): 6 percent
  - iShares MSCI EAFE Small Cap Index Fund (SCZ): 6 percent
  - Vanguard Emerging Markets ETF (VWO): 5 percent
  - SPRD Dow Jones Wilshire International Real Estate (RWX): 3 percent
- ✔ **U.S. bond indexes: 45 percent**
  - iShares Lehman Aggregate Bond Fund (AGG): 15 percent
  - iShares Lehman TIPS Bond Fund (TIP): 10 percent
  - SPDR Lehman New York Municipal Bond ETF (INY): 20 percent
- ✔ **Market-neutral funds: 10 percent**
  - Hussman Strategic Growth (HSGFX): 5 percent
  - Merger Fund (MERFX): 5 percent
- ✔ **Commodities index: 3 percent**
  - iPath Dow Jones-AIG Commodity Index Total Return ETN (DJP): 3 percent
- ✔ **Foreign bonds index: 2 percent**
  - PowerShares Emerging Markets Sovereign Debt Portfolio (PCY): 2 percent

Here are the key portfolio stats to keep in mind:

- ✔ The total expense ratio is 0.35 percent.
- ✔ The standard deviation is 4.2, indicating about half the volatility of the S&P 500.

Russell's "present and future" portfolio modeling technique

I find it makes enormous sense to map out today's portfolio, as well as tomorrow's, so that you know where your portfolio is headed. That way, you know which areas of your portfolio you're looking to fatten up, and which can stand to go on a diet. That information can come in very handy at times when you are either contributing fresh funds or needing to make a withdrawal. For example, say you currently have $500,000 invested. When you reach $650,000, you'll be that much closer to your ultimate goal — financial independence (retirement!) — and you figure (intelligently) that it will be a good time to turn down the risk. Your two-tier model portfolio may look like this:

The $500,000 portfolio you have today:

✔ U.S. stocks: 35 percent

✔ Foreign stocks: 30 percent

✔ REITs: 10 percent

✔ Bonds: 20 percent

✔ Commodities: 5 percent

The $650,000 portfolio you'll have, whenever:

✔ U.S. stocks: 30 percent

✔ Foreign stocks: 20 percent

✔ REITs: 5 percent

✔ Bonds: 40 percent

✔ Commodities: 5 percent

Your Personal Nest Egg

Using the sample portfolios in this chapter, I hope you can get a good feel for what your own index portfolio may look like. In this section, I give you a few more ideas for figuring out the details.

Looking over your financial situation carefully

As you begin to construct your own portfolio, ask yourself the following questions (which rarely come up in quick online questionnaires!). Based on your answers, adjust your portfolio toward more aggressive, more conservative, or perhaps just different allocations than you may find in the sample portfolios I present in this chapter. Under certain circumstances, you may want to build a portfolio that looks quite different from any of the ones I've shown you so far.

✔ **Is your job status shaky?** Your investment timeframe, which might normally allow for an aggressive portfolio, may not be as long as you think. You may need to tap your nest egg sooner than anticipated. If that's the case, you don't want everything in stocks, which could be down on the day you get your pink slip.

✔ **Are you expecting a fat inheritance?** You can take more risk, and hope for greater return, than someone who isn't expecting an inheritance.

✔ **Are you getting stock options or company stock in your 401(k)?** If you are overloaded with company stock, and you work for a large growth company, you may want a lesser amount of large growth stock in your portfolio than the next guy. Large growth stocks — which include your company stock — tend to move together.

✔ **Are you the nervous type?** Two people with very similar finances may not want the same portfolio. If you can't handle the heat, be true to yourself. There's no point losing sleep over an overly aggressive portfolio.

✔ **Are you a land baron?** If a lot of your net worth is tied up in real estate, lower (or even eliminate) your exposure to REITs. There's no point in property overkill.

✔ **Are you in a stratospheric tax bracket?** High taxes warrant a serious look at municipal bonds. All things being equal, you may want to tune down your allocation to tax-inefficient funds, such as REITs and high-dividend–paying funds.

Positioning your portfolio correctly

Remember, too, that where you put your funds can matter greatly over the long run. If you have both a tax-advantaged account, such as an IRA, and a non-retirement taxable account, you want the fixed income and high-dividend funds in the tax-advantaged accounts.

These funds are generally best in tax-advantaged retirement accounts:

✔ Taxable bonds
✔ REITs
✔ Value stocks (with high dividends)
✔ Non-indexed (actively managed) mutual funds

These funds are generally best in non-retirement taxable accounts:

✔ Municipal tax-free bonds
✔ Growth stocks
✔ International stocks

Part IV
Ensuring Happy Returns

The 5th Wave   By Rich Tennant

Looks like the market's about to take a downturn.

In this part . . .

Care and maintenance are the hot topics of this part of the book. I start with the assumption that you've digested the knowledge necessary to build a solid index portfolio, and you'd like to know what comes next.

In Chapter 16, I discuss the importance of having a portfolio plan and sticking to it. It's advice you've perhaps heard before, but I present it in a manner that makes it (I hope) both palatable and digestible. I fully realize that sitting tight on a portfolio through tough times requires resolve, and I invite you to read and reread this chapter as the years roll by. In Chapter 17, I talk about investment professionals of various shapes and sizes who may help you — or harm you! — in your index investing adventures to come. You want to make sure you can distinguish the helpers from the harmers.

Chapter 16

Buying and Holding: Boring, But It Really Works

. . . .

In This Chapter

▶ Embracing a long-term view of investing

▶ Tuning out the noise

▶ Knowing when you need to tinker

▶ Keeping an eye on Father Time

▶ Eyeballing economic trends

. . . .

*O*h yes, there can be a certain adrenaline rush to buying and selling securities. You watch the prices rise. And (gulp) fall. And then, perhaps, rise again. You carefully time your move. Fingers on the keyboard, eyes on the monitor, you race in for the kill . . . the quick and fat profit. Sometimes, when the going is good, you may just get your profit. Unfortunately, frenetic activity where stocks or bonds are concerned is wrought with peril. Over time, because trading costs money, and because you are (whether or not you know it) competing against pros, losses tend to exceed profits by a good margin.

Trust me on this, please. You'll find few frequent traders on Easy Street. Heck, even the pros themselves fail most of the time, as proven by the inability of actively managed funds to even match the indexes. (I discuss this topic in depth in earlier chapters.)

Indexes? Did someone just mention indexes? Index investing offers no big rush of adrenaline, but over time, profits tend to exceed losses. And that's why you, as a smart investor, have chosen to build an index portfolio.

I now wish to speak about your index portfolio's proper maintenance and feeding. An index portfolio, like a planted cactus, doesn't require all that much attention . . . hardly more than the patience to watch it grow, and some very occasional care.

On the following pages, I provide care instructions.

Keeping Your Eyes Firmly on the Future

Lest you have any doubt, I'm something of a traditional guy where it comes to index investing. While many of the newer index products on the market — namely, ETFs that track every conceivable market and submarket in every conceivable way — are designed for easy buying and selling, easy buying and selling is not such a good thing.

The tried and true, the proven-beyond-a-shadow-of-a-doubt strategy that ensures you'll be one of the most successful investors in your neighborhood, is a long-term, buy-and-hold strategy — a strategy that proved itself long before ETFs ever existed.

Index investing largely works because it equates to lower managerial expenses, lower trading costs, and lower taxes. The frequent trading of higher-priced index products can — and often does — easily negate all three of these advantages. On the other hand, wisely chosen index funds, allowed to do what they do best — earn interest or dividends and grow in price over time — allow you to tap into the surest money-making strategy you'll find anywhere.

Will you make money every month or every year as an index investor? No, of course not. That's where patience plays a key role.

Disaster-proofing your portfolio

It's easy to have patience when times are good. During a bull market, most people, indexers and active investors alike, not only put their money into the markets, they often put *too much* into the markets. During the bad times, however, people tend to panic. We've seen it time and time again: As stock prices plummet, investors move their money to cash (money-market funds, CDs, savings accounts, or *literally* cash . . . bills under the mattress). When stock prices rise again, investors move their money from cash and back to stocks. Over time, this is a losing formula. Even index investors who play this game lose. You're forever cashing out when things are bad (and prices are low) and buying back when things are good (and prices are high). Do the math!

To be a successful investor of any sort, you need to have a portfolio that you can live with in good times and bad . . . the kind of portfolio that you won't be inclined to abandon. This is the best way to prevent yourself from panicking (and lifting that mattress) when Wall Street hits the skids.

So be honest with yourself. If you think your blood pressure may shoot through the roof and sweat will form on your brow if your portfolio were to lose 10 percent in the next year, you may not really want an 80/20 (80 percent stock, 20 percent bonds) portfolio. You may be better off with a more sedate 60/40 portfolio.

A person's emotional makeup is critical to choosing the optimal portfolio.

Ignoring the hoopla and hype

Panicking during a bear market and throwing your portfolio all into cash isn't the only mistake an index investor can make. Many people have been known to have a solid plan in place, only to blow it by suddenly taking a gamble on, say, 5,000 shares of some high-tech company in Mexico City or Hong Kong that "Mad Money" host Jim Cramer or the brother-in-law who works in insurance assures will soon shoot through the ceiling. (Jimbo himself is way too smart to invest in this company, and the brother-in-law allegedly doesn't have the money, but that won't stop them from insisting that you take the plunge.)

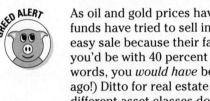

As oil and gold prices have risen in recent times, providers of commodity funds have tried to sell investors on their products. It can sometimes be an easy sale because their fancy charts and graphs "prove" how much better you'd be with 40 percent of your portfolio in their funds. (As I'm writing these words, you *would have* been better off if you bought their funds two years ago!) Ditto for real estate funds. Or for healthcare funds. Remember that different asset classes do better or worse during certain periods. You can't assume that past performance, especially short-term past performance, is at all indicative of what may happen tomorrow.

Because we as human beings are so susceptible to hype, I suggest you try to shield yourself from it as much as possible. Don't watch Jim Cramer. Shut off the TV when you hear his shouting. Don't pay attention to the myriad advertisements for actively managed funds (or narrow index funds) that tout the past few months' (or even the past few years') performance. Ignore altogether ads with testimonials ("JR from Denver") from people who claim to have made a mint actively trading and claim that you can do the same by subscribing to such-and-such newsletter.

Don't buy the hype.

Rebalancing on a Regular Basis

Even a cactus occasionally needs water. And even the best designed and carefully allocated index portfolio needs attention. The problem with letting things slide altogether is that one or several of your investments will do better than the rest. Your large cap stocks, for example, may do significantly better than your small cap stocks. Your foreign stocks may do better than your domestic stocks. Or your bonds may rise, and your stocks may fall. In any of these cases, your carefully constructed portfolio will find itself out of whack.

Failing to rebalance could mean that you are taking on added risk as your diversification dissolves and you become too heavily weighted in one or several types of investment. A second reason for rebalancing: It forces you, despite whatever your emotions are telling you, to sell off the recent overachievers and buy up the underachievers. Over the years, you'll find yourself buying low and selling high (the direct opposite of what most people do!). That process of buying low and selling high, sometimes known as the *rebalancing bonus,* may add as much as a full percentage point to your long-term annual average returns.

There are two ways to rebalance your portfolio. Fortunately, both methods are fairly easy to do, especially when your portfolio consists of wisely chosen index funds that represent crisp and clear asset classes.

The first, more common, method is to attack your portfolio allocations according to the calendar . . . say once a year, or every 18 months. The other strategy is to eyeball your portfolio more regularly, and rebalance if and when things get out of whack, regardless of whether that's a year from the last time you rebalanced or a week and a half. Both methods have their fans, and neither is necessarily better than the other. Which is better for you will depend on several factors.

Using the calendar to keep your portfolio on an even keel

If you use the calendar method, most financial advisors would suggest you rebalance either every year or every 18 months. I think that 18 months is fine for most folks. If you are living off your portfolio and need to raise regular cash, you may consider doing it every six months. The advantage to using the calendar is that it gives you a certain discipline and tends to result in less trading (with fewer trading costs and taxes) than using the as-needed basis. The calendar method also makes sure that you don't rebalance too often, which allows you to take advantage of the momentum that sometimes drives investments north over a period of months.

If you use the calendar method, I suggest that you consider buying or selling any piece of your portfolio (such as, for example, a large cap growth index fund) that has shrunk or grown more than 10 percent away from its target position. In other words, if your portfolio plan allocates 20 percent to large cap growth, consider buying or selling should your position be greater than 22 percent or fall short of 18 percent.

But don't be too rigid about that 10 percent plan. . . . Someone with a smaller portfolio, or someone with an ETF rather than a mutual fund portfolio, may want to use 15 percent. The smaller your portfolio, the smaller the positions, and the greater your trading costs may be. You obviously don't want to spend $10 to trade $100 worth of a single index ETF.

Adjusting your portfolio on an as-needed basis

The other way to attack the rebalancing issue is to ignore the calendar and do your juggling just as soon as you note a large enough swing to warrant a buy or sell. Doing it this way allows for a potentially larger rebalancing bonus but risks eating up that bonus with trading costs and added taxation. Plus, you may lose out on the momentum that drives some securities higher than they sometimes should probably go.

So which method of rebalancing is best?

The better method will depend on several factors:

- ✔ **How large is your portfolio?** Larger portfolios can be rebalanced with greater frequency.

- ✔ **Do you pay for trades, and if so, how much?** I would never make any trade that cost me more than, say, 1/5 of 1 percent of what I was trading. In other words, a $10 trading commission is okay to buy or sell $10,000 of a security (that's 1/10 of 1 percent), but I wouldn't incur a $10 commission to buy or sell $1,000 of a security (that's a full percentage point). Index mutual fund portfolios, provided there's no cost to trade, may be rebalanced more frequently. Ditto for an ETF portfolio if it's kept at (no commission) www.zecco.com or a brokerage house that charges you a nominal amount.

- ✔ **Are your investments in a taxable or tax-advantaged account?** If they're in a taxable account, you need to be more careful of short-term trades that could result in short-term capital gains taxes.

✔ **How volatile is your portfolio?** A portfolio of all bonds — one corporate bond index fund, one Treasury bond index fund, and one municipal bond index fund — requires rebalancing less often than a portfolio of tech stocks, commodities, and emerging-market stocks.

✔ **Are you taking money out or adding money regularly to the portfolio?** Either way, you may want to rebalance more often.

Tweaking Your Allocations as the Years Go By

If you've ever filled out one of those online, quick-and-dirty, build-your-own portfolio tools, you know that age is almost always the first question you are asked. Sometimes, it is the *only* question you are asked!

The common wisdom has it that the older you get, the more conservative your portfolio should be. There's some truth to that (see Part III), but age is only one factor that you want to look at in determining your optimal portfolio.

Bucking the common wisdom

So, what changes to your index portfolio *do* you want to make as you get older? I suggest that you make far fewer changes than the common wisdom dictates! Age itself doesn't mean, for example, that you want to rush from stock index funds to bond index funds.

Yes, you generally want a more conservative portfolio (more bonds and cash, less stock, less exposure to commodities) as you reach your ultimate financial goals, which, for most people, include having a portfolio large enough to not have to work for money. At that glorious point, after all, you start having more to lose than you have to gain.

A financial planning colleague of mine, William P. Bengen, CFP, has made something of a career out of crunching the numbers and figuring out what kinds of portfolios last the longest in all kinds of economic climates. What he finds is that those people with the most aggressive portfolios (say, 100 percent stock) should start to shave off 2 percentage points of stock each year as soon as they get within 15 years of retirement.

In other words, if you have 10 years till retirement, you may want as much as 90 percent stock, with 10 percent bonds. If you are within 5 years of retirement, you may consider 80 percent stock with 20 percent bonds.

Entering the golden years

What happens on the day you retire and start withdrawing money from your index portfolio? At that point, says Bengen, his exhaustive studies show that a portfolio of roughly 60 percent stock and 40 percent bonds is where you have the best chance of seeing your portfolio survive for the longest time. You'll have enough bonds to keep your portfolio afloat in times the stock market does poorly, and you'll have enough stock to keep your portfolio ahead of inflation and to supply you with the cash you need.

If you're fortunate enough to have a very healthy nest egg, I encourage you to tweak your portfolio upon retirement so that you have ten years of living expenses in high-quality bond index funds. If you have that, and only if you have that, consider getting more aggressive than Bengen's suggested 60/40 mix. Ten years of living expenses in quality bonds pretty much assures you that whatever the economic climate, you'll have enough to pay for the necessities of life.

Where do smart indexing retirees get their spending money from?

One costly mistake made by even the smartest investors is to confuse income with cash flow. A bond index fund generally produces much more income than a stock index fund. But a stock index fund generally produces greater long-term capital appreciation. For some reason, many retirees think that it is okay to touch the income from the bonds but not okay to touch the capital appreciation on the stocks. The explanation I've heard from some is this: "Well, Russell, if I sell off the stocks, I'm selling a productive asset. If I use just my bond income, I'm not." It sort of *sounds* logical, but it really isn't. Not at all.

If you are living off your portfolio, it makes the most sense to rebalance every six months or so, selling off whichever of your index funds have outperformed the others. If you started the six months with the bond funds at 30 percent, and now they are worth 35 percent of your portfolio, sell bonds. If stocks started at 70 percent of your portfolio and are now at 75 percent, sell stocks. That way, you keep your portfolio risk constant, you sell off your highest performing assets, and you raise the cash you need.

Don't differentiate so much between interest on bonds and capital appreciation on stocks. You want a portfolio with the highest possible *total* return. That generally means more stock and less bonds than you find in a typical conservative retiree's portfolio.

Gauging Economic Trends

Active investors are forever looking at economic indicators, trying to time the markets or figure out what kind of around-the-corner economic climate may warrant what kind of trading. As an index investor, you don't need to worry too much about economic indicators, most of which aren't terribly indicative of anything. But can you ignore the economy altogether? No, that may be going a tad far.

To what extent should index investors be concerned with economic trends?

Trends matter and matter greatly, but predicting trends is very difficult. I wouldn't attempt it often, if ever. However, here I show you a few economic indicators worth an occasional look, which may possibly prompt a tweak to your carefully constructed index portfolio.

Considering price/earning (P/E) ratios

All sorts of events and formulas have been used to predict stock market returns — you name it, from which league wins the World Series in any given year to U.S. presidential cycles to weather patterns in lower Manhattan. (There actually is *some* evidence that the market does better when the sun shines over Wall Street.) But by and large, these theories are bunk.

One fairly good predictor has been rather well studied, however, and that is prevailing *P/E ratios*. P/E stands for *price over earnings*:

P/E Ratio = Price per Share / Annual Earnings per Share

No, you can't use P/E ratios to forecast next Wednesday's stock market! But if you want to forecast market returns over, say, the next decade or so, knowing what P/E ratios are today may actually have some limited predictive value.

Price per share refers to the market price of any stock or basket of stocks. *Annual earnings per share* refers to the net income of a company or group of companies for the past 12 months, divided by the number of outstanding shares. In other words, P/E ratios measure how expensive a stock or group of stocks may be in relation to the earnings power of the company or companies behind the stock. As Yale researcher Robert Shiller put it, a high P/E is something of an indication of the market's irrational exuberance. A low P/E may indicate irrational despondency.

Shiller's studies and others show fairly conclusively that a low P/E for the overall stock market is a fairly good bellwether that the following decade will show better-than-average returns. And conversely, high P/Es, such as we saw in the late 1990s, indicate that the following decade may see less-than-average returns. (As I write this, it certainly looks like that prediction is going to pan out.)

Moral of story: You may want to tweak your portfolio, ever so slightly, toward a more aggressive stance if the market's overall P/E is low. And you may want to tweak it, ever so slightly, toward a more conservative position if the P/E is riding exceptionally high. The average P/E for the S&P 500 over the past several decades is about 15. It is, at the time of this writing, just about 15. In the late 1990s, it was up to about 32.

If, for example, your normal allocation would call for 65 percent stock, and the P/E for the market dips to 14 or even lower, you may want to up your stock allocation to 70 percent. If corporate earnings start to dip but market prices rise, and the P/E therefore climbs into the 20s, you may want to scale back to, say, 60 percent stock.

You may also want to very slightly overweight markets (Europe, for example) where the P/E is riding lower than elsewhere on the planet.

Want an easy way to find P/E ratios for the large indexes? Go to http://finance.yahoo.com, and search for an ETF that tracks the index you're interested in. No, the ETF and the index itself won't have the exact same P/E, but the number will be awfully close.

Note: You'll often see the notation *P/E (ttm)*. Those last three letters stand for *trailing twelve months*. That retrospective formula is the most common formula for determining P/E.

Here are a few ETFs that you may want to use to see how the P/E of the market stands.

ETF	*Ticker*	*Index tracked*
SPDR S&P 500 ETF	SPY	Large U.S. stocks
SPDR Dow Jones Wilshire Small Cap ETF	VB	Small U.S. stocks
Vanguard MSCI European ETF	VGK	European stocks
Vanguard MSCI Pacific ETF	VPL	Pacific country stocks
Vanguard Emerging Markets ETF	VWO	Emerging market stocks

Noticing the interest yield curve

Under most economic skies, the *interest curve* on bonds — the relation-ship between the long-term bond rates and short-term bond rates — slopes upward to the right. In other words, long-term bonds pay higher interest rates than short-term bonds do. That's the norm. But it isn't always so. Sometimes, such as was the case throughout most of 2007, the yield curve flattens. At very rare times, you may even see a higher return on short-term bonds than long-term bonds.

Don't be obsessed with the yield cure, but don't ignore it either.

Long-term bonds generally pay higher interest rates because the issuers are asking you to tie your money up for longer and to take additional risks by so doing. If the yield curve is flat, it makes less sense to invest in long-term bonds. But it still makes sense! If, for example, interest rates were to plum-met, the total return on your long-term bonds, regardless of interest pay-ments, would likely skyrocket.

So don't trash your long-term bonds, by any means, should the yield curve flatten. But you may possibly want to lighten up. If, for example, your normal allocation calls for one-third short-term bonds (available and recommended in index fund form) and two-thirds long-term bonds (also purchased as an index fund), you may want to tweak that allocation a bit. You could go, say, to three-quarters long-term bonds if long-term bonds are paying higher interest rates. If not, you may want to divide your bond portfolio in half, lessening the longer-term bonds for the time being and going with the less-volatile short-term index options.

Check out the yield curve on bonds by going to the free Bloomberg site: www.bloomberg.com/markets/rates.

Respecting reversion to the mean

One of the most powerful forces in both nature and finances is reversion to the mean. Say a particular industry sector or style of investment has returned an average of 10 percent a year for the past 100 years, but in the past three years it has jumped 100 percent. That comparison tells you something. If the asset class has returned an average of 15 percent a year for the past many decades but has languished in the past three years, that tells you something, too.

You can never tell *when* something will return to the mean. A certain asset class may outperform its norm for years on end (think tech stocks in the 1990s). But eventually, the forces of the universe seem to dictate that there will be a magnetic pull toward the mean.

What's that mean to you? Consider lightening up a wee bit on those portions of your portfolio that have soared beyond their norms for the past several years. Consider beefing up just a tad on those sectors that seem to have languished for so long. For example, if your REIT index fund were to lose 50 percent in a three-year period, you may consider giving it a 10 percent allocation in your stock portfolio rather than the normal 8 percent. If your small cap growth index fund has beaten the pants off all your other style index funds (large cap and value stocks) for the past two or three years running, you may give small growth a 6 percent allocation in your portfolio rather than the normal 8 percent.

Once again, I'm asking you to do the *opposite* of what most investors do!

It is hard to buy more of a fund that has lost money for you and to sell a recent winner, but by doing so, you'll fare way better than most investors!

Noting Positive Changes in the Indexing Industry

New index products have been popping up like mushrooms after a rainstorm. Although the index products I recommend in this book are the best the market has to offer, keep your eyes open (see Appendix C for indexing Web sites to visit), and take note when possibly superior products may hit the streets.

Costs, costs, costs

Remember that a key advantage to index investing is the low cost. Some of the index products I recommend in Part II and Part III may be faced with tough competition in the years to come. If two index funds look and feel very similar, and one costs half what the other costs . . . well, I don't need to tell you what to do.

Diversification opportunities

With more than 700 ETFs on the market, you'd think that every kind of worthwhile investment would be indexed by now. Not so. Oh, there are many *non-*worthwhile kinds of investments you can invest in! But as yet, for example, you have very limited offerings in the way of international small cap stocks and tax-free municipal bonds (especially state-specific municipal bonds). I expect a variety of ETFs in these areas in the near future. Keep your eyes open.

One investment product I'd love to see: An inflation-protected, tax-free, municipal bond index fund. It will come in time.

Chapter 17

Seeking Additional Assistance from Professionals . . . Carefully

In This Chapter

▶ Determining your need for help

▶ Avoiding scams

▶ Finding just the help you may need

S omehow, as a child during the Johnson administration, I got my hands on a small booklet that had a corny title — something like "Healthy Eating for a More Vibrant You." In this booklet were all kinds of helpful tips for eating healthy breakfasts, lunches, dinners, and snacks. It consisted largely of daily schedules, a sample of which I reproduce here. (Note: If you were born after 1970, you probably won't believe it, but "healthy eating" looked very different when we Boomers were kids; it really did include things like bacon and toast with butter.)

MONDAY

Breakfast

2 eggs

2 strips of bacon

1 glass of orange juice

1 slice of toast with butter

2–3 cups of delicious hot tea (lemon optional)

Morning snack

1 cup of pudding or four cookies

1–2 cups of tasty hot tea (milk optional)

Lunch

1 bologna or roast beef sandwich

1 slice of cheese

1 apple or pear

2–3 cups of scrumptious iced tea (sugar optional)

Anyway, you get the picture. The booklet was published — surprise! — by the American Tea Council, or something like that. And it bears a lot of resemblance to (and is no less silly than) what most often passes for investment advice these days. You tell me who is giving the advice and who is signing that person's paycheck, and I'll tell you what kinds of investments are being suggested.

News flash! Most investment professionals are something less than hog wild about low-cost index products. They just love costly actively managed funds — as much as the American Tea Council loves tea.

I'm not saying that there aren't good investment advisors out there, both knowledgeable and objective. I like to think that I'm one! I'm only saying that you are going to have to do some work to find a really good advisor, someone who knows his stuff and can share what he knows objectively. In this chapter, I outline the steps you can take to begin such a quest for such a good soul. I also help you to decide if you need a professional in the first place. Certainly, not everyone does. And finally, I give you a clue as to what you should be paying for help, if you need it.

Sizing Up Your Need for a Helping Hand

Using the tools available in this book, you can build yourself a first-class index portfolio, and you can maintain it. And you can probably do a great job. (Thank me later!) So why the heck would you even consider a professional's help? Here are four possible reasons:

✔ A good investment advisor can help you fine-tune your portfolio, possibly using state-of-the-art investment software, to build a slightly better index portfolio than you could do on your own. A competent investment advisor will look at your personal finances in the broadest sense (including everything from insurance policies to terms of your mortgage) and perhaps have a better idea than you do of just where your risk–return sweet spot should be — how much risk you should be taking for how much potential return.

✔ An investment advisor, like an exercise coach, can not only set you up with the best "exercises," but he or she can also help to monitor your progress and make sure that you stay the course. If you're paying someone to help with your portfolio, you're more apt to also pay attention to that portfolio! After you've hired a professional, there's no more procrastinating about your investments.

✔ An investment advisor can potentially help save you time and energy. Doing a portfolio right, rebalancing regularly, making sure you have the best index investment products available, tax harvesting at the end of the year . . . you may be able to do it all yourself, but a professional can save you a fair amount of effort. With a good investment advisor on your side, you can also save time by not having to constantly keep abreast of new financial products, new tax laws that may change your investment strategy, and so on.

✔ Many investment professionals (I'm thinking of true financial planners now) can not only help set up and maintain your portfolio, but may also be helpful in reducing your taxes, providing estate and insurance advice, finding a mortgage, and so on. Granted, you can pay for such types of advice separately — and perhaps you should — but in the real world, they often come as a package deal.

Assessing your knowledge and interest

The first thing you want to look at in deciding whether to hire an advisor is your level of ease with handling financial matters. Do you feel that you understood most of what you read in this book so far? Do you have a desire to get your hands dirty? Do you have the time and energy to keep track of your portfolio? If so, you may be a good candidate to handle your own index portfolio.

Also ask yourself if you believe that you really have the resolve it takes to be a good investor. If you are prone to rash decisions, making decisions based on emotion rather than reason, you may be better off having someone to hold your hand, especially during the rough times. Be honest with yourself.

Assessing your wealth

Plain and simple, if you have less than $50,000 to invest, I encourage you to build an index portfolio on your own using the information in this book. Between $50,000 and $150,000, you're in the in-between zone. If you have over $150,000, you may start to benefit by hiring a *fee-only* consultant to work with you on an hourly basis, at least to set up an initial portfolio. And before even considering handing your money over to an advisor to actually manage (an arrangement typically called "assets under management"), I would suggest that you have a portfolio of at least $200,000.

If you don't know what *fee-only* means, well, I explain that in just a moment.

Asking Where the Money Comes From

As someone determined to be an index investor, whether you know it or not, you've already eliminated about two-thirds of all the investment advisors in the nation. You won't want to work with them. They won't want to work with you. That's because a majority of investment professionals (at least 60 percent) work either entirely or partially on commission. Index investment products — at least *good* index investment products (good for YOU, that is) — don't charge high enough fees to afford anyone a commission.

Fee-only means that an advisor takes no commissions and works only for the money he or she charges you. A fee-only advisor is therefore much more likely to work with index funds than a commissioned advisor.

Now, just to completely confuse you, commissioned advisors may sometimes be referred to as *fee-basis* advisors. So here's what you must remember: *Fee-only* = no commissions. *Fee-basis* = commissions. Got that? Good!

Finding out how the advisor expects to be paid

If you wind up talking to a fee-basis or full commission advisor, you have a right to know exactly what kind of pay he or she is getting for selling you your investments. Ask! And don't settle for anything less than a specific number. Whatever that number is, just remember that *you* are paying for that commission. It may be indirect, but you are paying all the same.

Fee-only advisors will tell you what they charge up front. But even among fee-only advisors, there are differences in how they are paid. The vast majority of fee-only advisors charge in one of three ways:

- ✔ **Assets under management:** You pay a percentage of the size of your portfolio. This is usually a sliding scale. The more you have, generally, the lower the percentage. A typical fee may be 1 percent a year for assets under $500,000, 0.75 percent for assets $500,000 to $1,000,000, and 0.50 percent for assets greater than $1,000,000. Although these rates are typical, I also believe that they are too high.

You should never pay more than 0.50 percent for asset management alone. If a financial planner is also giving you regular advice on taxes, estate matters, insurance, and such, that's another story. But 1 percent for asset management is a high hurdle for you to jump.

Most advisors who charge based on a percentage of assets under management will expect to be paid four times a year.

> ✔ **Hourly basis:** Hourly fees generally range from $150 to $300 an hour. Some advisors require a minimum number of hours in order to meet with you — usually two to three hours.
>
> ✔ **Per job:** You may be asked to pay, say, $3,000 a year for portfolio management, regardless of portfolio size. Or you may pay $2,000 to have a portfolio set up and then an additional $1,500 a year for management. If the advisor does comprehensive financial planning (reviewing your insurances and wills and such), that work may be charged for separately.

Most fee-only advisors prefer to charge based on assets under management. I believe that most investors, and especially index investors, may be better off doing the grunt work themselves (filling out paperwork, making trades) and hiring the professional on an hourly basis to provide advice.

But good, hourly fee-only advisors are hard to find. There's more money to be had in taking assets under management. Also, hourly consultants (and I include myself here, although I also take assets under management) often get frustrated with clients who pay for good advice and then feel a need to be selective in the advice they choose to take. I know a number of hourly consultants who later decided to switch to strictly assets under management.

Eliminating biases that could harm you

A fee-only advisor may have his or her biases — we all do — but I firmly believe that you are more likely to get objective investment advice by paying for investment advice directly, rather than working through someone who earns a commission from what you decide to buy.

As I've already noted, most index investment products would earn little or no commission to advisors, and those that do pay a commission to advisors aren't going to be the best products for you.

I'm not saying that you can't get objective investment advice from someone who stands to make more money by steering you toward certain products, but the chances aren't in your favor. You may, in fact, wind up with "tea," "tea," and more "tea."

Using free services from a brokerage house

Large financial supermarkets often offer free investment advice to their customers, especially larger customers. What the heck . . . take it if it's free! But do realize that you'll be on the receiving end of a strong bias toward each brokerage house's own funds, and they generally won't be index funds.

Take whatever free advice you get for what it's worth.

Free lunch? C'mon

Landing a free lunch or dinner at a seminar given by an investment advisor is about as easy as finding dirt on a farm. Such seminars are a popular way for advisors to fish for new clients. As those of us in the profession know, however, the quality of the advice you get from an advisor is likely to be in direct inverse proportion to the quality of the meal. Lobster lunches equate to low-tide investments!

An advisor who shells out $150 per plate for a bunch of prospects is going to have to make

that money up somehow. He'll generally do it off the one or two suckers who go for the bait. Even if such an advisor puts you in index funds (unlikely, but possible), you'll be paying such astronomical fees that you won't possibly wind up ahead. More likely, your lunch or dinner host will put you into an investment such as an *equity-indexed annuity,* which (even though it has the word "index" in it) is the investment snake oil of the decade.

Sifting Through the Alphabet Soup

I don't want to scare you, but in addition to there being a lot of potential conflict of interest among financial advisors, there is also a lot of plain incompetence. Part of the reason: Regulations are lax. It takes little education and no real credentials to practice investment advising. All it took me, for example, was a Series 65 license in the state of Pennsylvania. I passed an exam that, if I recall, took less than one hour. It wasn't too difficult, either. And I have to pay the state, of course, a yearly fee to maintain my license. No big deal.

Looking up investment advisor John Doe, AAMS, AWMA, AFC, ETC

You don't *need* credentials to give investment advice, but investment advisors use more credentials than you can even count! *Hundreds* of credentials are available, and many of them — including a bunch of recent arrivals, many with the word "senior" or "retirement" in them — are next to worthless. They often require a weekend workshop and a short quiz, at most.

If you see credentials or letters after an advisor's name that you don't recognize, try the professional designations database at www.finra.org/designations. That's on the Web site of the Financial Industry Regulatory Authority. It gives you a thumbnail sketch of what each of the designations — AAMS, AWMA, AFC, C3DWP — means, and what kind of effort (or lack of effort) is required to get it.

Checking for competency and criminality

Some of the more popular credentials among investment advisors include the CFP, which stands for *Certified Financial Planner,* and the *CFA,* which stands for *Chartered Financial Analyst.* These are both pretty strong indicators that an investment advisor has some good investment knowledge. But they are not guarantees. Nor is an MBA (such as I have), a CPA (some accountants know very little about investments), or any other designation a guarantee of competency or impartiality.

Regardless of the credentials being offered, check to make sure an investment advisor is licensed, and check to see if he or she has any record of malpractice. Start by going to www.finra.org and clicking on the words "BrokerCheck." You'll find sometimes revealing histories of brokers and advisors. Alternatively, you can call the Financial Industry Regulatory Authority at 800-289-9999.

If you are about to hire an advisor who isn't licensed, you are taking a far greater risk than I would ever consider!

Protecting yourself from outright fraud

It's one thing to lose money in the stock market. It's another to have your nest egg ripped off by a squirrelly "investment advisor" who never intended to invest your money in anything but a new Hummer for himself. If you care to read about such blatant rip-offs, go to the Web site of the Securities and Exchange Commission — www.sec.gov — and click on "Litigation Releases" toward the bottom of the home page. You'll find hundreds of cases involving fly-by-night "advisors" who steal money from unwitting clients.

To protect yourself, don't ever sign a check or hand money over to anyone you don't know very well. Any money you invest — in index funds or otherwise — should be held by a brokerage house that is a member of the Securities

Investor Protection Corporation (SIPC). Unsure? Contact the SIPC Membership Department at 202-371-8300, or visit it on the Web at www.sipc.org. SIPC doesn't protect you against stock market crashes, but it does protect your assets should a custodian go under. And for that reason, SIPC makes sure that its members have some financial muscle and that Al Capone isn't running the store.

If you are giving an independent investment advisor permission to make trades for you, provide that advisor with *limited power of attorney,* and not *full power of attorney.* Limited power of attorney allows the advisor to make trades within your account on your behalf. Full power of attorney allows that advisor to make withdrawals — whether on your behalf, or not.

Shopping for the Best Advisor in Town

So where exactly do you start your search for such a gem as I describe in the preceding paragraphs — someone who is objective and competent and not too greedy?

You may want to start with the National Association of Personal Financial Advisors (I am a member) at www.napfa.org. Most fee-only advisors belong to this organization. On the Web site, you can plug in your home state and find advisors near you.

Unfortunately, unless you have lots of bucks and are looking for someone to actually manage your money (take assets under management), you may find it hard to locate a fee-only advisor. Two national networks of advisors that specialize in working with the non-wealthy and on an hourly or set-fee fashion include Alliance of Cambridge Advisors (www.cambridgeadvisors.com) and the Garrett Planning Network (www.garrettplanningnetwork.com).

Also check out the referral service provided free at www.indexshow.com. Click the icon at the top of the home page that says, "Yes, I want help with my 401(k), IRA, or portfolio."

You can also, of course, ask your friends and family members to recommend advisors. Be aware, however, that many people do a poor job of accurately judging the performance of their investment advisors. (They often look at last year's returns and judge their advisor by that. If the market's up, the advisor is good; if the market's down, he stinks.)

Finding an index kind of guy or gal

The future is unknowable — in life, in love, and especially in financial markets. You've decided to become an index investor because you realize the folly of trying to time markets and pick individual stocks. Now make sure, if you do hire an advisor, that the advisor shares your wisdom and philosophy.

You may know everything there is to know about index investing, but if your advisor is a rapid trader, you may rapidly lose your savings. Poke a potential advisor a bit to learn about his or her investing philosophy.

Asking the right questions, and getting the right answers

Start with the following questions to determine whether an advisor is a good match for an index investor such as yourself.

Question #1

What kind of investment returns can I expect you to generate for me over the next year? Five years? Ten years?

Good answer: "Well, I don't generate returns; the markets generate returns. Over the very long run, stocks have historically returned about 10 to 11 percent a year, and bonds, about half as much. The return on your portfolio will depend largely on what percentage of stocks and bonds we ultimately choose for your portfolio. Of course, future returns may differ from past returns, so I'm afraid we're a bit at the mercy of the markets."

Bad answer: "I can guarantee you at least 30 percent a year." (Run! Run!)

Question #2

How can you help me be less at the mercy of the markets and more in control of my own financial destiny?

Good answer: "I can do that by building you an optimally diversified portfolio with minimal costs. By so doing, I'll see that you get maximum return with minimal risk. You'll still be somewhat at the mercy of the markets, but regardless of what the markets do, you should still, over the long run, do better than the vast majority of investors, and see a positive return."

Bad answer: "I'll be keeping an eye on the markets for you every day. If things start to look ugly, I'll quickly move all your money into cash."

Question #3

So how exactly are you going to choose the best index funds to put me into?

Good answer: "All the index funds I use are chosen for their low costs, the broad and sensible indexes that they track, their tax efficiency, and their appropriateness to your portfolio. The total final mix will offer you a well-diversified portfolio with exposure to all major asset classes."

Bad answer: Anything else!

Part V
The Part of Tens

The 5th Wave   By Rich Tennant

"I like the value funds too, but right now we're looking into a more aggressive growth fund."

In this part . . .

*B*efore we finish our great indexing journey together, I leave you with the following three lists of ten indexing tidbits. I first provide you with ways to deal with the temptation to beat the market. Oh, yes, the temptation will come . . . and come again. Those who succumb to the temptation to beat the market often wind up getting beaten in the market! I then take you through ten ways to screw up a perfectly good index portfolio. It's the route that many of the sorely tempted take — a route you will successfully avoid. And finally, I finish up this section with ten Q&As with none other than John Bogle, the Father of Index Investing. Hear what Bogle has to say about the latest twists and turns, trials and tribulations in the world of index investing.

Chapter 18

Ten Ways to Deal with the Temptation to Beat the Market

· ·

In This Chapter

▶ Realizing that you will be lured

▶ Tuning out the noise

▶ Understanding benchmarks

▶ Swallowing a dose of humility

· ·

*Y*ou *know* that index investors wind up ahead the vast majority of the time. You've seen the numbers. You've read what the studies — studies prepared by hard-nosed academics in tweed jackets with leather elbow patches — say the odds are. You realize that you have, statistically speaking, almost no chance of beating the markets, at least not after expenses and taxes. You are resolute to remain true to your indexing strategies and allow the markets to work for you, knowing that you will beat the pants off most investors. You are content to be the tortoise, crawling over those poor hares. And yet . . . and yet . . . the sirens call.

Slick magazines call out to you from airport kiosks with promises of 50 percent returns. For a mere $5.25, you can find out which stocks are the hottest, which mutual funds are certain to kick ass, and which sectors are poised for certain explosion. The television is worse. Jim Cramer and others scream at you, eyes bulging, to buy, buy, buy . . . and they tell you exactly what to buy to retire next month rich, rich, rich. You open your daily paper and the finance column similarly is telling you where to place your bets, implying strongly that you're an idiot not to buy Microsoft, or Burger King, or Booger King, or whatever the stock du jour happens to be. Before you cash in your index funds and decide to get rich quick, please, please read this short chapter!

Here are ten things you should do the next time temptation starts to get the better of you.

Turn Off the TV

Yes, it's that simple! You don't need what they're selling you: not the get-rich-quick schemes, the junk food, or the gas-guzzling SUV. Shut out the noise. Cancel your subscription to *Wise Money* magazine. Stop reading the hot tips in your local paper. This will be hard to do, but it's possible! Of course, your shutting out the noise won't please the media advertisers — the brokerage houses and mutual fund companies — that help push so much of the money media drivel, but to heck with them.

Ask Yourself Who Is Doing the Pushing — and Why

Advertisers? Did I say advertisers? If you do pick up that magazine that, on pages 37 through 40, reveals the "Hot Funds for the New Year!," you should notice which fund companies are advertising on pages 48, 52, and the back cover. What a coincidence! Notice, too, how many other suckers are buying that same magazine in hopes of getting rich. If the truth were printed on the cover — "Indexing (Yawn) Is Still the Best Strategy" — how many people would reach into the kiosk to buy that magazine? Precious few. Indexing stories don't sell magazines. "Hot Funds!" stories sell magazines. "Become a Millionaire Tomorrow!" stories sell magazines.

Google the Past

A number of columnists and talking heads on TV make their living telling readers what to buy and what to sell, and they do it with such *conviction*. Oh yes, they have their reasons that you should buy Amalgamated Electronics and sell Acme Chili-and-Pudding Products this week. (It all has to do with consumer demand, interest rates, and China, you see.) Before you even *think* of taking any advice you read in the paper or see on TV, do an online search for the stock pickers' suggestions this time last year. You'll probably get as much indigestion as if you ate a bowl of Acme chili-and-pudding.

Remember the Rule of Appropriate Benchmarks

If a market prognosticator or a mutual fund manager claims to have a great track record and bases his success on "beating the S&P 500," that should raise your eyebrow right away. Remember that the S&P 500 represents 500 of America's largest corporations. Large companies tend to lag small companies when the markets are hot. So after a few months of stock market rise, many stock pickers, who generally pick the stocks of smaller, lesser-known companies, will seem successful. But just wait till the market goes down (as markets always do)! Beating the S&P 500 in the short-term is no big deal. Find out how this great prognosticator has done in the long run. If there is no long-run record, at the very least find out how this person's picks have done against *appropriate* benchmarks, which will often *not* be the S&P 500, but indexes that track either small value stocks or small growth stocks.

Understand the Ratings Claims

Ads for actively run mutual funds and mutual fund companies are rife with subtle misrepresentations that may give you the impression that indexing is for suckers. You should be aware of these subtle misrepresentations. Keep an eye open for them. Here's *misrepresentation #1*: "Eight out of ten of our funds achieved Morningstar/Lipper ratings of [insert impressive rating figures here]." Many mutual fund companies, especially the smaller ones, specialize in a certain kind of investment, such as bonds, foreign stocks, or real estate. If that particular kind of investment (asset class) happens to have done well in the past months, it can make a mutual fund company look genius. Don't buy it. Studies show that the single largest determinant of how well a particular investment does (up to 95 percent of how well that investment does) relates to the type of investment group (asset class) it belongs to.

Watch Out for Expiration Dates

Here's subtle *misrepresentation #2*: You pick up a magazine in September, and a particular mutual fund is showing you how well it did one year, three years, and five years prior to December of the previous year. Advertisers often hand-pick their starting and ending dates to make their returns appear as high as possible. If you see an ending date that looks suspiciously old, check to see how the fund has performed in the past few months. You may be in for a surprise.

Recognize Random Success

You may see an advertisement informing you that such-as-such fund beat such-and-such index over the past three years, five years, or whatever. Even if the index is an appropriate benchmark, such claims are still no guarantee that the fund's manager has any stock-picking abilities whatever. Keep in mind that there are thousands of such managers out there. Suppose they were flipping coins and trying to get all heads instead of trying to beat the indexes by picking stocks. Randomness tells us that of 6,000 managers flipping coins, 3,000 will get heads on the first flip. If they do the exercise again, 1,500 can be expected to get heads twice in a row. The third time, 750 will get heads. After five tosses, 187 of the managers will still have a perfect head-tossing record. Studies show that active managers with great track records tend to be far fewer than you would expect from randomness alone! Studies also show that star performers in any given year rarely exhibit such star performance the following year.

Pull Out Your Calculator

You wouldn't buy a car or a washing machine without wanting to know the full price, would you? Before plunking, say, $10,000 into a mutual fund that charges 1.5 percent a year in management expenses, punch out the numbers on your calculator: $10,000 × .15 = $150. Over the next ten years, you'll pay this manager ($150 x 10) $1,500 in the hopes he can beat the market for you. Keep in mind that it isn't really $1,500; it's much, much more. Every year, that money you pay the manager is denied the opportunity to grow for you. And that denied growth is compounded year in and year out. John Bogle (see Chapter 20) refers to the "tyranny of compounding costs." He reckons that over ten years, investing in the average actively managed mutual fund costs you about 21 percent of your possible gains. If you look at the real-world performance figures of actively managed funds verses index funds (provided on the cheat sheet at the front of this book), you'll see that Bogle's numbers are right on the mark.

Recognize That Someone, Somewhere Is Betting Against You

Most shares of stocks and most bonds — the vast majority in both cases — are bought and sold by professionals, men and women with fancy suits, lots of degrees, and incredible resources at their fingertips. Keep that in mind when your brother-in-law tells you to buy XYZ Corp. stock because he works with a gal whose husband once worked for XYZ, who says blah-blah-blah and $30 per share is a steal. When you go to buy your shares at $30, someone —

very likely one of those professionals in a fancy suit — will be selling those shares for $30. Why is that? If this stock "must go up," as your brother-in-law is telling you, why is there some professional out there betting otherwise? And what makes you think that your brother-in-law knows more than this professional, who probably tracks this stock full time and has a bevy of researchers?

Review the Facts

Remember that by index investing, you are not going to beat the market, but you *are* going to beat the performance of the vast majority of other investors. I hope I make that clear in the early chapters of this book. If you doubt me, flip through Part I. If that doesn't work, try a few other reads, including the seminal *A Random Walk Down Wall Street* by Burton G. Malkiel (W.W. Norton & Company) or John Bogle's *The Little Book of Common Sense Investing* (Wiley). Or flip to Appendix C of this book for suggestions as to many other sources for information on index investing. After all, the message that you can beat the markets is coming to you from many sources — you may need a few good tools to resist the temptation. But you can do it!

Chapter 19

Ten Ways to Screw Up a Perfectly Good Index Portfolio

*I*ndex investing doesn't require any kind of Herculean intellectual effort, but it does require some smarts. If you've read this book, you can do it — and you can do it very well! All you need at this point is not to fall prey to any of the ten foibles I describe in this chapter.

Chase Hot Sectors

As I'm writing this, people are lining up to buy commodities and emerging-market stocks, and they are turning largely to (highly advertised) exchange-traded funds (ETFs). When commodities and emerging markets cool, these same investors will sell, and then they'll look for whatever ETFs are hot at that time and buy those. Over the long run, these poor, confused investors will be buying high (as sectors heat up) and selling low (as they cool). Numerous studies show that individual investors tend to see much lower returns than the markets, or even the average funds. That's because they're chasing hot sectors. Don't!

Take Inappropriate Risks

Index funds remove some of the risk of investing, but there's still plenty left behind, especially when investing in stock index funds. Only the rare individual should have a portfolio of more than 80 percent stocks — even if those funds represent a highly diverse collection of stock indexes. Most people should have *at least* 30 percent non-stocks in a portfolio (bonds and cash, mostly). Yes, in the long run stocks will probably return more than those other asset classes — but don't get greedy! Regardless of your age, your income, or whatever else, you need diversification.

Invest in Nonsense

Some indexes and index funds just make limited sense. And some indexes and index funds, well, even to say "limited sense" would be a compliment! Some of the ETFs based on newfangled "fundamental indexes" seem promising, but exercise caution with anything that hasn't been road-tested. The index funds that truly scare me, however, are the leveraged indexes that promise you double the returns of the market, and the inverse indexes that promise you returns opposite the market. Some funds even offer double the inverse of the market. Forget about them. The leveraged funds and the inverse funds have been around for years and have left behind too many burnt investors to count. Steer clear, too, of index funds that track tiny markets (individual countries with populations smaller than Montana's) or thin slivers of markets (such as drug companies working on cancer cures).

Pay Too Much to the Fund Company

Part of the rationale for index investing is that it saves you money — or it should. Most index mutual funds and ETFs charge operating expenses of fractions of 1 percent; I list some of the more economical options throughout this book. Fill your portfolio with index mutual funds and ETFs from Vanguard, Fidelity, T. Rowe Price, Barclays, and State Street. Do not pay some of the ridiculous fees (in some cases 2 percent or more — and sometimes with an odious load on top of that) from the more expensive, what-the-market-will-bear companies like ProFunds, Rydex, JPMorgan, Morgan Stanley, and State Farm. This is one case where you most certainly will not get what you pay for . . . you'll be getting considerably less!

Fail to Change with the Times

Buying and holding, right along with indexing (they compliment each other so well!), is overall the best investment strategy. But don't take that to the extreme. The "perfect" portfolio for you today may not be right tomorrow. In particular, as we move on in years and presumably get closer to reaching our nest egg goals, it makes eminent sense to throttle down on the risk. After all, after you reach your financial goal, you'll find yourself with more to lose than to gain. Buy and hold, yes, but don't allow your portfolio to rust. Give it a good going-over every 18 months, at a minimum. (Rebalance at that point, as I discuss in Chapter 16.) Review your holdings, as well, anytime there has been a major life change (marriage, divorce, new career, your kid gets accepted into Princeton).

Put the Wrong Funds in the Wrong Accounts

Some index funds are much more tax-friendly than others. Put your stock index funds, which pay you mostly in appreciated share price and qualified dividends, into your taxable account. Stick your bond index funds, and your REIT funds, which pay you mostly through nonqualified dividends or interest payments, into your tax-advantaged accounts, such as your IRA or 401(k). Such proper placement can make a huge difference at tax time. If you have both U.S. and foreign index funds, the foreign index funds should be in your taxable account — not in a retirement account. That's because you get credit at year-end for any taxes paid to foreign governments, but only if the foreign-stock fund is held in your taxable account. If you keep those funds in your retirement account, you get no credit.

Allow Yourself to Get Eaten Alive by Little Charges

Even if you have your ETFs and index mutual funds in the most discounted of discount brokerages, those $5 or $10 charges can add up. ETFs are the more likely culprits to cost you more than you think over time. Regular, small deposits and withdrawals should not be made using ETFs. Most index mutual funds cost nothing to buy and sell, but there may be charges if you move money too often. Be sure to check with your brokerage house.

Get Scared and Head for the Hills

It's easy to say, "I'm an aggressive investor," but are you really? Could you stomach a 50 percent decline in the markets? A lot of people thought they were aggressive investors during the great bull market of the 1990s. But when the growly bear came out to snag them in 2000–2002, many of those investors suddenly lost their nerve and pulled their money from the markets faster than you could say *dot-com*. Of course, they then locked in their losses and were not present when the market popped back up in the few subsequent years. More recently, many investors dumped their financial stocks just as soon as the going got tough. My guess is that the financial market will pop back, and these people will have missed the boat. Be honest with yourself. If you are going to pull out of the market when the going gets rough, you really shouldn't be there now.

Pay Too Much for Investment Advice

Reading this book probably qualifies you as a do-it-yourselfer when it comes to your finances. But you may feel more comfortable seeking the advice of an expert. That's fine. A good investment counselor (such as, ahem, yours truly) will work with you on an hourly basis to set up your portfolio, determine reasonable goals, and set you on your way. Others may want to take your assets under management and put themselves on retainer. Some financial people will be happy to look at your portfolio alone; others will want to do a complete financial plan, examining not only your investments but also your insurance, your estate plans, and your will. What's a reasonable amount to pay for financial advice? If you're looking for primarily investment advice, I would draw the line at about 1 percent of your portfolio for the initial setup. If you're looking at ongoing management of your index portfolio, I would draw the line at about half a percent a year. I strongly urge you to hire a *fee-only* advisor (that means the advisor takes no commissions from third parties) and to run — don't walk, *run* — from any advisor who suggests you buy any index funds that involve paying a load.

Obsess

A big part of the appeal of index funds, to me, is that they allow you to relax. You don't have to worry about any manager absconding with your money, taking dumb bets, or moving your funds to someplace entirely inappropriate. In the long run, you know what your return will be: roughly that of the entire market. There's no point in checking your account balance every day, or even every week. Your money should be working for you . . . you should not be working for your money. So kick back and enjoy life. Golf! Take a bike ride! Go to the beach! Don't allow a basically automatic plan to consume your time and energy. Obsessing about your portfolio, even if your portfolio does well, is the ultimate investor screw-up!

Chapter 20

Ten Q & As with John Bogle, Father of Index Investing

*I*n 1974, John ("Jack") Bogle founded The Vanguard Group, and in 1975, he introduced the very first index mutual fund available to the public. For 22 years, he served as chairman and chief executive officer of Vanguard, introducing other index funds and shaking up the financial industry as no one has done before or since.

Today, Bogle is the president of Vanguard's Bogle Financial Markets Research Center, as well as a prolific author. He's written six books in all, most recently *The Battle for the Soul of Capitalism* (Yale University Press) and *The Little Book of Common Sense Investing* (Wiley). He is a frequent commentator on how the little guy (and big guys, too) should invest for success. *TIME* magazine named him one of the world's 100 most powerful and influential people. Some serious proponents of index investing refer to themselves as "Bogleheads."

Jack Bogle is the undisputed Father of Index Investing, and I am very pleased that he made the time to join me for an informative and provocative Q&A session on that very subject.

Q. It's now been more than three decades since you introduced the first index fund. Is there anything you know now about index investing that you wish you had known from the get-go?

A. There's really nothing major, no. Our very first fund — The First Index Investment Trust; it has since been renamed the Vanguard 500 Index fund and trades under the ticker VFINX — has tracked the market with great precision and has outperformed 80 to 85 percent of all active funds. That's what we figured would happen from the onset, and that's exactly what did happen . . . so the proof is in the pudding. I suppose if there is one thing that we could have done better, it was in the introduction of small cap indexing. We initially didn't realize how much turnover there would be as companies graduated to larger size, or failed, or merged with other companies. That made the first small cap index funds less tax efficient than we anticipated. But we've since made correction for that with much better indexes.

Q. What are some of the more positive developments in index investing that you've seen in recent days? And are there any index investing (or alleged index investing) abominations you've noted and care to comment on?

A. I'm pleased with the development of the total-market index fund. I'm quite displeased with the number of funds tracking narrow slices of the market. The real problems with index investing began with the advent of exchange-traded funds (ETFs). There are now approximately 700 of them, and only 15 of them are broad-market index funds. The rest tend to track narrow markets, such as industry sectors — technology, healthcare, energy, and such, and specific countries. I'm also not too happy with the number of so-called index funds that seek to beat the market with *fundamental* indexing, whether that means zeroing in on dividend payouts, company revenues, earnings, or whatever. A true index must be cap-weighted, with each company represented in proportion to its market value.

Another abomination is the introduction of all those ETFs that are leveraged and inverse. . . . The only way such funds will ever work for you is if you're one of those people (if they exist at all) who know in advance what the market is going to do each day.

Finally, although broad-market index ETFs can be wonderful buy-and-hold investments, they are being used too often as vehicles for speculation — bought today and sold tomorrow. That's not what indexing is all about. That's speculation. And it involves high costs and often considerable taxation. It's great for the brokerages and the creators of these funds, and maybe Uncle Sam, but it isn't so great for investors.

Q. What would you say is the number one misunderstanding that many people have about index investing?

A. It's almost too bad that we use the words *index investing,* because that in itself leads to misunderstanding. We should perhaps call it *all-market investing.* That would make it clear that the very best investment strategy is to capture the returns, not of narrow market sectors, but of the entire business world at a minimal cost. The way to do that is to invest in the entire market — U.S. and foreign — through low-cost, broad-market funds. Everything else is essentially speculation. Another common misconception is that indexing is safe. Broad-market investing does eliminate certain risks, that is true — the risks in individual stocks, of picking market sectors, and of actively managed funds. But there is still market risk, and that can be significant in and of itself.

Q. Despite the success of index investing — despite the *triumph* of index investing over the past decades — the vast majority of people still believe in active investing. Why the heck is that? And does it frustrate you?

A. Yes, that's true — broad-market index funds account for only about 12 percent of all money invested in the stock market. And, yes, that frustrates me! The number one reason why so many people still rely on active investing: The investment industry has done a great job, and continues to do a great job, of marketing. The fund marketers always have more information than the public, and they can always produce a few funds that have done better than the index, and then advertise the heck out of them. They sell their active funds, while index funds have to sell themselves.

The second reason: Index investing is counterintuitive, and at first blush, it seems un-American. Most people in this country believe that you get what you pay for, and it's hard for them to believe that the cheapest funds are really the best funds. It's similarly hard to believe that the best management of all is no management. And finally, people have way too high an opinion of their own investment prowess. . . . We all believe that we're smarter than our peers . . . we think we can do better. Of course, on average, we're all average!

Q. What's your prediction for the future of index investing over, say, the next 30 years?

A. My prediction is that true broad-market investing will be far larger than now. At present, it's about 12 percent of the entire stock market; I would think that we'll see that number at least double in the next 30 years. All that that requires is that investors get it — that they understand that costs are all-important, and that the promises of the "market beaters," as alluring as they are, are false promises.

Q. You mentioned fundamental indexing earlier. Some index fund providers today are using some rather radical methodologies for creating indexes, and these newfangled indexes have been catching on fast with many investors. You maintain, however, that the more traditional cap-weighted indexes are best. Why?

A. Oh, whenever anyone says that they've come up with a new system that will beat the market and work regardless of market conditions, I put a hand over my wallet! Many of the newer ETFs are tracking fundamental indexes that have beaten the traditional indexes in the past — but the ETFs were not created in the past. They were created only *after* the indexes they are tracking had done well. Their superlative track records exist only on paper, in a theoretical world. As time moves on, I'm quite certain that the outperformance we've seen from such *back testing* won't continue. In fact, just in the past year, we've seen many of those fundamentally weighted funds underperform the traditional indexes by a wide margin. That wasn't supposed to happen!

Q. Many of the index products today, particularly ETFs, are tracking things other than stocks and bonds, such as commodities and currencies. Do these asset classes belong in an average person's portfolio at all?

A. Stocks and bonds are productive assets. They are *investments* that earn an internal rate of return. Bonds pay interest. Stocks produce earnings growth and usually pay dividends, reflecting the return on capital invested by the companies that issue the stocks. Currencies and commodities are pure *speculations* that have no internal rate of return . . . they are not productive assets. They may produce short-term returns in certain economic environments, but over the long run, I wouldn't expect that to be the case. As such, they should play no significant role in the portfolio of a long-term serious investor.

Q. Some of the index fund providers today are charging operating expenses considerably higher than, say, Vanguard ever has. In fact, some are charging more than even active funds! Is there a limit to what one should ever pay for an index product? What should that limit be?

A. I would draw the line at 0.20 percent in yearly operating expenses for a broad-market index fund. There's not much reason to pay more than that, and some broad-market index funds charge a lot more. A firm like Morgan Stanley, for example, charges what the traffic will bear, getting away with murder, and their investors are losing greatly in the process. [Author's note: The Morgan Stanley S&P 500 Index fund, A class (SPIAX), charges a front load (commission) of 5.25 percent, a net expense ratio of 0.64 percent, and a 12b-1 fee (ongoing marketing fee) of 0.24 percent.] It's absurd. The whole success of indexing depends on low cost. And there's no reason to charge a lot of money for an index fund, as the fund requires no management. In the case of international developed-world funds, I'd draw the line at 0.30 percent. And in the case of emerging markets, I wouldn't pay more than 0.40 percent. That's not to say that costs should be your only consideration in choosing an index fund — you also want a fund issued by a solid company with good people at the helm — but costs should always be paramount.

Q. Let's talk for a minute about the Big Picture. Ultimately, the returns on stock indexes are tied to the success of businesses operating within our capitalistic system. How is our economic system doing? You expressed some serious concerns in *The Battle for the Soul of Capitalism.* **Do indexed portfolios of stocks and bonds still make sense, given some of the problems we're seeing today?**

A. I feel that capitalism, for all its problems, is still strong. And our economy is very resilient. We're gotten through recessions, depressions, and war. And we'll get through the challenges we're seeing today. I have enormous confidence in our youngest generation. The returns on capital and the performance of the markets, in the long run, should continue to be fairly similar to what they've been in the past. But with the dividend yield on stocks today less than half of the long-term norm (2.3 percent versus about 5 percent), future returns on stocks will likely be lower than history might suggest.

But I see changes, and not all good ones, including greater global competition and a higher failure rate of companies, that forewarn of more turbulent markets. That turbulence will make it more important to index than ever. More than ever, you want to own a piece of *all* companies. By keeping your costs low and resisting the urge to speculate, you'll let the system work for you in the long run — and I don't think the system will let you down.

Q. Thank you very much for your time, Jack. And thank you for all that you've done for the common investor. I have only one last question: What's it like to be a living legend?

A. I travel much of the time, and I meet with a lot of people. I get many positive comments, and it makes me feel very good to know that I've helped people meet their financial goals. But a legend? Someday, perhaps, I'll get to that point where I feel like a legend, soak that up, and really enjoy it. But for right now, I'm simply too busy trying to get my message out there to take much time to reflect. As Sophocles said, "One must wait until the evening to see how splendid the day has been." I may be 79, but I don't see this as the evening of my life . . . not yet. It's still day.

Part VI
Appendixes

The 5th Wave   By Rich Tennant

"She had a great first year with index investing. Another one like it, and she can buy the matching desk.

In this part . . .

Welcome to the end of *Index Investing For Dummies*. In this part, I give you some very useful reference material, including a handy list of index mutual funds (courtesy of Morningstar) and a similarly handy list of index exchange-traded funds (courtesy of ETFguide.com). Both lists, but particularly the list of ETFs, can be expected to change over time, which is exactly why I also provide you with a list of Web resources that you can use to keep as up-to-date as possible on any developments in index investing.

Appendix A

A Select List of Index Mutual Funds

....

Morningstar graciously provided me with a complete list of index mutual funds for this book. For space purposes, and also to eliminate index funds that I'd rather you don't invest in anyway, I've removed the following types of funds from the comprehensive list:

- ✔ Funds with expense ratios greater than 0.70 percent
- ✔ Funds that require ridiculously high minimums and are used primarily by institutions
- ✔ Very small index funds from small companies that may be difficult to purchase and probably aren't worth the effort anyway
- ✔ Funds with odious *loads* (commissions paid to brokers)

In the end, what you see here is a list of what I consider to be acceptable index mutual funds available to individual investors. My faves are outlined throughout the book.

The information listed in this appendix is © Morningstar, Inc. All rights reserved. The information contained herein: (1) is proprietary to Morningstar and/or its content providers; (2) may not be copied or distributed; and (3) is not warranted to be accurate, complete, or timely. Neither Morningstar nor its content providers are responsible for any damages or losses arising from any use of this information. Past performance is no guarantee of future results.

Large Cap Stock Fund	Ticker Symbol	Fund Category	Expense Ratio
Fidelity Spartan U.S. Equity Index Advantage	FUSVX	Large blend	0.06
Fidelity Spartan 500 Index Advantage	FSMAX	Large blend	0.07
Fidelity Spartan Total Market Index Advantage	FSTVX	Large blend	0.07

Large Cap Stock Fund	Ticker Symbol	Fund Category	Expense Ratio
Vanguard 500 Index Admiral	VFIAX	Large blend	0.07
Vanguard Total Stock Market Index Admiral	VTSAX	Large blend	0.07
Vanguard Large Cap Index Admiral	VLCAX	Large blend	0.08
E*TRADE S&P 500 Index	ETSPX	Large blend	0.09
Fidelity Spartan U.S. Equity Index Investor	FUSEX	Large blend	0.09
Vanguard Tax-Managed Capital Appreciation Admiral	VTCLX	Large blend	0.09
Vanguard Tax-Managed Growth & Income Admiral	VTGLX	Large blend	0.09
Fidelity Spartan 500 Index Investor	FSMKX	Large blend	0.10
Fidelity Spartan Total Market Index Investor	FSTMX	Large blend	0.10
Vanguard Growth Index Admiral	VIGAX	Large growth	0.10
Vanguard Value Index Admiral	VVIAX	Large value	0.10
Bridgeway Blue-Chip 35 Index	BRLIX	Large blend	0.15
Vanguard 500 Index	VFINX	Large blend	0.15
Vanguard Tax-Managed Capital Appreciation	VMCAX	Large blend	0.15
Vanguard Tax-Managed Growth & Income	VTGIX	Large blend	0.15
Vanguard Total Stock Market Index	VTSMX	Large blend	0.15
Fidelity 100 Index	FOHIX	Large blend	0.19
Schwab S&P 500 Index Select	SWPPX	Large blend	0.19
Barclays Global Investors S&P 500 Stock	WFSPX	Large blend	0.20

Large Cap Stock Fund	*Ticker Symbol*	*Fund Category*	*Expense Ratio*
Dreyfus Basic S&P 500 Stock Index	DSPIX	Large blend	0.20
Schwab S&P 500 Index e.Shares	SWPEX	Large blend	0.20
Vanguard Large Cap Index	VLACX	Large blend	0.20
Vanguard Value Index	VIVAX	Large value	0.20
Vanguard Growth Index	VIGRX	Large growth	0.22
Vanguard FTSE Social Index Investor	VFTSX	Large blend	0.24
Vanguard Consumer Staples Index Admiral	VCSAX	Large blend	0.26
Vanguard Industrials Index Admiral	VINAX	Large blend	0.26
Vanguard Consumer Discretionary Index Admiral	VCDAX	Large growth	0.27
Schwab 1000 Index Select	SNXSX	Large blend	0.33
Schwab S&P 500 Index Investor	SWPIX	Large blend	0.35
T. Rowe Price Equity Index 500	PREIX	Large blend	0.35
Fidelity Nasdaq Composite Index	FNCMX	Large growth	0.35
Schwab Total Stock Market Index Select	SWTSX	Large blend	0.37
T. Rowe Price Total Equity Market Index	POMIX	Large blend	0.40
Vanguard Dividend Appreciation Index Investor	VDAIX	Large blend	0.40
Vanguard High Dividend Yield Index Investor	VHDYX	Large value	0.40
Schwab Fundamental US Large Company Index TM Select	SFLSX	Large value	0.44
Schwab 1000 Index Investor	SNXFX	Large blend	0.48
Dreyfus S&P 500 Index	PEOPX	Large blend	0.50

Large Cap Stock Fund	Ticker Symbol	Fund Category	Expense Ratio
Schwab Total Stock Market Index Investor	SWTIX	Large blend	0.52
Schwab Fundamental US Large Company Index TM Investor	SFLVX	Large value	0.59

Mid Cap Stock Fund	Ticker Symbol	Fund Category	Expense Ratio
Fidelity Spartan Extended Market Index Advantage	FSEVX	Mid cap blend	0.07
Fidelity Spartan Extended Market Index Investor	FSEMX	Mid cap blend	0.09
Vanguard Extended Market Index Admiral	VEXAX	Mid cap blend	0.09
Vanguard Mid Capitalization Index Admiral	VIMAX	Mid cap blend	0.10
Vanguard Mid Capitalization Index	VIMSX	Mid cap blend	0.21
Vanguard Extended Market Index	VEXMX	Mid cap blend	0.24
Vanguard Mid-Cap Growth Index Investor	VMGIX	Mid cap growth	0.24
Vanguard Mid-Cap Value Index Investor	VMVIX	Mid cap value	0.24
T. Rowe Price Extended Equity Market Index	PEXMX	Mid cap blend	0.40
Dreyfus MidCap Index	PESPX	Mid cap blend	0.50

Small Cap Stock Fund	Ticker Symbol	Category	Expense Ratio
Vanguard Small Cap Index Admiral	VSMAX	Small blend	0.11
Vanguard Tax-Managed Small Cap Investor	VTMSX	Small blend	0.12
E*TRADE Russell 2000 Index	ETRUX	Small blend	0.22
Vanguard Small Cap Index	NAESX	Small blend	0.22
Vanguard Small Cap Growth Index	VISGX	Small growth	0.22

Small Cap Stock Fund	Ticker Symbol	Category	Expense Ratio
Vanguard Small Cap Value Index	VISVX	Small value	0.22
Schwab Small Cap Index Investor	SWSMX	Small blend	0.42
Schwab Small Cap Index Select	SWSSX	Small blend	0.42
Schwab Fundamental US Small-Mid Company Index TM Select	SFSSX	Small blend	0.44
Dreyfus Small Cap Stock Index	DISSX	Small blend	0.50
Schwab Fundamental US Small-Mid Company Index TM Investor	SFSVX	Small blend	0.59

Industry Sector Stock Fund	Ticker Symbol	Category	Expense Ratio
Vanguard REIT Index Admiral	VGSLX	Specialty — real estate	0.10
Vanguard REIT Index	VGSIX	Specialty — real estate	0.20
Vanguard Financials Index Admiral	VFAIX	Specialty — financial	0.26
Vanguard Health Care Index Admiral	VHCIX	Specialty — health	0.26
Vanguard Energy Index Admiral	VENAX	Specialty — natural resources	0.26
Vanguard Materials Index Admiral	VMIAX	Specialty — natural resources	0.26
Vanguard Information Technology IndexAdmiral	VITAX	Specialty — technology	0.26
Vanguard Utilities Index Admiral	VUIAX	Specialty — utilities	0.26
Vanguard Telecom Services Index Admiral	VTCAX	Specialty — communications	0.27
E*TRADE Technology Index	ETTIX	Specialty — technology	0.60

Balanced Fund (Stocks and Bonds)	Ticker Symbol	Category	Expense Ratio
Vanguard Balanced Index Admiral	VBIAX	Moderate allocation	0.10
Vanguard Balanced Index	VBINX	Moderate allocation	0.19

Global & International Stock Fund	Ticker Symbol	Category	Expense Ratio
Fidelity Spartan International Index Advantage	FSIVX	Foreign Large Blend	0.07
E*TRADE International Index	ETINX	Foreign Large Blend	0.09
Fidelity Spartan International Index Investor	FSIIX	Foreign Large Blend	0.10
Vanguard European Stock Index Admiral	VEUSX	Europe Stock	0.12
Vanguard Pacific Stock Index Admiral	VPADX	Japan Stock	0.12
Vanguard Tax-Managed International	VTMGX	Foreign Large Blend	0.15
Vanguard Developed Markets Index	VDMIX	Foreign Large Blend	0.22
Vanguard European Stock Index	VEURX	Europe Stock	0.22
Vanguard Pacific Stock Index	VPACX	Japan Stock	0.22
Vanguard Total International Stock Index	VGTSX	Foreign Large Blend	0.27
Vanguard FTSE All-World ex-US Index Investor	VFWIX	Foreign Large Blend	0.40
Schwab Fundamental International Large Company Index TM Select	SFNSX	Foreign Large Blend	0.44
Schwab International Index Select	SWISX	Foreign Large Blend	0.50
T. Rowe Price International Equity Index	PIEQX	Foreign Large Blend	0.50

Global & International Stock Fund	Ticker Symbol	Category	Expense Ratio
Schwab Fundamental International Large Company Index TM Investor	SFNVX	Foreign Large Blend	0.59
Dreyfus International Stock Index	DIISX	Foreign Large Blend	0.60
Schwab International Index Investor	SWINX	Foreign Large Blend	0.69

Emerging Markets Fund	Ticker Symbol	Category	Expense Ratio
Vanguard Emerging Markets Stock Index Admiral	VEMAX	Diversified emerging markets	0.25
Vanguard Emerging Markets Stock Index	VEIEX	Diversified emerging markets	0.37

Fixed Income Fund	Ticker Symbol	Category	Expense Ratio
Fidelity Spartan Intermediate Treasury Bond Index Fidelity Advantage	FIBAX	Intermediate government	0.10
Vanguard Intermediate-Term Bond Index Admiral	VBILX	Intermediate-term bond	0.10
Vanguard Total Bond Market Index Admiral	VBTLX	Intermediate-term bond	0.10
Fidelity Spartan Long-Term Treasury Bond Index Fidelity Advantage	FLBAX	Long government	0.10
Fidelity Spartan Short-Term Treasury Bond Index Fidelity Advantage	FSBAX	Short government	0.10
Vanguard Short-Term Bond Index Admiral	VBIRX	Short-term bond	0.10
Dreyfus Bond Market Index Basic	DBIRX	Intermediate-term bond	0.15
Vanguard Intermediate-Term Bond Index	VBIIX	Intermediate-term bond	0.18
Vanguard Long-Term Bond Index	VBLTX	Long-term bond	0.18

Fixed Income Fund	*Ticker Symbol*	*Category*	*Expense Ratio*
Vanguard Short-Term Bond Index	VBISX	Short-term bond	0.18
Vanguard Total Bond Market Index	VBMFX	Intermediate-term bond	0.19
Fidelity Spartan Intermediate Treasury Bond Index Investor	FIBIX	Intermediate government	0.20
Fidelity Spartan Long-Term Treasury Bond Index Investor	FLBIX	Long government	0.20
Fidelity Spartan Short-Term Treasury Bond Index Investor	FSBIX	Short government	0.20
Barclays Global Investors Bond Index	WFBIX	Intermediate-term bond	0.23
T. Rowe Price U.S. Bond Index	PBDIX	Intermediate-term bond	0.30
Fidelity U.S. Bond Index	FBIDX	Intermediate-term bond	0.31
Dreyfus Bond Market Index Investor	DBMIX	Intermediate-term bond	0.40
Schwab Total Bond Market	SWLBX	Intermediate-term bond	0.53
Schwab Short-Term Bond Market	SWBDX	Short-term bond	0.56

Appendix B

A Select List of Exchange-Traded Funds

· ·

*T*o create this list, I started with a complete list of exchange-traded funds, provided to me by the kind courtesy of the folks at www.etfguide.com. Because that list is long and forever growing, and because not everything on it is worthy of your consideration, I've pared it down a bit.

The list that follows is a great starting point to do your ETF shopping. The following categories of ETFs have been eliminated:

✔ ETFs with expense ratios of greater than 0.70 percent

✔ Leveraged and inverse ETFs

✔ Currency ETFs

✔ ETFs that track extremely narrow indexes

✔ Single-country indexes, except for Japan and the U.K. (the second- and third-largest stock markets in the world)

✔ Commodity ETFs, except for a few select funds that may make sense in certain portfolios. Important note: This category includes exchange-traded notes, which are not exactly ETFs. Read Chapter 9 before you invest. A few of these have expense ratios as high as 0.75 percent.

What's left behind are by and large the building blocks — along with perhaps index mutual funds (see Appendix A) — that you want to use to create your index portfolio.

This list is printed with permission of www.etfguide.com (© 2008).

Broad Market U.S. Stock ETFs	Ticker Symbol	Expense Ratio
Vanguard Total Stock Market ETF	VTI	0.07%
Vanguard Extended Market ETF	VXF	0.08%
iShares Dow Jones U.S. Total Market	IYY	0.20%
iShares Russell 3000	IWV	0.20%

Broad Market U.S. Stock ETFs	Ticker Symbol	Expense Ratio
iShares S&P 1500	ISI	0.20%
PowerShares QQQ Trust	QQQQ	0.20%
SPDR DJ Wilshire Total Market ETF	TMW	0.20%
iShares NYSE Composite	NYC	0.25%
iShares Russell 3000 Growth	IWZ	0.25%
iShares Russell 3000 Value	IWW	0.25%
WisdomTree Total Earnings Fund	EXT	0.28%
WisdomTree Total Dividend Fund	DTD	0.28%
Fidelity Nasdaq Composite	ONEQ	0.30%
WisdomTree Low P/E Fund	EZY	0.38%
WisdomTree High-Yield Equity Fund	DHS	0.38%
PowerShares Dividend Achievers	PFM	0.50%
PowerShares Dynamic OTC Portfolio	PEY	0.50%
PowerShares High Growth Rate Dividend Achievers	PHJ	0.50%

Large Cap U.S. Stock ETFs	Ticker Symbol	Expense Ratio
Vanguard Large Cap ETF	VV	0.07%
iShares S&P 500	IVV	0.09%
SPDR S&P 500 ETF	SPY	0.10%
Vanguard Growth ETF	VUG	0.11%
Vanguard Value ETF	VTV	0.11%
Vanguard Mega Cap 300 ETF	MGC	0.13%
Vanguard Mega Cap 300 Growth ETF	MGK	0.13%
Vanguard Mega Cap 300 Value ETF	MGV	0.13%
iShares Russell 1000	IWB	0.15%
Dow Diamonds	DIA	0.18%
iShares S&P 500 Growth	IVW	0.18%
iShares S&P 500 Value	IVE	0.18%
iShares Morningstar Large Core	JKD	0.20%
iShares Russell 1000 Growth	IWF	0.20%
iShares Russell 1000 Value	IWD	0.20%

Large Cap U.S. Stock ETFs	Ticker Symbol	Expense Ratio
iShares S&P 100	OEF	0.20%
iShares NYSE 100 Index	NY	0.20%
Rydex Russell Top 50 Index	XLG	0.20%
SPDR DJ Wilshire Large Cap ETF	ELR	0.20%
SPDR DJ Wilshire Large Cap Growth ETF	ELG	0.20%
SPDR DJ Wilshire Large Cap Value ETF	ELV	0.20%
iShares Morningstar Large Growth	JKE	0.25%
iShares Morningstar Large Value	JKF	0.25%
Vanguard High Dividend Yield ETF	VYM	0.25%
Vanguard Dividend Appreciation ETF	VIG	0.28%
WisdomTree Earnings 500 Fund	EPS	0.28%
WisdomTree Large Cap Dividend Fund	DLN	0.28%
Rydex S&P 500 Pure Growth	RPG	0.35%
Rydex S&P 500 Pure Value	RPV	0.35%
SPDR S&P Dividend ETF	SDY	0.35%
WisdomTree Earnings Top 100 Fund	EEZ	0.38%
WisdomTree Dividend Top 100 Fund	DTN	0.38%
Rydex S&P 500 Equal Weight	RSP	0.40%
First Trust Morningstar Dividend Leaders Index	FDL	0.45%
RevenueShares Large Cap Fund	RWL	0.49%
iShares KLD Select Social Index	KLD	0.50%
iShares KLD 400 Social Index	DSI	0.50%
Claymore/Great Companies Large-Cap Growth Index	XGC	0.60%
Claymore Zacks Yield Hog	CVY	0.60%
PowerShares Dynamic Aggressive Growth	PGZ	0.60%
PowerShares Dynamic Deep Value	PVM	0.60%
PowerShares Dynamic Large Cap Portfolio	PJF	0.60%
PowerShares Dynamic Large Cap Growth	PWB	0.60%
PowerShares Dynamic Large Cap Value	PWV	0.60%
First Trust DB Strategic Value Index	FDV	0.65%

Mid Cap U.S. Stock ETFs	Ticker Symbol	Expense Ratio
Vanguard Mid Cap ETF	VO	0.13%
Vanguard Mid Cap Growth ETF	VOT	0.13%
Vanguard Mid Cap Value ETF	VOE	0.13%
iShares Russell Mid Cap	IWR	0.20%
iShares S&P 400 Mid Cap	IJH	0.20%
iShares S&P 400 Value	IJJ	0.20%
iShares Morningstar Mid Core	JKG	0.25%
iShares Russell Mid Cap Growth	IWP	0.25%
iShares Russell Mid Cap Value	IWS	0.25%
iShares S&P 400 Growth	IJK	0.25%
SPDR S&P 400	MDY	0.25%
SPDR DJ Wilshire Mid Cap ETF	EMM	0.25%
SPDR DJ Wilshire Mid Cap Growth ETF	EMG	0.25%
SPDR DJ Wilshire Mid Cap Value ETF	EMV	0.25%
iShares Morningstar Mid Growth	JKH	0.30%
iShares Morningstar Mid Value	JKI	0.30%
Rydex S&P 400 Mid Cap Pure Growth	RFG	0.35%
Rydex S&P 400 Mid Cap Pure Value	RFV	0.35%
WisdomTree MidCap Earnings Fund	EZM	0.38%
WisdomTree MidCap Dividend Fund	DON	0.38%
RevenueShares Mid Cap Fund	RWK	0.54%
Claymore/Zacks Mid Cap Core	CZA	0.60%
PowerShares Dynamic Mid Cap Portfolio	PJG	0.60%
PowerShares Dynamic Mid Cap Growth	PWJ	0.60%
PowerShares Dynamic Mid Cap Value	PWP	0.60%
First Trust Mid Cap Core AlphaDEX Fund	FNX	0.70%
Small Cap U.S. Stock ETFs	**Ticker Symbol**	**Expense Ratio**
Vanguard Small Cap ETF	VB	0.10%
Vanguard Small Cap Growth ETF	VBK	0.12%
Vanguard Small Cap Value ETF	VBR	0.12%

Small Cap U.S. Stock ETFs	Ticker Symbol	Expense Ratio
iShares Russell 2000	IWM	0.20%
iShares S&P 600 Small Cap	IJR	0.20%
iShares Morningstar Small Core	JKJ	0.25%
iShares Russell 2000 Growth	IWO	0.25%
iShares Russell 2000 Value	IWN	0.25%
iShares S&P 600 Growth	IJT	0.25%
iShares S&P 600 Value	IJS	0.25%
SPDR DJ Wilshire Small Cap ETF	DSC	0.25%
SPDR DJ Wilshire Small Cap Growth ETF	DSG	0.25%
SPDR DJ Wilshire Small Cap Value ETF	DSV	0.25%
iShares Morningstar Small Growth	JKK	0.30%
iShares Morningstar Small Value	JKL	0.30%
Rydex S&P 600 Small Cap Pure Growth	RZG	0.35%
Rydex S&P 600 Small Cap Pure Value	RZV	0.35%
WisdomTree SmallCap Earnings Fund	EES	0.38%
WisdomTree SmallCap Dividend Fund	DES	0.38%
iShares MSCI EAFE Small Cap Index Fund	SCZ	0.40%
RevenueShares Small Cap Fund	RWJ	0.54%
Claymore Sabrient Stealth	STH	0.60%
iShares Russell Microcap	IWC	0.60%
PowerShares Dynamic Small Cap Portfolio	PJM	0.60%
PowerShares Dynamic Small Cap Growth	PWT	0.60%
PowerShares Dynamic Small Cap Value	PWY	0.60%
PowerShares Zacks Microcap	PZI	0.60%
PowerShares Zacks Small Cap Portfolio	PZJ	0.60%
First Trust Dow Jones Select Microcap	FDM	0.60%
First Trust Small Cap Core AlphaDEX Fund	FYX	0.70%
U.S. Industry & Sector Stock ETFs	**Ticker Symbol**	**Expense Ratio**
Vanguard REIT ETF	VNQ	0.12%
Vanguard Consumer Discretionary ETF	VCR	0.22%

U.S. Industry & Sector Stock ETFs	*Ticker Symbol*	*Expense Ratio*
Vanguard Consumer Staples ETF	VDC	0.22%
Vanguard Energy ETF	VDE	0.22%
Vanguard Financials ETF	VFH	0.22%
Vanguard Health Care ETF	VHT	0.22%
Vanguard Industrials ETF	VIS	0.22%
Vanguard Information Technology ETF	VGT	0.22%
Vanguard Materials ETF	VAW	0.22%
Vanguard Telecommunications ETF	VOX	0.22%
Vanguard Utilities ETF	VPU	0.22%
Consumer Staples Select Sector SPDR	XLP	0.23%
Consumer Discretionary Select Sector SPDR	XLY	0.23%
Energy Select Sector SPDR	XLE	0.23%
Financial Select Sector SPDR	XLF	0.23%
Healthcare Select Sector SPDR	XLV	0.23%
Industrial Select Sector SPDR	XLI	0.23%
Materials Select Sector SPDR	XLB	0.23%
Technology Select Sector SPDR	XLK	0.23%
Utilities Select Sector SPDR	XLU	0.23%
DJ Wilshire REIT ETF	RWR	0.25%
iShares Cohen & Steers Realty Majors	ICF	0.35%
KBW Bank ETF	KBE	0.35%
KBW Regional Bank ETF	KRE	0.35%
KBW Capital Markets ETF	KCE	0.35%
KBW Insurance ETF	KIE	0.35%
SPDR S&P Biotech ETF	XBI	0.35%
SPDR S&P Homebuilders ETF	XHB	0.35%
SPDR S&P Metals & Mining ETF	XME	0.35%
SPDR S&P Pharmaceuticals ETF	XPH	0.35%
SPDR S&P Retail ETF	XRT	0.35%
SPDR S&P Semiconductor ETF	XSD	0.35%
SPDR S&P Oil & Gas Equipment & Services ETF	XES	0.35%

U.S. Industry & Sector Stock ETFs	Ticker Symbol	Expense Ratio
SPDR S&P Oil & Gas Exploration & Production ETF	XOP	0.35%
Claymore/Morningstar Information Super Sector Index ETF	MZN	0.40%
Claymore/Morningstar Services Super Sector Index ETF	MZO	0.40%
Claymore/Morningstar Manufacturing Super Sector Index ETF	MZG	0.40%
iShares Dow Jones U.S. Consumer Goods	IYK	0.48%
iShares Dow Jones U.S. Energy	IYE	0.48%
iShares Dow Jones U.S. Financial	IYF	0.48%
iShares Dow Jones U.S. Financial Services	IYG	0.48%
iShares Dow Jones U.S. Healthcare	IYH	0.48%
iShares Dow Jones U.S. Industrial	IYJ	0.48%
iShares Dow Jones U.S. Real Estate	IYR	0.48%
iShares Dow Jones U.S. Technology	IYW	0.48%
iShares Dow Jones U.S. Telecommunications	IYZ	0.48%
iShares Dow Jones U.S. Transportation	IYT	0.48%
iShares Dow Jones U.S. Utilities	IDU	0.48%
iShares Dow Jones U.S. Oil & Gas Exploration/Production	IEO	0.48%
iShares Dow Jones U.S. Oil Equipment & Services	IEZ	0.48%
iShares Dow Jones U.S. Pharmaceuticals	IHE	0.48%
iShares Dow Jones U.S. Healthcare Providers	IHF	0.48%
iShares Dow Jones U.S. Medical Devices	IHI	0.48%
iShares Dow Jones U.S. Broker/Dealers	IAI	0.48%
iShares Dow Jones U.S. Insurance	IAK	0.48%
iShares Dow Jones U.S. Regional Banks	IAT	0.48%
iShares Dow Jones U.S. Aerospace & Defense	ITA	0.48%
iShares Dow Jones U.S. Home Construction	ITB	0.48%
iShares FTSE EPRA/NAREIT Global Real Estate ex-U.S. Index Fund	IFGL	0.48%
iShares FTSE EPRA/NAREIT Asia Index Fund	IFAS	0.48%

U.S. Industry & Sector Stock ETFs	Ticker Symbol	Expense Ratio
iShares FTSE EPRA/NAREIT Europe Index Fund	IFEU	0.48%
iShares FTSE EPRA/NAREIT North America Index Fund	IFNA	0.48%
iShares FTSE NAREIT Industrial/Office	FIO	0.48%
iShares FTSE NAREIT Mortgage REITs	REM	0.48%
iShares FTSE NAREIT Real Estate 50	FTY	0.48%
iShares FTSE NAREIT Residential	REZ	0.48%
iShares FTSE NAREIT Retail	RTL	0.48%
iShares Nasdaq Biotechnology	IBB	0.48%
iShares S&P North American Technology-Multimedia Networking Index Fund	IGN	0.48%
iShares S&P North American Technology-Semiconductors Index Fund	IGW	0.48%
iShares S&P North American Technology-Software Index Fund	IGV	0.48%
iShares S&P North American Technology Sector Index Fund	IGM	0.48%
iShares S&P North American Natural Resources Sector Fund	IGE	0.50%
NYSE Arca Tech 100	NXT	0.50%
Rydex S&P Equal Weight Consumer Discretionary	RCD	0.50%
Rydex S&P Equal Weight Consumer Staples	RHS	0.50%
Rydex S&P Equal Weight Energy	RYE	0.50%
Rydex S&P Equal Weight Financial Services	RYF	0.50%
Rydex S&P Equal Weight Healthcare	RYH	0.50%
Rydex S&P Equal Weight Industrial	RGI	0.50%
Rydex S&P Equal Weight Materials	RTM	0.50%
Rydex S&P Equal Weight Technology	RYT	0.50%
Rydex S&P Equal Weight Utilities	RYU	0.50%
Morgan Stanley Technology ETF	MTK	0.50%
Claymore/Zacks Sector Rotation	XRO	0.60%
PowerShares Aerospace & Defense	PPA	0.60%
PowerShares Cleantech	PZD	0.60%

U.S. Industry & Sector Stock ETFs	Ticker Symbol	Expense Ratio
PowerShares Dynamic Pharmaceuticals	PJP	0.60%
PowerShares Dynamic Biotechnology & Genome	PBE	0.60%
PowerShares Dynamic Food & Beverage	PBJ	0.60%
PowerShares Dynamic Leisure & Entertainment	PEJ	0.60%
PowerShares Dynamic Media	PBS	0.60%
PowerShares Dynamic Networking	PXQ	0.60%
PowerShares Dynamic Semiconductor	PSI	0.60%
PowerShares Dynamic Software	PSJ	0.60%
PowerShares Dynamic Banking	PJB	0.60%
PowerShares Dynamic Basic Materials	PYZ	0.60%
PowerShares Dynamic Building & Construction	PKB	0.60%
PowerShares Dynamic Consumer Discretionary	PEZ	0.60%
PowerShares Dynamic Consumer Staples	PSL	0.60%
PowerShares Dynamic Energy	PXI	0.60%
PowerShares Dynamic Energy & Exploration	PXE	0.60%
PowerShares Dynamic Financial	PFI	0.60%
PowerShares Dynamic Hardware & Consumer Electronics	PHW	0.60%
PowerShares Dynamic Healthcare	PTH	0.60%
PowerShares Dynamic Healthcare Services	PTJ	0.60%
PowerShares Dynamic Industrials	PRN	0.60%
PowerShares Dynamic Insurance	PIC	0.60%
PowerShares Dynamic Retail	PMR	0.60%
PowerShares Dynamic Oil & Gas	PXJ	0.60%
PowerShares Dynamic Technology	PTF	0.60%
PowerShares Dynamic Telecommunications & Wireless	PTE	0.60%
PowerShares Dynamic Utilities	PUI	0.60%
PowerShares FTSE RAFI Basic Materials	PRFM	0.60%

U.S. Industry & Sector Stock ETFs	Ticker Symbol	Expense Ratio
PowerShares FTSE RAFI Consumer Goods Sector Portfolio	PRFG	0.60%
PowerShares FTSE RAFI Consumer Services Sector Portfolio	PRFS	0.60%
PowerShares FTSE RAFI Energy Sector Portfolio	PRFE	0.60%
PowerShares FTSE RAFI Financials Sector Portfolio	PRFF	0.60%
PowerShares FTSE RAFI Health Care Sector Portfolio	PRFH	0.60%
PowerShares FTSE RAFI Industrials Sector Portfolio	PRFN	0.60%
PowerShares FTSE RAFI Telecommunications & Technology Portfolio	PRFQ	0.60%
PowerShares FTSE RAFI Utilities Sector Sector Portfolio	PRFU	0.60%
PowerShares LUX Nanotech	PXN	0.60%
PowerShares NASDAQ Internet Portfolio	PNQI	0.60%
PowerShares WilderHill Clean Energy	PBW	0.60%
PowerShares WilderHill Progressive Energy	PUW	0.60%
PowerShares Water Resources	PHO	0.60%
Claymore/Clear Global Timber Index	CUT	0.65%
Claymore Solar ETF	TAN	0.65%
Market Vectors Coal ETF	KOL	0.65%
Market Vectors Gaming ETF	BJK	0.65%
Market Vectors Solar Energy ETF	KWT	0.65%
Global & International Stock ETFs (Developed World)	**Ticker Symbol**	**Expense Ratio**
Vanguard Europe Pacific ETF	VEA	0.15%
Vanguard MSCI European ETF	VGK	0.18%
Vanguard MSCI Pacific ETF	VPL	0.18%
iShares MSCI Kokusai Index	TOK	0.25%
Vanguard FTSE All World ex-US	VEU	0.25%
Vanguard Total World Stock Index ETF	VT	0.25%

Global & International Stock ETFs (Developed World)	Ticker Symbol	Expense Ratio
PowerShares BLDRs Developed Markets 100 ADR	ADRD	0.30%
PowerShares BLDRs Europe 100 ADR	ADRU	0.30%
PowerShares BLDRs Asia 50 ADR	ADRA	0.30%
DJ STOXX 50 ETF	FEU	0.31%
DJ EURO STOXX 50 ETF	FEZ	0.32%
iShares MSCI ACWI ex US Index Fund	ASWX	0.35%
iShares MSCI ACWI Index Fund	ACWI	0.35%
iShares MSCI EAFE	EFA	0.35%
SPDR MSCI ACWI ex-US ETF	CWI	0.35%
SPDR S&P World ex-US ETF	GWL	0.35%
iShares MSCI EAFE Value Index	EFV	0.40%
iShares MSCI EAFE Growth Index	EFG	0.40%
iShares S&P Global 100	IOO	0.40%
SPDR S&P International Dividend ETF	DWX	0.45%
SPDR S&P International Mid Cap ETF	MDD	0.45%
NETS TOPIX Index Fund (Japan)	TYI	0.47%
NETS FTSE 100 Index Fund (United Kingdom)	LDN	0.47%
iShares S&P Global Clean Energy Index Fund	ICLN	0.48%
iShares S&P Global Consumer Discretionary	RXI	0.48%
iShares S&P Global Consumer Staples	KXI	0.48%
iShares S&P Global Energy	IXC	0.48%
iShares S&P Global Financials	IXG	0.48%
iShares S&P Global Healthcare	IXJ	0.48%
iShares S&P Global Industrials	EXI	0.48%
iShares S&P Global Infrastructure	IGF	0.48%
iShares S&P Global Materials	MXI	0.48%
iShares S&P Global Nuclear Energy Index Fund	NUCL	0.48%
iShares S&P Global Technology	IXN	0.48%
iShares S&P Global Telecommunications	IXP	0.48%
iShares S&P Global Timber & Forestry Index Fund	WOOD	0.48%

Global & International Stock ETFs (Developed World)	Ticker Symbol	Expense Ratio
iShares S&P Global Utilities	JXI	0.48%
WisdomTree DIEFA Fund	DWM	0.48%
WisdomTree Europe Total Dividend Fund	DEB	0.48%
WisdomTree Japan Total Dividend Fund	DXJ	0.48%
WisdomTree International LargeCap Dividend Fund	DOL	0.48%
WisdomTree Pacific ex-Japan Total Dividend	DND	0.48%
iShares Dow Jones EPAC Select Dividend	IDV	0.50%
iShares FTSE Developed Small Cap ex-North America IF	IFSM	0.50%
iShares MSCI Pacific ex-Japan	EPP	0.50%
iShares S&P Asia 50	AIA	0.50%
iShares S&P TOPIX 150	ITF	0.50%
PowerShares International Dividend Achievers	PID	0.50%
SPDR DJ Global Titans ETF	DGT	0.50%
SPDR DJ Wilshire Global Real Estate ETF	RWO	0.50%
SPDR S&P International Consumer Discretionary Sector ETF	IPD	0.50%
SPDR S&P International Consumer Staples Sector ETF	IPS	0.50%
SPDR S&P International Financial Sector ETF	IPF	0.50%
SPDR S&P International Health Care Sector ETF	IRY	0.50%
SPDR S&P International Industrial Sector ETF	IPN	0.50%
SPDR S&P International Materials Sector ETF	IRV	0.50%
SPDR S&P International Technology Sector ETF	IPK	0.50%
SPDR S&P International Telecommunications Sector ETF	IST	0.50%
SPDR S&P International Utilities Sector ETF	IPU	0.50%
SPDR S&P International Energy Sector ETF	IPW	0.50%
iShares MSCI United Kingdom	EWU	0.51%
iShares MSCI Japan	EWJ	0.52%

Global & International Stock ETFs (Developed World)	Ticker Symbol	Expense Ratio
iShares MSCI EMU	EZU	0.54%
Cohen & Steers Global Realty Majors ETF	GRI	0.55%
Market Vectors Gold Miners ETF	GDX	0.55%
Market Vectors Environmental Services ETF	EVX	0.55%
Market Vectors Steel ETF	SLX	0.55%
WisdomTree DIEFA High Yielding Equity Fund	DTH	0.58%
WisdomTree Europe High Yielding Equity Fund	DEW	0.58%
WisdomTree Europe SmallCap Dividend Fund	DFE	0.58%
WisdomTree Japan High-Yielding Equity Fund	DNL	0.58%
WisdomTree Japan SmallCap Dividend Fund	DFJ	0.58%
WisdomTree International Dividend Top 100 Fund	DOO	0.58%
WisdomTree International MidCap Dividend Fund	DIM	0.58%
WisdomTree International Small Cap Dividend Fund	DLS	0.58%
WisdomTree International Basic Materials	DBN	0.58%
WisdomTree International Communications	DGG	0.58%
WisdomTree International Consumer Cyclical	DPC	0.58%
WisdomTree International Consumer Non-Cyclical	DPN	0.58%
WisdomTree International Energy	DKA	0.58%
WisdomTree International Financial	DRF	0.58%
WisdomTree International Health Care	DBR	0.58%
WisdomTree International Industrial	DDI	0.58%
WisdomTree International Real Estate Fund	DRW	0.58%
WisdomTree International Technology	DBT	0.58%
WisdomTree International Utilities	DBU	0.58%
WisdomTree Pacific ex-Japan High-Yielding Equity	DNH	0.58%
SPDR DJ Wilshire International Real Estate ETF	RWX	0.59%
First Trust DJ Global Select Dividend Index Fund	FGD	0.60%

Global & International Stock ETFs (Developed World)	Ticker Symbol	Expense Ratio
First Trust DJ STOXX Select Dividend 30 Index Fund	FDD	0.60%
iShares S&P Europe 350	IEV	0.60%
SPDR FTSE/Macquarie Global Infrastructure 100 ETF	GII	0.60%
International Small Cap ETF	GWX	0.60%
Claymore/AlphaShares China Real Estate ETF	TAO	0.65%
Claymore/Clear Global Exchanges, Brokers & Asset Mgrs	EXB	0.65%
Claymore/Delta Global Shipping Index ETF	SEA	0.65%
Claymore/SWM Canadian Energy Income	ENY	0.65%
Claymore/Robeco Developed International Equity	EEN	0.65%
Claymore S&P Global Water ETF	CGW	0.65%
Claymore/Zacks Country Rotation ETF	CRO	0.65%
Market Vectors Global Alternative Energy ETF	GEX	0.65%
Market Vectors Agribusiness ETF	MOO	0.65%
Market Vectors Nuclear Energy ETF	NLR	0.65%

Emerging Markets ETFs	Ticker Symbol	Expense Ratio
PowerShares BLDRS Emerging Markets 50 ADR	ADRE	0.30%
Vanguard Emerging Markets ETF	VWO	0.30%
SPDR S&P BRIC 40 ETF	BIK	0.40%
iShares S&P Latin America 40	ILF	0.50%
SPDR Claymore/BNY BRIC ETF	EEB	0.60%
First Trust ISE ChIndia	FNI	0.60%
SPDR S&P Emerging Markets	GMM	0.60%
SPDR S&P Emerging Latin America	GML	0.60%
SPDR S&P Emerging Middle East & Africa	GAF	0.60%
SPDR S&P Emerging Europe	GUR	0.60%
SPDR S&P Emerging Asia Pacific	GMF	0.60%
WisdomTree Emerging Markets High Yielding Index	DEM	0.63%

Emerging Markets ETFs	*Ticker Symbol*	*Expense Ratio*
Claymore/BNY Mellon Frontier Markets ETF	FRN	0.65%
SPDR S&P Emerging Markets Small Cap	EWX	0.65%

Fixed Income ETFs	*Ticker Symbol*	*Expense Ratio*
Vanguard Intermediate Term Bond ETF	BIV	0.11%
Vanguard Long Term Bond ETF	BLV	0.11%
Vanguard Short Term Bond ETF	BSV	0.11%
Vanguard Total Bond Market ETF	BND	0.11%
SPDR Lehman 1-3 Month T-Bill ETF	BIL	0.13%
SPDR Lehman Aggregate Bond ETF	LAG	0.13%
SPDR Lehman Intermediate Term Treasury ETF	ITE	0.13%
SPDR Lehman Long Term Treasury ETF	TLO	0.13%
Vanguard Extended Duration	EDV	0.14%
iShares Lehman Short Treasury Bond	SHV	0.15%
iShares Lehman 1-3 YR Treasury Bond	SHY	0.15%
iShares Lehman 3-7 YR Treasury Bond	IEI	0.15%
iShares Lehman 7-10 YR Treasury Bond	IEF	0.15%
iShares Lehman 10-20 YR Treasury Bond	TLH	0.15%
iShares Lehman 20+ YR Treasury Bond	TLT	0.15%
iShares iBoxx $ Investment Grade Corporate Bond	LQD	0.15%
SPDR Barclays TIPS ETF	IPE	0.18%
iShares Lehman Aggregate Bond	AGG	0.20%
iShares 1-3 YR Credit Bond	CSJ	0.20%
iShares Lehman Credit Bond	CFT	0.20%
iShares Lehman Intermediate Credit Bond	CIU	0.20%
iShares Lehman Intermediate Government/Credit Bond	GVI	0.20%
iShares Lehman Government/Credit Bond	GBF	0.20%
iShares Lehman TIPS Bond	TIP	0.20%
Market Vectors Lehman AMT-Free Interim Municipal	ITM	0.20%

Fixed Income ETFs	Ticker Symbol	Expense Ratio
SPDR Lehman California Municipal Bond ETF	CXA	0.20%
SPDR Lehman Municipal Bond ETF	TFI	0.20%
SPDR Lehman New York Municipal Bond ETF	INY	0.20%
SPDR Lehman Short Term Municipal Bond ETF	SHM	0.20%
Market Vectors Lehman AMT-Free Long Municipal	MLN	0.24%
iShares Lehman MBS Fixed Rate Bond	MBB	0.25%
iShares S&P National Municipal Bond Fund	MUB	0.25%
iShares S&P California Municipal Bond Fund	CMF	0.25%
iShares S&P New York Municipal Bond Fund	NYF	0.25%
PowerShares 1-30 Laddered Treasury Portfolio	PLW	0.25%
PowerShares VRDO Tax Free Weekly Portfolio	PVI	0.25%
WisdomTree U.S. Current Income Fund	USY	0.25%
Claymore U.S. Capital Markets Bond ETF	UBD	0.27%
Claymore U.S. Micro-Term Fixed Income ETF	PQY	0.27%
PowerShares Insured California Municipal Bond Portfolio	PWZ	0.28%
PowerShares Insured New York Municipal Bond Portfolio	PZT	0.28%
PowerShares Insured National Municipal Bond Portfolio	PZA	0.28%
SPDR Lehman High Yield Bond ETF	JNK	0.40%
iShares S&P US Preferred Stock Index	PFF	0.48%
iShares iBoxx $ High Yield Corporate Bond	HYG	0.50%
PowerShares Emerging Markets Sovereign Debt Portfolio	PCY	0.50%
PowerShares High Yield Corporate Bond Portfolio	PHB	0.50%
PowerShares Preferred Portfolio	PGX	0.50%
SPDR Lehman International Treasury Bond ETF	BWX	0.50%
SPDR DB International Government Inflation Protected Bond ETF	WIP	0.50%

Fixed Income ETFs	*Ticker Symbol*	*Expense Ratio*
iShares JP Morgan USD Emerging Markets Bond Fund	EMB	0.60%
PowerShares Financial Preferred Portfolio	PGF	0.60%
Market Vectors Lehman AMT-Free Short Municipal	SMB	0.65%

Commodities		
iShares Comex Gold Trust	IAU	0.40%
SPDR Gold Trust	GLD	0.40%
iShares Silver Trust	SLV	0.50%
United States 12 Month Oil	USL	0.60%
E-TRACS UBS Bloomberg CMCI Agriculture Index ETN	UAG	0.65%
iPath Dow Jones AIG Commodity Index Total Return ETN	DJP	0.75%
iPath GSCI Total Return Index ETN	GSP	0.75%
iPath GS Crude Oil Total Return Index ETN	OIL	0.75%
iShares S&P GSCI Commodity Index Trust	GSG	0.75%

Appendix C

Helpful Web Resources for the Smart Index Investor

. . . .

*T*imes change, indexes change, index products (sometimes for better, sometimes for worse) continue to proliferate. Make sure you stay up to speed by popping in now and then to some of these Web sites.

Web Sites with an Index Investing Focus

www.bogleheads.org: Not only the official fan club of John Bogle, father of index investing, but also a place to engage in intelligent conversation with some ardent fans of index investing, as well as a few very knowledgeable investors and advisors.

www.efficientfrontier.com: The Web site of finance guru William Bernstein. Bernstein presents a scientific look at index investing, with some rather weighty discussions. Lots of good food for thought.

www.etfconnect.com: Quotes, yields, and ETF nuts-n-bolts information (expense ratios, performance records, and so on). A search function allows you to rummage through the world of ETFs to find one that fits your specific needs. The sponsor is Nuveen Investments, a provider of closed-end mutual funds. Purposely, there is a blurring of the lines between closed-end mutual funds and ETFs. They are not the same!

www.etfguide.com: A good, quick summary of the entire ETF world — what's hot, what's not, and why. It contains a complete listing of all ETFs available, along with ticker symbols.

www.etftrends.com: A gossip column of sorts for ETF enthusiasts. There's chit-chat about new ETFs on the market, ETFs pending approval of the SEC, behind-the-scenes industry workings, rumors, and ripoffs.

www.etfzone.com: Discussion, data, news, and more . . . practically everything you want to know about ETFs, and then some.

`http://finance.yahoo.com/etf`: Features a search function with intimate details on individual funds, an ETF glossary, and regularly updated news and commentary.

`http://finance.yahoo.com/funds`: Focuses on mutual funds, with all sorts of helpful shopping tools.

`www.indexfunds.com`: A commercial Web site from a guy, Mark Hebner, who wants to manage your money (in index funds, of course). But he is also an index-investing evangelist and packs his Web site with scads of information, both old and new, on the virtues of indexing.

`www.indexshow.com`: Would you believe that there's a syndicated radio show about index investing? Check out the stations, the schedule, and the topics by logging on here.

`www.indexuniverse.com`: See "Breaking News" for the most up-to-date information on ETFs and index mutual funds. The commentary section features some of the most intelligent discussion of indexing you'll encounter anywhere.

`www.morningstar.com`: (Click either the ETF icon or the Funds icon on the blue bar at the top of screen.) Thorough information on individual funds, along with Morningstar's trademarked rating system. (One star is bad, five stars is grand.)

`www.seekingalpha.com`: Tons of information, some good, some bad. I like the ETF selector, which divides up the ever-growing world of ETFs into manageable chunks.

General Investing News, Advice, and Education

`www.bankrate.com`: Compare rates on all sorts of fixed-income investments. Get the latest lowdown on CD rates, mortgages, and home-equity loans.

`www.bloomberg.com`: Rather hardcore financial data, news of Corporate America, and sporadic dirt on CEOs being sued by their ex-wives.

`www.cnnfn.com`: Get your daily dose of everything markets-related, including pre-market trading quotes, currency exchange rates, and bond yields.

`www.dinkytown.com`: Financial calculators of every sort imaginable.

`http://finance.yahoo.com`: Surf your heart out . . . tons of information on financial markets. There's also a section that allows you input data on your own portfolio and track its performance.

`www.finra.org/fundanalyzer`: Compare the expenses of up to three ETFs, mutual funds, or share classes of the same mutual fund.

`www.marketwatch.com`: An encyclopedia of investment information, updated daily. Links to blogs and podcasts allow you spend hours and hours reading or listening to news about the markets, if you care to.

`www.moneychimp.com`: For the beginning to the more advanced investor, this site with a silly name offers quick and mostly accurate hits on a number of important investment subjects.

`www.morningstar.com`: Exclusive ratings of funds, and much more. Morningstar offers many premium services. If you're going to subscribe to any, you may, as a serious index investor, consider the *ETFInvestor* newsletter ($150/year).

`www.riskgrades.com`: A novel way of looking at investment risk and return, much simpler than standard deviation.

`www.socialinvest.org`: A wealth of information on socially responsible investing.

Financial Supermarkets

Otherwise known as large brokerage houses, here are some places where you can buy, sell, and house your index funds.

`www.fidelity.com`: Or telephone Fidelity at 800-544-8888.

`www.schwab.com`: Or telephone Charles Schwab at 866-232-9890.

`www.amtd.com`: Or telephone TD Ameritrade at 800-454-9272.

`www.troweprice.com`: Or telephone T. Rowe Price at 800-638-5660.

`www.vanguard.com`: Or telephone Vanguard at 800-662-7447.

`www.zecco.com`: Or telephone Zecco at 877-700-7862.

Index Fund Providers: Exchange-Traded Funds

Here are the big players in ETFs (which also happen to be those I tend to most often recommend):

- Barclays Global Investors iShares: www.ishares.com
- State Street Global Advisors (SSgA): www.ssgafunds.com
- Vanguard ETFs: www.vanguard.com/etf

And here are the smaller players:

- Claymore Securities: www.claymore.com
- Currency Shares: www.currencyshares.com
- Deutsche Bank: www.dbcfund.db.com
- First Trust: www.ftportfolios.com
- Invesco PowerShares: www.invescopowershares.com
- Merrill Lynch HOLDRS: www.holdrs.com
- Northern Trust Corp. (NETS): www.netsetfs.com
- Pimco ETFs: www.allianzinvestors.com
- ProShares: www.proshares.com
- Rydex Investments: www.rydexfunds.com
- Van Eck Global: www.vaneck.com
- WisdomTree: www.wisdomtree.com

Index Fund Providers: Mutual Funds

The largest producers of index mutual funds also tend to be financial supermarkets where you may want to open a brokerage account to keep your entire portfolio:

- www.fidelity.com
- www.schwab.com
- www.tiaacref.com
- www.troweprice.com
- www.vanguard.com

Stock Exchanges

This is where the action happens if you happen to be investing in ETFs rather than index mutual funds.

www.amex.com: Almost half of all ETFs are listed on the American Stock Exchange. Bland Web site, but it provides all the ETF basics.

www.nyse.com: Those ETFS that aren't listed on the AMEX are by and large traded on the New York Stock Exchange. Surprisingly, there isn't a lot of ETF information on the Web site, but there is a wealth of general information about the world of finance.

www.nasdaq.com: Despite the fact that not many ETFs are listed on the NASDAQ, there are some very cool things on this Web site. Check out especially the "ETF Dynamic Heatmap."

The People Who Create the Indexes

In case you want to get to the nuts and bolts of it all . . .

- ✔ www.djindexes.com
- ✔ www.ftse.com
- ✔ www.lehman.com
- ✔ www.mscibarra.com
- ✔ www.russell.com
- ✔ www.standardandpoors.com
- ✔ www.wilshire.com

Best Retirement Calculators

www.firecalc.com: FIRE is short for Financial Independence/Retire Early, and this free Web site (feel free to contribute!) is one of the best you'll find. There's lots more here than a calculator, including some pretty good general investment advice, and even a forum where you can chat with others about retiring young, if that's your thing.

www.moneychimp.com/articles/volatility/retirement.htm: Moneychimp is a funny name, but it's a great Web site full of all kinds of financial calculators. For some funny reason, there's a ridiculously simple and simpleminded retirement calculator featured on the home page. The better calculator is buried deeper within. Make sure you use the link provided here.

www3.troweprice.com/ric/RIC/: Many of the financial supermarkets offer silly retirement calculators; T. Rowe Price's uses Monte Carlo simulations and is presented in an easy-to-read fashion. (RIC stands for Retirement Income Calculator.)

Where to Find a Financial Planner

www.cfp.net: The Certified Financial Planning Board of Standards, which lists Certified Financial Planners (CFPs) nationwide. The CFP designation assures that the person has a fair amount of education and experience, and passed a wicked ten-hour exam.

www.cfainstitute.org: CFA Institute is where you want to go to find a Chartered Financial Analyst (CFA), which is not as well known but is very similar to a CFP.

www.fpanet.org: Financial Planning Association is the nation's largest organization of financial planners. It doesn't take much to join.

www.napfa.org: National Association of Personal Financial Advisors is the association for *fee-onlys*: financial people who don't take commissions but rather work for a straight fee. About four out of ten financial planners are fee-onlys.

www.cambridgeadvisors.com: A national network of fee-onlys who are eager to work with middle-class folk.

www.garrettplanningnetwork.com: A list of 250 or so financial advisors who charge for services on an hourly, as-needed basis.

The Author Himself . . . At Your Service

Two URLs — www.globalportfolios.net and www.russellwild.com — will get you to the same place: the author's own fashionable Web site.

Index

ProFunds UltraShort NASDAQ-100 mutual
fund, 131
ProShares, 130, 318
pumping short-term performers, 49

• *Q* •

quality of bonds, 135–136

• *R* •

RAFI (Research Affiliates Fundamental
Index), 229, 230
random success, 274
A Random Walk Down Wall Street (Malkiel,
Burton G.), 28, 275
ratings claims, understanding, 273
real estate investment trusts (REITs)
above average returns for, 156–157
asset allocation for, 189
avoiding niche areas, 164
for diversifying investments, 125
ETF picks, 161–164
indexes for, 156
international, 156, 158, 164
low stock market correlation of, 157,
158–159
mutual fund picks, 159–161
percentage to invest in, 164, 205
tax liabilities of, 158
unique qualities of, 158–159
rebalancing your portfolio
on as-needed basis, 251
bonus for, 187
calendar method for, 250–251
choosing a method for, 251–252
with commodities, 154
diversification allowing for, 187
importance of, 250, 279
overview, 137–138
Red Rocks Listed Private Equity Index, 167
Remember icon, 6
Research Affiliates Fundamental Index
(RAFI), 229, 230
research costs, not paid on index funds, 13

retirement calculators
caveats for, 192–193
limitations of, 194–195
Monte Carlo simulations with, 193–194
Web sites, 194, 319–320
retirement planning
calculators for, 192–195, 319–320
cash flow versus income, 253
determining amount to save, 192
getting index funds in your 401(k),
183–184
portfolio for, 244
rolling over, 184
20x rule for, 192
reversion to the mean, 222, 256–257
risk. *See also* volatility
compensation for systemic, 98
determining amount to take, 191
inappropriate, avoiding, 278
for large cap versus small cap funds,
202–203
lessened by diversification, 15
nonsystemic versus systemic, 97
Sharpe Ratio for, 202–203
with stock index funds, 100
for value versus growth stocks, 203–204
Russell, 90–91, 319
Russell 1000 index, 90
Russell 2000 index, 90, 98, 99
Russell 3000 index, 90
Russell/Nomura indexes, 90
Rydex Investments
equal-weighted index fund offerings, 67
inverse index ETFs from, 68
S&P equal-weighted indexes used by, 85
Web site, 318
Rydex Russell Top 50 ETF (XLG), 107–108
Rydex S&P Equal Weight Consumer
Discretionary ETF (RCD), 67
Rydex S&P Equal Weight Consumer Staples
ETF (RHS), 67
Rydex S&P Equal Weight Energy ETF
(RYE), 67
Rydex S&P Equal Weight Financials ETF
(RYF), 67
Rydex S&P Equal Weight Index ETF
(RSP), 67, 230

BUSINESS, CAREERS & PERSONAL FINANCE

0-7645-9847-3

0-7645-2431-3

Also available:

- Business Plans Kit For Dummies
  0-7645-9794-9
- Economics For Dummies
  0-7645-5726-2
- Grant Writing For Dummies
  0-7645-8416-2
- Home Buying For Dummies
  0-7645-5331-3
- Managing For Dummies
  0-7645-1771-6
- Marketing For Dummies
  0-7645-5600-2

- Personal Finance For Dummies
  0-7645-2590-5*
- Resumes For Dummies
  0-7645-5471-9
- Selling For Dummies
  0-7645-5363-1
- Six Sigma For Dummies
  0-7645-6798-5
- Small Business Kit For Dummies
  0-7645-5984-2
- Starting an eBay Business For Dummies
  0-7645-6924-4
- Your Dream Career For Dummies
  0-7645-9795-7

HOME & BUSINESS COMPUTER BASICS

0-470-05432-8

0-471-75421-8

Also available:

- Cleaning Windows Vista For Dummies
  0-471-78293-9
- Excel 2007 For Dummies
  0-470-03737-7
- Mac OS X Tiger For Dummies
  0-7645-7675-5
- MacBook For Dummies
  0-470-04859-X
- Macs For Dummies
  0-470-04849-2
- Office 2007 For Dummies
  0-470-00923-3

- Outlook 2007 For Dummies
  0-470-03830-6
- PCs For Dummies
  0-7645-8958-X
- Salesforce.com For Dummies
  0-470-04893-X
- Upgrading & Fixing Laptops For Dummies
  0-7645-8959-8
- Word 2007 For Dummies
  0-470-03658-3
- Quicken 2007 For Dummies
  0-470-04600-7

FOOD, HOME, GARDEN, HOBBIES, MUSIC & PETS

0-7645-8404-9

0-7645-9904-6

Also available:

- Candy Making For Dummies
  0-7645-9734-5
- Card Games For Dummies
  0-7645-9910-0
- Crocheting For Dummies
  0-7645-4151-X
- Dog Training For Dummies
  0-7645-8418-9
- Healthy Carb Cookbook For Dummies
  0-7645-8476-6
- Home Maintenance For Dummies
  0-7645-5215-5

- Horses For Dummies
  0-7645-9797-3
- Jewelry Making & Beading For Dummies
  0-7645-2571-9
- Orchids For Dummies
  0-7645-6759-4
- Puppies For Dummies
  0-7645-5255-4
- Rock Guitar For Dummies
  0-7645-5356-9
- Sewing For Dummies
  0-7645-6847-7
- Singing For Dummies
  0-7645-2475-5

INTERNET & DIGITAL MEDIA

0-470-04529-9

0-470-04894-8

Also available:

- Blogging For Dummies
  0-471-77084-1
- Digital Photography For Dummies
  0-7645-9802-3
- Digital Photography All-in-One Desk Reference For Dummies
  0-470-03743-1
- Digital SLR Cameras and Photography For Dummies
  0-7645-9803-1
- eBay Business All-in-One Desk Reference For Dummies
  0-7645-8438-3
- HDTV For Dummies
  0-470-09673-X

- Home Entertainment PCs For Dummies
  0-470-05523-5
- MySpace For Dummies
  0-470-09529-6
- Search Engine Optimization For Dummies
  0-471-97998-8
- Skype For Dummies
  0-470-04891-3
- The Internet For Dummies
  0-7645-8996-2
- Wiring Your Digital Home For Dummies
  0-471-91830-X

SPORTS, FITNESS, PARENTING, RELIGION & SPIRITUALITY

0-471-76871-5

0-7645-7841-3

Also available:

- Catholicism For Dummies
  0-7645-5391-7
- Exercise Balls For Dummies
  0-7645-5623-1
- Fitness For Dummies
  0-7645-7851-0
- Football For Dummies
  0-7645-3936-1
- Judaism For Dummies
  0-7645-5299-6
- Potty Training For Dummies
  0-7645-5417-4
- Buddhism For Dummies
  0-7645-5359-3

- Pregnancy For Dummies
  0-7645-4483-7 †
- Ten Minute Tone-Ups For Dummies
  0-7645-7207-5
- NASCAR For Dummies
  0-7645-7681-X
- Religion For Dummies
  0-7645-5264-3
- Soccer For Dummies
  0-7645-5229-5
- Women in the Bible For Dummies
  0-7645-8475-8

TRAVEL

0-7645-7749-2

0-7645-6945-7

Also available:

- Alaska For Dummies
  0-7645-7746-8
- Cruise Vacations For Dummies
  0-7645-6941-4
- England For Dummies
  0-7645-4276-1
- Europe For Dummies
  0-7645-7529-5
- Germany For Dummies
  0-7645-7823-5
- Hawaii For Dummies
  0-7645-7402-7

- Italy For Dummies
  0-7645-7386-1
- Las Vegas For Dummies
  0-7645-7382-9
- London For Dummies
  0-7645-4277-X
- Paris For Dummies
  0-7645-7630-5
- RV Vacations For Dummies
  0-7645-4442-X
- Walt Disney World & Orlando
  For Dummies
  0-7645-9660-8

GRAPHICS, DESIGN & WEB DEVELOPMENT

0-7645-8815-X

0-7645-9571-7

Also available:

- 3D Game Animation For Dummies
  0-7645-8789-7
- AutoCAD 2006 For Dummies
  0-7645-8925-3
- Building a Web Site For Dummies
  0-7645-7144-3
- Creating Web Pages For Dummies
  0-470-08030-2
- Creating Web Pages All-in-One Desk
  Reference For Dummies
  0-7645-4345-8
- Dreamweaver 8 For Dummies
  0-7645-9649-7

- InDesign CS2 For Dummies
  0-7645-9572-5
- Macromedia Flash 8 For Dummies
  0-7645-9691-8
- Photoshop CS2 and Digital
  Photography For Dummies
  0-7645-9580-6
- Photoshop Elements 4 For Dummies
  0-471-77483-9
- Syndicating Web Sites with RSS Feeds
  For Dummies
  0-7645-8848-6
- Yahoo! SiteBuilder For Dummies
  0-7645-9800-7

NETWORKING, SECURITY, PROGRAMMING & DATABASES

0-7645-7728-X

0-471-74940-0

Also available:

- Access 2007 For Dummies
  0-470-04612-0
- ASP.NET 2 For Dummies
  0-7645-7907-X
- C# 2005 For Dummies
  0-7645-9704-3
- Hacking For Dummies
  0-470-05235-X
- Hacking Wireless Networks
  For Dummies
  0-7645-9730-2
- Java For Dummies
  0-470-08716-1

- Microsoft SQL Server 2005 For Dummies
  0-7645-7755-7
- Networking All-in-One Desk Reference
  For Dummies
  0-7645-9939-9
- Preventing Identity Theft For Dummies
  0-7645-7336-5
- Telecom For Dummies
  0-471-77085-X
- Visual Studio 2005 All-in-One Desk
  Reference For Dummies
  0-7645-9775-2
- XML For Dummies
  0-7645-8845-1